2nd edition

Solutions

Pre-Intermediate Student's Book

Tim Falla   Paul A Davies

OXFORD

UNIVERSITY PRESS

1 All about you

THIS UNIT INCLUDES

Vocabulary ▪ personality adjectives ▪ negative prefixes: *un-*, *in-*, *im-*, *ir-* and *dis-*
Grammar ▪ present simple and continuous ▪ verbs not used in continuous tenses
▪ verb + infinitive or *-ing* form
Speaking ▪ talking about personality ▪ expressing likes and dislikes
Writing ▪ a personal profile

1A   VOCABULARY AND LISTENING Personality

I can describe someone's personality.

1 SPEAKING Do you know the film and TV characters in the photos? Match four of them with descriptions a–d.

a She's generous and kind. Her husband is quite lazy and rude, so she has to be patient.

b He's nasty and dishonest. He's also very clever – but not in a good way.

c She's shy and quiet. But she's also very strong and determined.

d He's strong and confident – almost arrogant. He's usually serious, but he can be funny.

2 🎧 1.02 VOCABULARY Complete the pairs of opposites with the blue adjectives from the descriptions in exercise 1. Then listen, repeat and check.

Personality adjectives			
1 mean	*generous*	7 stupid	_____
2 honest	_____	8 shy	_____
3 hard-working	_____	9 funny	_____
4 weak	_____	10 polite	_____
5 talkative	_____	11 impatient	_____
6 modest	_____	12 nice	_____

3 Choose two film or TV characters that you know. What adjectives can you use to describe them?

⟫⟫ **VOCABULARY BUILDER (PART 1): PAGE 124** ⟪⟪

4 🎧 1.03 Listen to the dialogues. Match each person with an adjective. There are two adjectives that you do not need.

arrogant   funny   generous   impatient   lazy   shy

1 Martha _____   3 Sam _____
2 Ryan _____   4 Julie _____

5 Choose three adjectives to describe someone you like or do not like and three adjectives to describe you. Can you give reasons for your choices?

6 SPEAKING Work in pairs. Describe yourself or a person you like to your partner.

> I really like Sarah. She's kind and funny.

> I think I'm quite generous. I'm also sometimes a bit lazy.

⟫⟫ **VOCABULARY BUILDER (PART 2): PAGE 124** ⟪⟪

1 SPEAKING Describe the scene in the picture. What are the people doing? Use the verbs below.

chat dance drink eat hold laugh listen look at sit smile stand wear

> A boy is drinking orange juice.

2 🎧 1.04 Read and listen to the dialogue. Underline examples of the present simple and present continuous.

Alice Hi, Matt. Are you having a good time?
Matt Not really. I don't know anyone here.
Alice Do you know Sam?
Matt No. Who's he?
Alice *She*. She lives next door to me. She's over there. She's wearing a yellow top.
Matt Is she dancing?
Alice No, that's Zoe. Sam's standing by the door. She isn't talking to anyone. Do you want me to introduce you?
Matt OK.

3 Complete the table with the correct form of the verb *wear*.

Present simple	
affirmative	She always ¹_____ dresses.
negative	He ²_____ trainers to school.
interrogative	³_____ you _____ a tie to school?

Present continuous	
affirmative	She ⁴_____ a blue cap.
negative	He ⁵_____ a jacket.
interrogative	⁶_____ you _____ a vest?

4 Complete rules 1–4 in the *Learn this!* box with the correct tenses.

> LEARN THIS!
>
> 1 We use the _____ for something that always, regularly or never happens.
> 2 We use the _____ for something that is happening now.
> 3 We use the _____ for a fact that is always true.
> 4 We don't normally use the _____ with certain verbs, e.g. *believe, hate, like, love, need, know, prefer, want*.
> 5 We also use the present continuous for arrangements in the future, e.g. *I'm meeting John at 10 a.m.*

>>> GRAMMAR BUILDER 1B: PAGE 104 <<<

5 Complete the dialogue. Use the present simple or present continuous form of the verbs in brackets.

Matt So, ¹_____ (you / enjoy) the party?
Sam Yes, it's really good.
Matt Hey, I ²_____ (like) your shoes, Sam. They're cool.
Sam Thanks. They hurt my feet, though. That's why I ³_____ (not dance). You ⁴_____ (wear) trainers. They're much better for dancing.
Alice Hey, you two. ⁵_____ (you / want) to dance?
Sam No, thanks, Alice. Matt, you go ahead and dance.
Matt Uh, no thanks.
Alice But you ⁶_____ (love) dancing, Matt.
Matt Er, yes, but I ⁷_____ (not like) this band.
Sam Really? I ⁸_____ (love) them. Actually, I ⁹_____ (go) to see them next month and I've got a spare ticket. Do you want to come, Alice?
Alice Yes, please!

6 🎧 1.05 Listen and check.

7 SPEAKING Work in pairs. Look at the table. Ask and answer a question for each verb. Use the present simple or present continuous, a noun and a time phrase.

Verbs	Nouns	Time phrases
go	the housework	after school
speak	a dress	every day
wear	English	at the moment
do	a computer	today
use	to the cinema	next month
	on holiday	at weekends
	this book	this weekend

> Are you going on holiday next month?

> No, I'm not. Do you speak English every day?

1 SPEAKING Look at the photos. What can you see? What are the people doing?

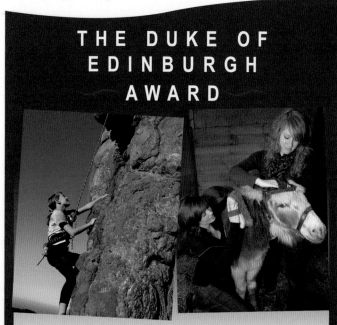

THE DUKE OF EDINBURGH AWARD

Would you like to learn to rock climb? Or spend time working at an animal sanctuary? That's what Andrea Black and Jenny Smith are doing as part of their Duke of Edinburgh Award programme.

The award encourages young people to do exciting cultural, social and adventure activities in their free time. The Queen's husband, the Duke of Edinburgh, started the award in 1956. He started it because he wanted young people to learn to help themselves and other people.

The award is for people aged 14–25, and there are three levels: Bronze, for those aged 14 or over, Silver for over 15s, and Gold for over 16s. You have to complete four activities to achieve the award:

- go on an expedition (e.g. hiking, kayaking or climbing)
- learn a new practical or social skill (anything from painting to podcasting!)
- take on a physical challenge (e.g. learn or improve at a sport)
- do voluntary work, helping people or the environment (e.g. work with disabled or elderly people, or raise money for a charity)

Young people usually do the award at a Duke of Edinburgh club at their school or at a local youth group. They decide what they are going to do, and write a plan. It usually takes between one and three years to finish an award.

2 🎧 1.06 Read the text quickly. What is the Duke of Edinburgh Award? Choose the correct answer.

a an award for the most active young person in the UK
b a programme of challenging activities for young people
c an opportunity for young people to learn new skills and make some money

3 Read the text again. Answer the questions.

1 Who started the award?
2 Why did he start the award?
3 How many levels of award are there?
4 How old do you have to be to get a Gold award?
5 How many activities do participants have to complete?
6 Who plans which activities the participants do?

4 VOCABULARY Complete the phrases from the text with the verbs below.

do   do   learn   go on   spend   write

1 _____ voluntary work   4 _____ time
2 _____ an expedition   5 _____ an activity
3 _____ a plan   6 _____ a new skill

5 🎧 1.07 Listen to four people who are taking part in the Duke of Edinburgh Award. Match the speakers with the four parts of the programme.

1 Jasmine   a physical challenge
2 Nathan   b new skill
3 Caitlin   c expedition
4 Dominic   d voluntary work

6 🎧 1.07 Listen again and write *J, N, C* or *D*. Who:

1 is learning to make something? _____
2 is learning what life is like for people in other countries? _____
3 might continue with the activity later in life? _____
4 is spending most of the time outdoors? _____
5 is learning to work in a team? _____ and _____
6 feels stronger? _____ and _____

7 Imagine you are going to do the Duke of Edinburgh Award. What would you do for your four activities: Expedition, Skill, Physical and Volunteering? Give reasons.

8 SPEAKING Work in pairs. Tell your partner about your plans and reasons.

> For my expedition, I'd like to ... because I want to ...

> For my skill, I'd like to learn how to ... , so I'm planning to ...

1D GRAMMAR Verb + infinitive or -ing form

I can identify and use different verb patterns.

1 **SPEAKING** Work in pairs. Ask and answer the questions. Make a note of your answers.

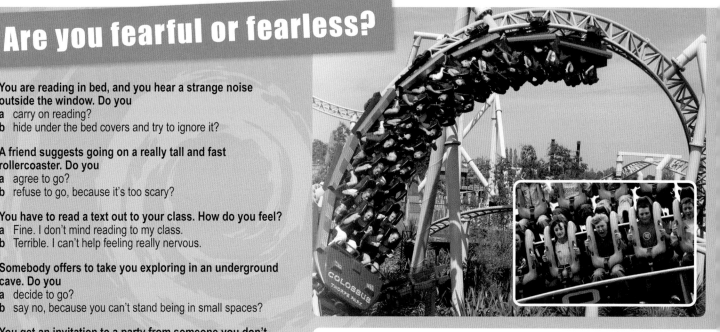

Are you fearful or fearless?

1 You are reading in bed, and you hear a strange noise outside the window. Do you
   a carry on reading?
   b hide under the bed covers and try to ignore it?

2 A friend suggests going on a really tall and fast rollercoaster. Do you
   a agree to go?
   b refuse to go, because it's too scary?

3 You have to read a text out to your class. How do you feel?
   a Fine. I don't mind reading to my class.
   b Terrible. I can't help feeling really nervous.

4 Somebody offers to take you exploring in an underground cave. Do you
   a decide to go?
   b say no, because you can't stand being in small spaces?

5 You get an invitation to a party from someone you don't know very well. Do you
   a accept the invitation and look forward to meeting some new people?
   b pretend to be busy?

2 Look at your answers and count the a's and b's. Are you fearless (mostly a's) or fearful (mostly b's)?

3 Read the *Learn this!* box. Underline all the verbs in the questionnaire that are followed by the infinitive or -*ing* form of another verb.

4 Complete the table with the verbs that you underlined in the questionnaire.

5 Add these verbs to the correct group in the *Learn this!* box. Check in a dictionary if necessary.

avoid   expect   fancy   hope   promise   spend time

LEARN THIS!

1 Some verbs are followed by the infinitive of another verb.
   She's pretending to be asleep.

2 Some verbs are followed by the -*ing* form of another verb.
   Danny suggested going out tonight.

Verb + infinitive	Verb + -*ing* form
pretend	suggest

6 Complete the sentences. Use the infinitive or -*ing* form of the verbs below.

talk   be   buy   make   lend   pass   send   watch

1 He promised _____ me a text message as soon as his plane arrived.
2 If you suffer from claustrophobia, you can't stand _____ in small spaces.
3 Sam is very talkative. She carries on _____ even when no one is listening to her!
4 Harry is very funny. He can't help _____ jokes all the time!
5 Liam is working hard. He expects _____ all his exams in the summer.
6 I don't really fancy _____ TV this evening.
7 John is so mean! He refused _____ me £1 for a coffee!
8 My grandparents offered _____ me a computer, which was very generous of them.

>>> GRAMMAR BUILDER 1D: PAGE 104 <<<

7 Complete the sentences. Use the infinitive or -*ing* form and true information about yourself.

1 I usually avoid …	**6** I sometimes pretend …
2 I really can't stand …	**7** I never look forward to …
3 I don't mind …	**8** I can't help …
4 I spend a lot of time …	**9** I often decide …
5 I really want …	**10** I never agree …

8 **SPEAKING** Work in pairs. Read your sentences to your partner. Does he/she have any similar sentences?

1 🎧 1.08 **VOCABULARY** Listen and match the music extracts with six of the musical styles below.

blues   classical   country and western
heavy metal   indie   jazz   pop   R&B   rap
reggae   rock 'n' roll   soul

2 **SPEAKING** Look at the photos. What kind of music do you think these people listen to? What type of personality do you think they have? Use the adjectives below to help you.

arrogant   confident   friendly   funny   generous
hard-working   impatient   lazy   modest   polite
quiet   rude   serious   shy   talkative   unfriendly

> I think the person in photo 1 listens to … I think he's probably …

3 🎧 1.09 Read the article. Compare the results of the research with your ideas from exercise 2.

WHAT DOES YOUR MUSICAL TASTE SAY ABOUT YOU?

A ☐ We often have stereotypical images of rockers as rebellious, classical music fans as quiet and modest, and lovers of rap as talkative and outgoing. But is it really true that our musical tastes show our personality? According to recent research from a university in Edinburgh, it is.

B ☐ Professor North, who did the research, says that people often express their identity through the kind of music they listen to, the kind of clothes they wear and their hobbies and interests. So it isn't surprising that people's taste in music says something about their personality.

C ☐ The researchers interviewed more than 36,000 people from around the world, asked them about their musical tastes and gave them personality tests. But did the research show that our stereotypical images are right? Here are some of the results:

- Lovers of indie music aren't very confident, gentle or hard-working, but they are very creative.
- Country and western fans are hard-working and not shy.
- Rap fans are outgoing and confident.
- Fans of pop songs aren't creative, but are hard-working, gentle and outgoing.
- The best fan to be is a soul fan, because they are creative, confident, outgoing and gentle!

D ☐ Perhaps the most surprising result was that classical music fans and heavy metal fans have very similar personalities. People think of heavy metal fans as being very sad and unhappy. But like classical fans, they are in fact easy-going and creative, and not very outgoing.

E ☐ Professor North says that the results explain why so many people are good friends with people who like the same music. Heavy metal fans in Sweden have more in common with heavy metal fans in Brazil than with, say, Swedish fans of pop.

F ☐ The results also explain why some of us are so passionate about what we listen to, since music is likely to be closely linked to our personality. However, the research doesn't say what people who listen to lots of different types of music are like. Perhaps they are perfectly balanced! So, what does your music say about you?

4 Match paragraphs A–F in the article with sentences 1–7. There is one sentence that you do not need.

1 The research described the personalities of groups of music fans.
2 One result from the research was very unexpected.
3 Are our traditional images of music fans true?
4 We like to make friends with people who enjoy the same music as us.
5 Music can change your personality in many ways.
6 There are lots of different things that show our personality.
7 We have very strong feelings about the kind of music we like and don't like.

5 **VOCABULARY** Match the highlighted adjectives in the text with the definitions below.

1 has a good imagination and can make new things
2 very friendly and interested in other people
3 calm and relaxed; not easily worried
4 not doing what your parents, teachers, etc. want you to do
5 having very strong feelings
6 kind and calm

6 🎧 1.10 Listen to the song. What is the musical style?

7 🎧 1.10 Listen again and complete the song with the words below.

despair   dreams   explosion (x2)   eyes   love   robot
romance   shoulders (x2)   tunes

8 **SPEAKING** Work in pairs. Discuss the questions.

1 What kind of music do you like, and do you think it shows your personality?
2 Do you have lots of friends with the same musical tastes as you?
3 In which of these ways do you show your personality? Can you give examples?

clothes   music   language   hobbies and interests
places you go in your free time

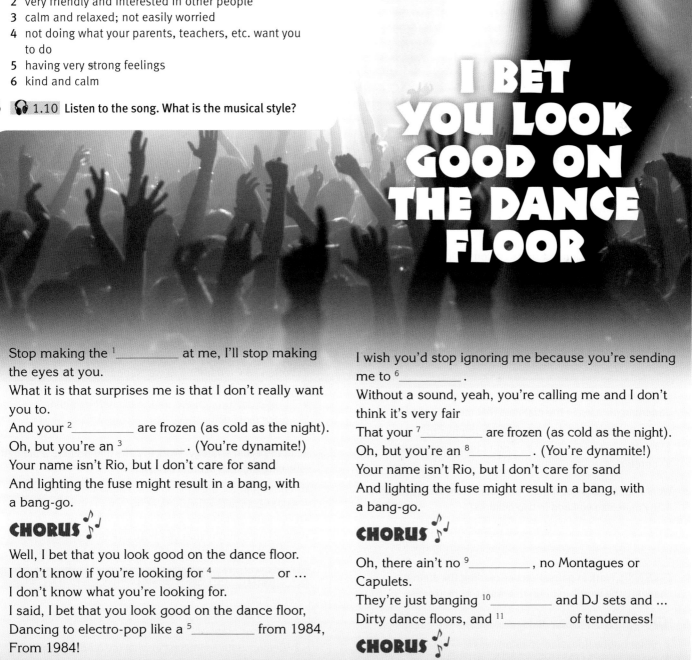

I BET YOU LOOK GOOD ON THE DANCE FLOOR

Stop making the ¹_____ at me, I'll stop making the eyes at you.
What it is that surprises me is that I don't really want you to.
And your ²_____ are frozen (as cold as the night).
Oh, but you're an ³_____ . (You're dynamite!)
Your name isn't Rio, but I don't care for sand
And lighting the fuse might result in a bang, with a bang-go.

CHORUS 🎵

Well, I bet that you look good on the dance floor.
I don't know if you're looking for ⁴_____ or …
I don't know what you're looking for.
I said, I bet that you look good on the dance floor,
Dancing to electro-pop like a ⁵_____ from 1984,
From 1984!

I wish you'd stop ignoring me because you're sending me to ⁶_____ .
Without a sound, yeah, you're calling me and I don't think it's very fair
That your ⁷_____ are frozen (as cold as the night).
Oh, but you're an ⁸_____ . (You're dynamite!)
Your name isn't Rio, but I don't care for sand
And lighting the fuse might result in a bang, with a bang-go.

CHORUS 🎵

Oh, there ain't no ⁹_____ , no Montagues or Capulets.
They're just banging ¹⁰_____ and DJ sets and …
Dirty dance floors, and ¹¹_____ of tenderness!

CHORUS 🎵

I can exchange information about hobbies.

1 🎧 1.11 Read and listen to the dialogue. Are Beth and Jamie good friends? How do you know?

Beth So, what do you like doing in your free time, Jamie?

Jamie I love playing sport. How about you?

Beth Oh, I can't stand playing sport. I prefer watching TV.

Jamie Really? I'm not that keen on watching TV. I'd rather chat to my friends online. What else do you like doing?

Beth I quite like drawing. And I enjoy going to the cinema.

Jamie Me too! Do you fancy going to the cinema this evening?

Beth Yeah – sounds good!

2 Underline phrases in the dialogue that mean:

1 I really like …
2 I hate …
3 I prefer …
4 Would you like to … ?
5 I don't like … very much

3 Work in pairs. Look at the list of hobbies and interests. How many more can you add in two minutes?

dancing   eating out   listening to music   playing chess
playing computer games   shopping   surfing the Net

4 SPEAKING Work in pairs. Practise reading the dialogue, changing the words in blue. Use words from exercise 3.

5 🎧 1.12 Listen to four dialogues. Answer the questions.

1 What hobby does each pair discuss?
2 Which pairs of speakers make a social arrangement?

6 🎧 1.13 Complete the sentences with the words below. Listen again and check.

absolutely   a bit   big   fan   fond   into   much

1 I'm not really a _____ .
2 I _____ prefer war films.
3 I'm a _____ fan of YouTube.
4 I _____ love blogs.
5 I think the lives of celebrities are _____ boring.
6 I'm _____ of reading.
7 I'm really _____ sci-fi books.

7 Put the words in the correct order to make questions. Then ask and answer in pairs.

1 into / what / you / are / ?
2 like / do / at / doing / weekends / what / you / ?
3 you / do / what / doing / like / else / ?
4 Take That / do / you / of / what / think / ?
5 you / into / are / films / of / kind / what / ?

8 🎧 1.14 **PRONUNCIATION** Read the speaking strategy. Then listen to eight dialogues and repeat the replies. Try to copy the intonation.

SPEAKING STRATEGY

In a conversation, react to what the other person says using phrases such as:
That's interesting!   Really?   Cool!   No way! Me too!
Me neither.   Do you?   Wow! Are you?   Can you?

9 SPEAKING Work in pairs. Take turns to say and react to the sentences.

1 I'm not really into heavy metal.
2 I often go windsurfing at weekends.
3 I can't stand chocolate.
4 I prefer chatting on the phone to chatting online.
5 I quite like gymnastics.

10 Read the exam strategy. Work in pairs and prepare a dialogue following the instructions below.

You have met for the first time in a new class at school.
• Ask and answer questions about your hobbies.
• Give your opinion on your partner's hobbies.
• Agree on a hobby that you both like doing.
• Suggest meeting this weekend to do the hobby together.

EXAM STRATEGY

Remember!
1 When you talk about what you like and dislike, use different phrases.
2 Demonstrate an interest in what the other person says.

11 SPEAKING Act out your dialogue to the class.

1 Read the profiles. Which information do *both* of the profiles contain? Tick the boxes.

1 their home town ☐
2 their personality ☐
3 the type of people they like ☐
4 the type of people they don't like ☐
5 their hobbies ☐
6 their ambitions ☐

Ross

My name is Ross. I'm 17 years old and I live in Boston in the USA. I'm quite a friendly person and rather sensitive. At least I think so! My friends say I'm sometimes slightly impatient and I can be a bit lazy about schoolwork! I like being around really confident people and also people who share the same interests as me. I enjoy outdoor activities. I do a lot of surfing and swimming, and a bit of rock-climbing too.

Abigail

Hi! I'm Abigail. I'm 16 years old and my home is in San Diego, California. I'm pretty hard-working and very loyal. I get on well with funny people. I'm quite an ambitious person: I want to study medicine at university. I'm not very tolerant of lazy people. I'm interested in books and I spend a lot of time reading. My hobbies are chess and computer games, and I'm crazy about rock music.

2 **SPEAKING** Work in pairs. What do you have in common with Ross and/or Abigail? Tell your partner.

> I'm the same age as Ross.

> I'm hardworking, like Abigail.

3 **VOCABULARY** Underline the personality adjectives in the profiles. Are they positive or negative?

4 Complete the phrases for talking about hobbies and interests. Use the words below.

do   enjoy   hobbies   interested   crazy

1 I'm _____ in …
2 I _____ …
3 I'm _____ about …
4 I _____ a bit of / a lot of …
5 My _____ are …

5 Find a phrase in each profile that means '*I like to be with*'.

6 Read the *Learn this!* box. Circle all the modifying adverbs in the profiles. Translate them.

Modifying adverbs
We use modifying adverbs to make the meaning of adjectives stronger or weaker.
very   slightly   a bit (informal)   *quite   pretty   rather*
It can sound too negative in English to use 'not' with an adjective, so we often use 'not very' instead – but the meaning is the same as 'not'.
He's not very friendly. (= He's not friendly.)

7 Look at the modifying adverbs in the profiles in exercise 1. Choose the correct words in the rules.

1 Modifying adverbs usually go **before** / **after** the adjective.
2 The modifying adverb **quite** / **very** goes before *a/an* when there is a noun.
3 *a bit* and *slightly* are used with adjectives with a **positive** / **negative** meaning.

8 Add the modifying adverbs in brackets to the sentences.

1 I'm creative. I'm ambitious. (pretty / not very)
2 My best friend is confident but impatient. (rather / a bit)
3 My brother is serious and shy. (pretty / slightly)
4 He's a friendly person, but he's arrogant. (very / a bit)
5 She's an honest person. She's sensitive. (quite / not very)

9 Write a personal profile about yourself. Include:

• basic information about yourself (name, age, etc.).
• some information about your personality.
• what type of people you like and/or don't like.
• information about your hobbies and interests.

CHECK YOUR WORK

Have you:
☐ included the information in the task in exercise 9?
☐ used some modifying adverbs?
☐ checked your spelling and grammar?

Speaking

1 **Get ready to SPEAK** Match 1–5 with A–E to make true sentences about the photo.

1 The girl on the left
2 The girl on the right
3 The group of people in the foreground
4 The girls in the middle
5 The boy in the background

A is wearing a red top.
B are smiling.
C is wearing a pink top.
D is wearing a green and white striped T-shirt.
E are sitting on a sofa.

2 🎧 1.15 Listen to Maria describing the photo. Complete the sentences with the words below.

guess look perhaps shows sure think view

1 I _____ they are in a café or maybe a hotel.
2 I _____ that they are about seventeen or eighteen years old.
3 The photo _____ them chatting and smiling.
4 In my _____ they are friends because they _____ very relaxed and they are laughing.
5 I'm not _____ why they are so happy.
6 _____ they are celebrating a special occasion, like a birthday.

3 Do the exam task.

SPEAKING exam task

Describe the photo in exercise 1 and answer the questions.

1 How do you think the people in the picture are feeling? What makes you think this?
2 What other sorts of activities do young people do with their friends to relax?
3 Tell us about the last time you were out with your friends.

Listening

4 🎧 1.16 Do the exam task.

LISTENING exam task

Listen to six people introducing themselves. Complete the table.

	Age	Country	Hobbies
Laura			
Martin			
Emre			
Lottie			
Greg			
Brigitta			

Use of English

5 Do the exam task.

USE OF ENGLISH exam task

Complete the text. Use one word only for each gap.

My name's Harriet. I'm seventeen years [1]_____ .
I spend a lot [2]_____ time reading magazines, and I'm very interested [3]_____ photography. My best friend is Zoe. She's [4]_____ the same class as me at school. We always sit [5]_____ to each other. She's very friendly and she always helps me [6]_____ my homework. There [7]_____ four people in my family: my mum, my dad, my brother [8]_____ me. My brother's name [9]_____ George. [10]_____ main hobby is listening [11]_____ music, and he's also a [12]_____ fan of computer games.

Get Ready for your Exam

Reading

6 `Get ready to READ` Work in pairs. Ask and answer the questions.

1 Do you like being on your own? Why?/Why not?
2 Do you think animals make good friends? Why?/Why not?

7 Check the meaning of the adjectives. Then find six pairs with opposite meanings.

afraid alive brave bright dark dead exciting
friendly terrible uninteresting unkind wonderful

8 Do the exam task.

READING exam task

Read the text. Decide if the sentences (1–6) are true (T) or false (F). Put ✗ in the appropriate space in the table.

Conradin was ten years old and was often ill.

'The boy is not strong,' said the doctor. 'He will not live much longer.' But the doctor did not know about Conradin's imagination. In Conradin's lonely, loveless world, his imagination was the only thing that kept him alive.

Conradin's parents were dead and he lived with his aunt. The aunt did not like Conradin and was often unkind to him. Conradin hated her with all his heart, but he obeyed her quietly and took his medicine without arguing. Mostly he kept out of her way. She had no place in his world. His real, everyday life in his aunt's colourless, comfortless house was narrow and uninteresting. But inside his small, dark head exciting and violent thoughts ran wild. In the bright world of his imagination Conradin was strong and brave. It was a wonderful world, and the aunt was locked out of it.

The garden was no fun. There was nothing interesting to do. He was forbidden to pick the flowers. He was forbidden to eat the fruit. He was forbidden to play on the grass. But behind some trees, in a forgotten corner of the garden, there was an old shed.

Nobody used the shed, and Conradin took it for his own. To him it became something between a playroom and a church. He filled it with ghosts and animals from his imagination. But there were also two living things in the shed. In one corner lived an old, untidy-looking chicken. Conradin had no people to love, and this chicken was the boy's dearest friend. And in a dark, secret place at the back of the shed was a large wooden box with bars across the front. This was the home of a very large ferret with long, dangerous teeth and claws. Conradin had bought the ferret and its box from the friendly boy who lived in the village.

It cost him all his money but Conradin did not mind. He was most terribly afraid of the ferret, but he loved it with all his heart. *Sredni Vashtar* by Saki

	T	F
1 Conradin's health was very poor.		
2 The boy had a good relationship with his aunt.		
3 The boy was not allowed to play in the garden.		
4 A lot of animals lived in the shed.		
5 The ferret was a gift from Conradin's friend.		
6 The text is about a boy who uses his imagination to escape from the real world.		

Speaking

9 `Get ready to SPEAK` Work in pairs. Ask and answer the questions.

1 What do you like doing in your free time?
2 What places do you like going to with your friends?

10 Read the speaking exam task in exercise 12.

11 🎧 1.17 Listen to a student doing the exam task. Complete the sentences with the words below.

don't fancy let's prefer really shall sounds want

1 Do you _____ doing something on Saturday?
2 Why _____ we go out?
3 I'm _____ not into heavy metal.
4 OK, then. _____ go and see his band.
5 _____ we invite Jack and Martha?
6 I'd _____ to go with just you, really.
7 And what do you _____ to do after the concert?
8 OK, then. _____ good.

12 Now do the exam task.

SPEAKING exam task

You and your friend are going to a concert next Saturday. Discuss the details of the trip. Include information about the following points:

• Your preferences about kinds of music
• The cost of the tickets
• The possibility of bringing other friends with you
• Plans after the concert

THIS UNIT INCLUDES

Vocabulary ▪ sports ▪ *play/go/do* + sport ▪ collocations: sports and games ▪ free-time activities ▪ sports equipment
Grammar ▪ past simple ▪ contrast: past simple and past continuous
Speaking ▪ talking about favourite sports ▪ talking about the past ▪ narrating a story
Writing ▪ an informal thank-you letter

2A VOCABULARY AND LISTENING A question of sport

I can talk about sports I like.

1 Look at the photos. Can you name these sportspeople and their sports?

2 🎧 1.18 Match the icons (1–18) with the words below. Then listen, repeat and check.

<u>Sports</u> archery athletics badminton baseball basketball boxing cricket fencing ice hockey karate netball rowing ski jumping snowboarding surfing volleyball wrestling weightlifting

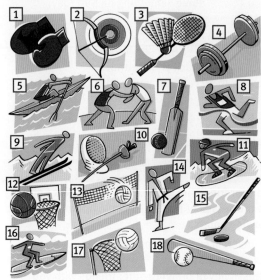

3 Work in pairs. Put the sports from exercise 2 into these groups. Some sports can go in more than one group.

A winter sports
B combat sports
C team sports
D indoor sports
E outdoor sports

4 In pairs, add more sports to the groups in exercise 3. Then compare answers with the class. Who has added the most?

5 Read the *Learn this!* box. Then match the sports from exercise 2 with the correct verb (*play*, *go* or *do*).

▶▶▶ **VOCABULARY BUILDER (PART 1): PAGE 125** ◀◀◀

LEARN THIS!

We normally use:
play with team sports and ball sports.
play badminton
go with sports ending in *-ing*.
go cycling
do with individual sports not ending in *-ing*.
do gymnastics
Note: We use *do* with combat sports even if they end in *-ing*.
do karate, do boxing

6 🎧 1.19 Listen to eight commentaries and identify the sports. Choose from the sports in exercise 2.

7 SPEAKING Work in pairs. Ask and answer the questions.

1 Which sports do you enjoy watching? Who are your favourite players and teams?
2 Which sports do you enjoy doing? When do you do them?
3 Which sports do you find boring? Can you explain why?

▶▶▶ **VOCABULARY BUILDER (PART 2): PAGE 125** ◀◀◀

1 Read the text and choose the correct answers.

1 Aldermaston FC **won** / **lost** every match between May 2009 and March 2010.

2 Aldermaston **won** / **lost** / **drew** the match against Warminster.

Some people call AFC Aldermaston the worst football team in Britain. Between May 2009 and March 2010 they didn't win a single match. In fact, they lost 40 matches in a row. Then, on 12th April 2010, they played Warminster Town. They were desperate to win – and they scored in the first half! The fans went wild! Did they win the match? No, they didn't. Unfortunately, Warminster equalised in the second half, and it was a 1–1 draw. But at least Aldermaston didn't lose again!

2 Underline the following past simple forms in the text.

1 three affirmative regular verbs

2 two forms of *be* (one singular and one plural)

3 two affirmative irregular verbs

4 two negative forms and an interrogative form

3 Complete the table with the correct past simple form of *play*, *go* or *do*.

Past simple
affirmative
I ¹_____ volleyball in the park last Sunday.
We ²_____ swimming yesterday.
negative
My brother ³_____ karate at school last year.
interrogative
⁴_____ they ⁵_____ skiing in the mountains?

LOOK OUT!

We don't use *did* or *didn't* with the past simple negative and interrogative form of *be*.

Fred wasn't at the match. Were you?

⟫⟫ GRAMMAR BUILDER 2B: PAGE 106 ⟪⟪

4 🎧 1.20 PRONUNCIATION Listen and repeat the past simple forms. How is the *-ed* ending pronounced? Write the correct sound next to each verb: /d/, /t/ or /ɪd/.

1 played _/d/_   5 scored _____

2 expected _____   6 voted _____

3 finished _____   7 faced _____

4 stopped _____   8 watched _____

5 🎧 1.21 Complete the text. Use the past simple form of the verbs in brackets. Then listen and check.

The tortoise and the hare?

In 2001, 22-year-old Trevor Misipeka _arrived_ (arrive) at Edmonton in Canada to compete in the World Athletics Championship. He ¹_____ (want) to take part in the shot put, but a new rule ²_____ (make) this impossible. Two days before the competition, he ³_____ (have) to find a new event! He ⁴_____ (decide) on the 100 metres, because the new rule ⁵_____ (not apply) to running.

At 135 kilos, he ⁶_____ (not have) the body of a sprinter, but he ⁷_____ (try) his best. So how ⁸_____ he _____ (do)? Well, unfortunately, Trevor didn't win. In fact, he ⁹_____ (come) last. The newspapers ¹⁰_____ (give) him a nickname: Trevor the Tortoise. But he ¹¹_____ (not be) sad about his time of 14.28 seconds. 'That's my personal best,' he ¹²_____ (say).

6 Complete the questions about the story.

1 Where _____ take place in 2001?

In Edmonton, Canada.

2 Which event _____ to do?

The shot put.

3 Why _____ to find a new event?

Because of a new rule.

4 Which event _____ to do?

The 100 metres.

5 _____ the race?

No, he didn't.

6 _____ about his time of 14:28?

No, he wasn't.

7 Write two true sentences and one false sentence about what you did last weekend.

I played basketball in the park with my sister.

8 SPEAKING Tell the class your sentences. The class votes on which sentence they think is false.

1 SPEAKING Look at the photo. How would you describe this sport?

a messy   b cold   c slow   d tiring

2 🎧 1.22 Read the text. Is bog snorkelling only popular with British people?

DARK, COLD AND SCARY

The British seem to enjoy unusual sports more than most other nationalities. But the Bog Snorkelling Championship is one of the strangest. It takes place every year in Wales. The competitors have to swim 110 metres through cold, dark, muddy water – without using their arms! And they have to keep their faces in the water at all times, breathing through a snorkel.

Who would want to compete in a horrible event like that? Well, in fact more than 100 people enter it each year, many of them from other countries. Dan Morgan from Wales is the current champion. He finished the course in 1 minute 30 seconds – a world record.

Is bog snorkelling really so nasty? Sheelagh Tompkins, the woman who started the tournament, says yes. 'It's dark and you can't see, and that's scary.' So why do the British enjoy such unusual sports? Perhaps it's because we have a chance of winning!

3 VOCABULARY Match the highlighted words in the text with the definitions below.

1 to take part (in a competition)
2 a sports competition
3 the winner of a competition or event
4 the best time (distance, score, etc.) ever
5 the route of a race
6 people who take part in an event

4 Read the text again. Answer the questions.

1 Where does the competition take place?
2 How far do the competitors have to swim?
3 How many competitors enter each year?
4 What is the fastest ever time?
5 Who started the competition?
6 Why is it frightening, according to Sheelagh Tompkins?

5 🎧 1.23 Listen to the radio programme. Do you believe that this event can be exciting? Why?/Why not?

6 🎧 1.23 Listen again and choose the correct answers.

1 People in Congham are excited because the World Snail Racing Championship
 a is starting soon.
 b is taking place there for the first time.
 c includes competitors from different countries.

2 Which is the correct track: a, b or c?

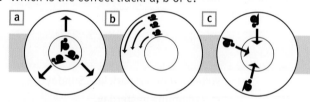

3 What is the name of the fastest snail ever?
 a Flash   b Archie   c Speedy

4 How has Jack tried to prepare his snail for the race?
 a by giving the snail a good name
 b by spending a lot of time with his snail
 c by trying to keep his snail happy

5 How does Flash do in the race?
 a He wins.   b He nearly wins.   c He comes last.

7 SPEAKING Work in pairs. Cover the text and describe the photo in exercise 1.

8 PROJECT Work in groups. Find information about an unusual sporting event in your own country or abroad. Make notes about:

• where the event takes place and when/how often.
• what the name of event is and what happens at the event.
• whether you would like to take part in the event and why/why not.

9 SPEAKING Present the information you found to the class.

1 Read the text. What is unusual about this team photo?

Karl Power

In 2001, Manchester United were preparing for a Champions League football match. The sun was shining and the crowd were cheering. While a photographer was taking a photo of the team, a strange thing happened. A man walked onto the pitch and joined them. The players weren't looking and didn't say anything. He was wearing the Manchester United kit, but he wasn't a player. Who was he? Why was he standing with the team? Eventually, the truth came out: the man was a practical joker called Karl Power.

2 Look at the past continuous forms in the text. Then complete the table with the correct form of the verb *be*.

Past continuous
affirmative
I ¹_____ reading. We ²_____ listening.
negative
It ³_____ snowing. They ⁴_____ playing.
interrogative
⁵_____ you sleeping? What ⁶_____ he doing?

3 Read the *Learn this!* box. Find one example of the uses 1–3 in the text in exercise 1.

LEARN THIS!

1 We use the **past continuous** to describe a scene in the past.
   It was raining. The wind was blowing.
2 We use the **past simple** for a sequence of actions or events that happened one after the other.
   I sat down, opened my book and started to read.
3 We use the **past continuous** and the **past simple** together to describe a sudden event that interrupted a longer one.
   While I was having lunch, my cousin phoned.
        ↑   ↑
   longer action   interruption
4 We use the **past continuous** to describe an event that was in progress at a specific moment in the past.
   At 7.30 this morning, I was waiting for the bus.

⟫⟫⟫ **GRAMMAR BUILDER 2D: PAGE 106** ⟪⟪⟪

4 🎧 1.24 Complete the text. Use the past simple or past continuous form of the verbs in brackets. Then listen and check.

In 1904, in the middle of a summer afternoon, Fred Lorz *was running* (run) the Olympic marathon. The sun ¹_____ (shine) and it was very hot. Nine miles into the race, Fred ²_____ (feel) tired, so he ³_____ (decide) to stop. While he ⁴_____ (sit) next to the road, his manager ⁵_____ (drive) past, ⁶_____ (stop) his car, and Lorz ⁷_____ (get) in. But eleven miles later, the car ⁸_____ (break) down, so Lorz ⁹_____ (start) running again. He ¹⁰_____ (come) first in the race, but while he ¹¹_____ (get) his gold medal, a spectator ¹²_____ (complain). Lorz ¹³_____ (give) back the medal immediately, and said 'It ¹⁴_____ (be) just a joke!'

5 Look at the cartoon story and answer the questions. Use the words in brackets to help you.

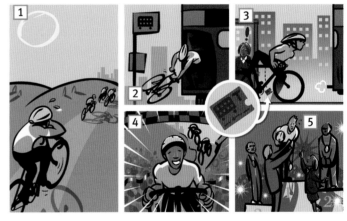

1 What was the weather like? (the sun / shine, hot) What was the cyclist doing? (compete / in a race, lose)
2 Where did the cyclist go? (a bus stop) What did the bus do? (stop) What did the cyclist do? (get on)
3 What was the cyclist doing? (get off the bus) What did he drop? (ticket) Who saw him? (a girl)
4 Who finished the course first? (the cheat) What were the crowd doing? (cheer)
5 What was the man getting? (a medal) What did the girl give him? (a bus ticket)

6 SPEAKING Work in pairs. Look at the cartoon story again for one more minute. Close your books and tell the story to your partner. Use the past simple and past continuous.

The sun was shining. It was a hot day. A cyclist was ...

1 Read the exam strategy. Look at the photos and the title of the text. What do you think happened to Bethany Hamilton?

EXAM STRATEGY

In order to get an idea of what the text is about, read the title and the first few lines of text.

2 🎧 1.25 Read the first three paragraphs and check your ideas.

3 Read the text. Put the events in the correct order.

a ☐ The shark swam away.

b ☐ Ten weeks later she took part in a surfing competition.

c ☐ She started to swim back to the beach.

d ☐ Bethany decided to go surfing with some friends.

e ☐ Her friends saw the blood and came to help her.

f ☐ While she was waiting for a wave, a shark attacked her.

Surfing superstar!

On the morning of 31 October 2003, Bethany Hamilton and some friends decided to go surfing. The sky was clear, the sun was shining and it was a perfect day for enjoying the big waves near the island of
5 Kauai, Hawaii.

The 13-year-old surfing star was lying sideways on her surfboard about 300 metres from the shore with her left arm in the clear, blue water. Her friends were floating nearby, looking out to sea. They were all
10 waiting for the next big wave.

Suddenly a five-metre tiger shark appeared just below the surface and attacked her. It bit her left arm and shook her violently backwards and forwards. Bethany saw the water around her turn red. She held on to
15 her board and the shark swam away – but it took her arm with it. It also took a piece of her board. Luckily for Bethany, the shark attacked only once. It all happened so fast that she didn't even scream.

In her mind, Bethany repeated: 'Get to the beach.
20 Get to the beach.' She started to paddle towards it with one arm. Her friends didn't know about the shark attack – they thought at first that she was joking. Then they saw the blood and quickly came to help. It took fifteen minutes to reach the shore.
25 They called the emergency services and Bethany eventually got to hospital.

Bethany's parents are both keen surfers. As a baby, Bethany liked to splash in the shallow water. She started surfing at the age of five. By thirteen, she was
30 one of the best teenage surfers in the world, and was planning to become a professional surfer. Then the shark attack happened.

The really incredible thing about Bethany is that only ten weeks later she was surfing again in a
35 competition. Less than a year after the accident she won first place in a surfing competition in Hawaii. Before the accident, a lot of professional surfers thought that Bethany was going to be the women's world champion one day. After the accident, they
40 haven't changed their minds.

4 Are the sentences true or false? Correct the false sentences.

1 Bethany was standing on her surfboard when the shark attacked her.
2 Her friends were close to her when the shark bit her.
3 Bethany lost her surfboard in the attack.
4 The shark attacked her again a few minutes later.
5 Immediately after the attack, she wanted to stay in the water.
6 Bethany is not the only person in her family who likes surfing.
7 Ten weeks later, Bethany won a surfing competition.
8 A lot of professional surfers still think Bethany can be a champion surfer.

5 Find the past simple form of these verbs in the text.

1 bite (line 12)
2 shake (line 13)
3 see (line 14)
4 hold (line 14)
5 swim (line 15)
6 take (line 15)
7 think (line 22)
8 come (line 23)
9 win (line 36)

6 **VOCABULARY** Find these words highlighted in the text. Are they nouns or verbs? Write *n* or *v* next to each word.

shore   floating   wave   surface   paddle   splash

7 Complete the sentences. Use the correct form of the words in exercise 6.

1 I hate going swimming with my brothers – they always _____ me!
2 The east coast is not good for surfing because the _____ are too small.
3 You need to lie on the surfboard and _____ with your hands.
4 We stood on the _____ and watched the boats go past.
5 An empty canoe was _____ down the river.
6 She accidentally dropped her phone into the river and watched it disappear below the _____ .

8 Work in pairs. Prepare an interview with Bethany.

Student A: You are the interviewer. Prepare five questions for Bethany using the prompts below.

Student B: You are Bethany. Prepare your answers to the questions below using the information in the text and your own words.

1 what / weather / like / 31 October 2003?
2 what / you / doing / when / shark / attack?
3 what / your friends / do?
4 how important / surfing / in your life / before shark attack?
5 how important / surfing / in your life / now?

9 **SPEAKING** Work in pairs. Act out your interview to the class.

What was the weather like on 31 October 2003?

1 🎧 1.26 Listen and complete the dialogue with the words below. Where were Amy and Finlay on Sunday?

go   play   see   what   what   where

Finlay	Hi Amy. How was your weekend?
Amy	It was good. I went to the cinema on Saturday.
Finlay	¹_____ did you ²_____ ?
Amy	The new Ben Stiller film.
Finlay	Cool. What did you do on Sunday?
Amy	Nothing much. I stayed at home and revised. What about you? What did you get up to at the weekend?
Finlay	I went out with some friends on Saturday.
Amy	³_____ did you ⁴_____ ?
Finlay	To the skate park.
Amy	No way! What about on Sunday?
Finlay	I played computer games at home.
Amy	⁵_____ did you ⁶_____ ?
Finlay	*BioShock*. It was great!

2 SPEAKING Work in pairs. Practise reading the dialogue, changing the words in blue. Use your own ideas.

3 Find two phrases in the dialogue for reacting with interest (see page 10).

4 🎧 1.27 Listen to four teenagers talking about their weekends and answer the questions. Write *Ella*, *Abi*, *Daisy* or *Chloe*.

a Who made something? _____
b Who celebrated something? _____
c Who broke something? _____
d Who lost something? _____

SPEAKING STRATEGY

When you ask someone about what they did or what happened, ask follow-up questions to find out more information and to keep the conversation going.
A *What did you do last night?*
B *I phoned a friend.*
A *Really? Who did you phone?*

5 🎧 1.27 Read the speaking strategy. Then listen again and complete the follow-up questions.

1 Who _____ you play _____ ?
2 Did _____ _____ ?
3 _____ did you _____ ?
4 Do you _____ go out for _____ ?
5 What _____ you _____ ?
6 Did you _____ and find it?
7 _____ did _____ make?
8 _____ was it?

LOOK OUT!

When a *Wh-* question includes a preposition, the preposition usually goes at the end.
Who did you go with?   What did you listen to?

6 Read the *Look out!* box. Which follow-up question in exercise 5 ends with a preposition?

7 Work in pairs. Choose three different activities each and write a sentence about each one using the past simple.

I cooked dinner for my family last night.

Free-time activities   cook dinner
go away for the weekend   go bowling/dancing
go to a party/theme park   have a barbecue
play volleyball   see a show   visit relatives

8 Look at your partner's sentences and write one or two follow-up questions for each one. Do not show your partner.

9 SPEAKING Work in pairs. Take turns to be A and B.
Student A: Read one of your sentences from exercise 7.
Student B: Ask your follow-up question(s) from exercise 8.
Student A: Answer your partner's follow-up question(s).

I cooked dinner for my family last night.

Really? What did you make?

Spaghetti Bolognese.

10 Work in pairs. Prepare a dialogue about what you did last weekend. Use follow-up questions and phrases for reacting with interest. Include the following information:
• Say what you did on Saturday and Sunday.
• Say where you went and who you were with.
• Say whether you enjoyed it.

11 SPEAKING Act out your dialogue to the class.

I can write an informal thank-you letter.

1 Read the letter. What two birthday presents did Connor get? Choose from the items in the photos below.

weights

badminton net

bowling ball

baseball bat   tennis racket

12 Westfield Drive
Bromley BR13 6TF
21st August 2012

Dear Uncle Harry,
I hope you are well. Thanks so much for the presents
you sent me for my birthday. I love them – they're
brilliant! When I was opening them I thought they were
bowling balls. I'm glad that they weren't! I use them
every day before school and I reckon I'm stronger
already. My dad told me that using weights is a good
way to get fit too. Maybe you should buy some for him!

I really enjoyed my birthday. We had a barbecue in
the garden and loads of friends came round. It was a
laugh! My best mate gave me a baseball bat. We don't
play baseball at school, but there are teams at the
local gym.

See you soon, I hope. And thanks again for the weights.

Lots of love,
Connor

PS Mum and Dad send their love too.

2 Find informal words and phrases in the letter that mean:

1 thank you   4 lots of
2 very good   5 fun
3 I think   6 best friend

3 Rewrite these sentences in a more informal style.

1 I think my best friend is fun.
2 Thank you for the book. It's very good.
3 I got lots of very good presents for my birthday.
4 I think there are lots of very good places to visit near here.
5 Thank you for inviting me to your party. It was fun!

4 Put what Connor says in the correct paragraph in the chart below, and in the correct order.

a He says he enjoyed his birthday.
b He says what one of his friends gave him.
c He thanks his uncle for the present.
d He says what he did on his birthday.
e He thanks his uncle again for the present.
f He gives his opinion of his uncle's present.
g He says when he uses his uncle's present.

Paragraph 1	Paragraph 2	Paragraph 3
1 _____	4 _____	7 _____
2 _____	5 _____	
3 _____	6 _____	

WRITING STRATEGY

An informal letter
1 Begin with *Dear* then add the name of the recipient.
2 Ask how the person you are writing to is or express your hope that he/she is well e.g. *How are you?* or *I hope you are well.*
3 You are allowed to use short forms (e.g. *it's*, *you're*, *I'll*) and colloquial expressions.
4 Put one of the following expressions at the end of the letter: *Love, Lots of love, Best wishes, Bye for now.* Then sign it with your name.
5 If, after having finished the letter, you need to add something, do it in post scriptum. Start a new paragraph with *PS*.

5 Read the writing strategy. Answer the questions about Connor's letter.

1 What phrases does he use to open and close his letter?
2 Which four different contractions does he use?
3 What information does he add after his name?

6 You have just received a birthday present in the post from your English friend. Write a letter (120–150 words) to your friend.

• Thank your friend for the gift.
• Say why you like the gift and how you use it.
• Say what happened on your birthday.
• Tell your friend what other presents you received.

CHECK YOUR WORK

Have you:
☐ included the information in the task in exercise 6?
☐ used informal expressions and contractions?
☐ written 120–150 words?
☐ checked your spelling and grammar?

Unit 1

1 Complete the reactions with the adjectives below.

arrogant generous hard-working impatient mean shy

1 'I'm paying for your ticket.' 'Thanks, that's _____ .'
2 'Hurry up! It's nearly 7.30!' 'Don't be _____ !'
3 'She looks nice.' 'Don't be _____ . Go and talk to her!'
4 'Gavin is really ugly.' 'No, he isn't. Don't be _____ !'
5 'I'm more intelligent than you.' 'You're very _____ !'
6 'I'm a teacher and I've also got a weekend job.'
   'Wow! You're _____ .'

Mark: ___ /6

2 Solve the anagrams and write the musical styles.

1 RB& _____
2 arp _____
3 roncuty _____
4 ouls _____
5 elbus _____
6 sillacasc _____

Mark: ___ /6

3 Complete the email. Use the present simple or continuous form of the verbs below.

cook do hate have shine write

Hi Jason!
I ¹_____ this email in the garden. The sun ²_____ and it's very warm. It's summer at last! I'm so happy – I ³_____ winter. What about you? What ⁴_____ you _____ ?
We ⁵_____ a barbecue on Saturday. Why don't you come?
Dad always ⁶_____ too much food.

Mark: ___ /6

4 Complete the sentences. Use the infinitive or -ing form of the verbs in brackets.

1 My brother is pretending _____ (be) a footballer.
2 I spend a lot of time _____ (play) computer games.
3 Sarah can't help _____ (be) impatient.
4 We decided _____ (spend) the weekend in London.
5 I don't fancy _____ (walk) home.
6 My dad suggested _____ (have) dinner in a restaurant.

Mark: ___ /6

5 Put the lines of the dialogue in the correct order.

a ☐ I like playing chess. How about you?
b ☐ Me too. Do you fancy a game this weekend?
c ☐ Let's meet in the park at midday.
d ☐ What do you like doing in your free time?
e ☐ Yes. That sounds good. What time?
f ☐ Really? I don't really like chess, but I quite like tennis.

Mark: ___ /6

Total: ___ /30

Unit 2

6 Match 1–6 with a–f to make sports.

1 basket   a lifting
2 ice   b boarding
3 weight   c ball
4 ski   d ball
5 base   e hockey
6 snow   f jumping

Mark: ___ /6

7 Complete the free-time activities with the verbs below.

cook go have play see visit

1 _____ to a party   4 _____ a show
2 _____ relatives   5 _____ a barbecue
3 _____ dinner   6 _____ volleyball

Mark: ___ /6

8 Rewrite the sentences using the affirmative (✓) or interrogative (?) form.

1 She didn't win the race. (✓)
2 I didn't get your email. (✓)
3 You weren't at school yesterday. (?)
4 It didn't snow last winter. (✓)
5 The bus didn't stop in the town centre. (?)
6 They didn't come to my party. (?)

Mark: ___ /6

9 Complete the text. Use the past simple or continuous form of the verbs in brackets.

One afternoon at the races, riders and their horses ¹_____ (get) ready for a race. The conditions were terrible – the sun ²_____ (not shine) and there was thick fog. A few metres after the start, one of the riders suddenly ³_____ (ride) across the middle of the track to the finish line. Why ⁴_____ (he/do) this? It wasn't a mistake: he knew exactly what he ⁵_____ (do)! However, the other riders ⁶_____ (see) him cheating and his prize was a ten-year ban!

Mark: ___ /6

10 Write the missing words to complete the dialogue.

Joe Hi! ¹_____ was your weekend?
Ann It was fine, thanks. I ²_____ shopping on Saturday.
Joe What did you ³_____ ?
Ann A new top. What about ⁴_____ ? What did you get up to?
Joe Nothing ⁵_____ . I played computer games on Sunday.
Ann ⁶_____ did you play with?
Joe A friend in Hong Kong. We played online.

Mark: ___ /6

Total: ___ /30

Lead-in

1 Look at the photo. Would you like to spend a holiday here?

Reading

2 Read the text quickly. What kind of text is it?

a a magazine article   c an informal letter
b a publicity leaflet   d a newspaper report

3 Read the text again. Match paragraphs A–E with headings 1–6. There is one heading that you do not need.

1 Great entertainment   4 Comfortable accommodation
2 An ideal location   5 Keeping fit
3 Food and drink   6 Our team

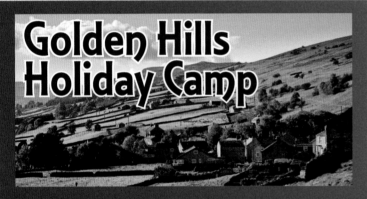

A Golden Hills is a modern, well-equipped holiday camp on the edge of the Yorkshire Dales in the north of England. It's a perfect base for exploring the beautiful scenery of the Dales and for visiting nearby places like Leeds and Harrogate.

B The camp has excellent sports facilities. There is an indoor swimming pool and an outdoor pool (May–September), as well as a gym with regular aerobics classes. And for guests who are looking for a physical challenge, we can help organise activities like rock-climbing and kayaking.

C We provide high-quality entertainment five nights a week, all year round. Every Friday and Saturday night there is a two-hour show from one of the best singers or comedians in the area. On Mondays and Wednesdays, it's karaoke. And Thursday night is quiz night!

D You can buy food and other necessities at the small supermarket next to reception. If you don't fancy cooking, snacks are available all day at the bar, and during the summer months, there is a barbecue every Friday and Saturday evening. Several take-away restaurants in the area will deliver to the camp – ask for details at reception.

E We have twenty full-time members of staff, including a general manager and a deputy manager. They are hard-working, patient and polite, and are happy to deal with questions or problems at any time.

Speaking

4 Read the job advert. Work in pairs. Ask and answer the questions below.

Golden Hills Holiday Camp!
STAFF WANTED

Applicants must be good at dealing with the public. We are particularly interested in employing people who:

* speak foreign languages
* can play and organise sports
* have experience of working in a bar or café
* have computer skills

For details of how to apply, visit **Golden-Hills.com**.

1 What personal qualities do the staff at a holiday camp need? Which of these qualities do you have?
2 Do you think working at a holiday camp would be fun? Why?/Why not?

Listening

5 🎧 1.28 Listen to Anna talking to some employees at Golden Hills Holiday Camp. Tick ✓ the employees (1–6) she talks to or mentions in the chart.

Employee	Talks to?	Mentions?
1 Steve, bar manager		
2 Maggie, general manager		
3 Jack, IT expert		
4 Sue, cleaner		
5 Dani, fitness instructor		
6 Tom, security guard		

6 🎧 1.28 Listen again. Are the sentences true or false?
1 Anna has got a job in the bar.
2 Jack started his job about six months ago.
3 Jack thinks Maggie is lazy.
4 Anna enjoys swimming.
5 The gym is closed on Sundays.
6 Jack never goes to the gym.

Writing

7 Ellie, a student from England, is starting at your school. Write a note welcoming her and giving this information.

* what time lessons start and finish
* what sports or hobbies you can do
* where you can buy food and drink
* what some of the staff are called, and their jobs

3A VOCABULARY AND LISTENING Landscapes

I can describe a place in the town or country.

1 SPEAKING Look at the pictures. Where would you prefer to live? Why?

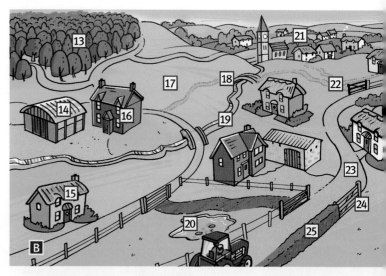

2 🎧 1.29 VOCABULARY Match items 1–25 in the pictures with the words below. Then listen and check.

Urban landscapes

billboard _____   bus stop _____
pavement _____   pedestrian crossing _____
postbox _____   road sign _____
roadworks _____   roundabout _____
rubbish bin _____   street lamp _____
telegraph pole _____   traffic lights _____

Rural landscapes

barn _____   bridge _____
cottage _____   farmhouse _____
field _____   footpath _____
gate _____   hedge _____
lane _____   pond _____
stream _____   village _____
wood _____

3 Label the pictures with the prepositions below.

Prepositions of movement across   over   past   through   along

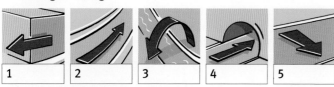

4 🎧 1.30 Listen to a walker asking a farmer for directions. Mark the route on picture B above.

5 🎧 1.30 Listen again. Complete the directions with the words below.

across   along   end   follow   on   onto   past   right   straight   through

1 Go _____ this lane.
2 Go _____ the pond.
3 Go _____ the gate _____ your left.
4 Go _____ the field – just _____ the footpath.
5 Turn right _____ the lane.
6 Then go _____ on.
7 Take the first _____ .
8 Walk to the _____ of the road.

⟫⟫⟫ VOCABULARY BUILDER (PART 1): PAGE 126 ⟪⟪⟪

6 SPEAKING Work in pairs. Take turns to be A and B.

Student A: Give directions to two other places in picture B.
Student B: Follow the directions on the picture.

> Walk across the field to …

⟫⟫⟫ VOCABULARY BUILDER (PART 2): PAGE 126 ⟪⟪⟪

I can talk about quantities.

1 SPEAKING What do you think an eco-town is?

2 Read the advertisement for Greenton. In which paragraph (1–3) can you find out:

a what to do in Greenton?   b what an eco-town is?
c how to get more information?

Move to Greenton

1 Greenton is an 'eco-town' so there aren't any cars in the town centre. There isn't much pollution because everyone cycles or walks. In fact, there aren't many cleaner towns in the world – and there's some beautiful scenery to explore just outside the town too.

2 You'll always be busy in Greenton. There are a lot of cafés and nightclubs, and some great shops. If you don't want to spend any money, why not spend a little time relaxing by the river instead?

3 If you have any questions about Greenton, why not spend a few minutes exploring our website? Or better still, come and visit!

3 Find two examples of *some* and three examples of *any* in the text. Then complete the rules in the *Learn this!* box.

1 We use _____ in affirmative sentences.
2 We use _____ in negative sentences and questions.

4 🎧 1.32 Martin is asking about renting a flat. Complete the dialogue with *some* or *any*. Then listen and check.

Martin   Are there ¹_____ one-bedroom flats to rent in the centre of Greenton?
Agent   Yes, but they're very expensive. There are ²_____ really nice flats just outside the town.
Martin   Have you got ³_____ pictures of them?
Agent   Yes, I have. Look. And the rent isn't high: £500 a month.
Martin   Nice. Are there ⁴_____ shops nearby?
Agent   Yes, there are ⁵_____ shops about 200 metres away.
Martin   Great! I can't see ⁶_____ disadvantages!
Agent   Do you have ⁷_____ pets?
Martin   Well, I've got ⁸_____ fish.
Agent   That's fine. There won't be ⁹_____ problems with fish.

5 Look at the words in blue in the text in exercise 2. Which are plural countable nouns? Which are uncountable nouns?

6 Find *a little, a few, many, much* and *a lot of* in the text in exercise 2. Then complete the table.

With uncountable nouns	With plural countable nouns
a lot of	3 _____
1 _____	4 _____
2 _____	5 _____

LOOK OUT!

We often use *much* and *many* in negative sentences and questions. We don't often use them in affirmative sentences. We use *a lot of* (or *lots of*) in both affirmative and negative sentences.

▶▶▶ GRAMMAR BUILDER 3B: PAGE 108 ◀◀◀

7 Read the notice. Choose the correct words.

One-bedroom flat   £1,100 / month

¹**A few / Much** new one-bedroom flats are now available near the centre of Greenton. These flats all offer ²**a few / a lot of** space, and there are ³**a lot of / a little** good reasons to live in this area. There are ⁴**a few / a little** shops in the same street and ⁵**much / a lot of** shops in the nearby shopping centre. There are ⁶**a lot of / a little** offices in the area, but there aren't ⁷**a few / many** restaurants or nightclubs, so there isn't ⁸**much / many** noise at night.

Come and have a look!

8 PROJECT Work in small groups. Prepare and present a short advertisement for your town or village. Use some of these words: *some, any, much, many, a lot of, a little* and *a few*. You can use the ideas below to help you.

cafés   cinemas   nightclubs   parks   pollution
scenery   shops   traffic

There are a few …   You can find some …

1 **SPEAKING** Describe the photo. What do you think the people are doing?

2 🎧 1.33 Read the text. Match the headings (1–5) with paragraphs A–C. There are two headings that you do not need.

1 A country divided   4 The future of fox hunts
2 A royal sport   5 The history of hunting
3 The end of fox hunts?

3 **VOCABULARY** Find these words highlighted in the text. Use them to complete the sentences below.

ban cruel damage economy illegal law out-dated
respect upper-class

1 You shouldn't hurt animals – it's _____ .
2 In the past, only _____ families could afford to have holidays abroad.
3 My dad doesn't want my sister to become a pilot. He has very _____ views about jobs for women!
4 Tourism is good for a town's _____ . Tourists spend a lot of money!
5 You can't steal things. It's against the _____ .
6 He hit a tree and did a lot of _____ to his car.
7 When you're visiting a foreign country, you should _____ its customs and traditions.
8 It's _____ to drive without a licence.
9 The government is going to _____ smoking in public buildings.

4 🎧 1.34 Listen to four teenagers talking about hunting. Who agrees and who disagrees with the ban?

a Olivia   b Rory   c Jake   d Christine

5 🎧 1.34 Listen again. Match two opinions with each speaker. Write *O, R, J* or *C*.

1 Killing animals for fun is always wrong.
2 People from towns don't understand rural traditions.
3 Fishing is just as cruel as fox-hunting.
4 Hunting damages fields and hedges.
5 We should respect traditional activities even if only a few people do them.
6 Other ways of killing foxes are crueller than hunting.
7 Only very rich people are interested in hunting.
8 In the past, people didn't care about animal rights, but they do now.

6 **SPEAKING** Work in pairs. Tell your partner whether you agree or disagree with the opinions in exercise 5. Give reasons where possible.

✤ Fox-hunting ✤

A ☐ Hunting is a very old activity. Hundreds of years ago, kings and their families hunted deer. In the 1800s, fox-hunting became more popular. The hunters used groups of dogs to chase the foxes while they followed on horses. They wore special clothes for hunting: bright jackets – usually red – black boots and black hats. This tradition continued through the 1800s and 1900s, especially in rural areas.

B ☐ However, many people in the UK were unhappy about the tradition of fox-hunting. It was especially unpopular among people who lived in cities. They thought it was a cruel and out-dated activity and argued that it is wrong to kill animals for fun. The government agreed, and on 15 September 2004, they made a new law to ban hunting with dogs. The traditional fox hunts had to stop. They were now illegal.

C ☐ Some people in the countryside feel very strongly that the hunting ban is unfair. They argue that the government stopped the hunts only because they disliked upper-class rural traditions.
They say that:

• foxes eat farm animals so farmers need help to protect their animals.
• in the countryside, 60% of people want fox-hunting to continue. We should respect rural traditions, and not allow people from cities to stop them.
• fox hunts created jobs for people, so the ban does a lot of damage to the economy in the countryside.

Some people even try to continue the tradition of hunting by using dogs and horses to chase a sock with a special smell, but it isn't the same.

So, which is more important: respecting a rural tradition or protecting foxes? It's still a question that divides town and country in Britain.

3D GRAMMAR Articles

I can correctly use 'a/an' and 'the' with nouns.

1 Look at the photo. Would you like to live in this town? Why?/Why not?

2 Read the text and the *Learn this!* box. Then match the rules in the *Learn this!* box with the words in blue.

I live in a city on the south coast of Croatia. The city is called Dubrovnik. It's a beautiful place, and I love living by the sea. My dad's a tour guide. He's got a boat for tourists. I usually help on the boat during the summer.

> ### LEARN THIS!
> 1 We use *a* or *an* when we talk about something for the first time.
> *They've got a swimming pool.*
>
> 2 We use *the* when we talk about something again.
> *There's a cinema and a café. The café is cheap.*
>
> 3 We use *a* or *an* when we say what someone's job is, or when we describe what somebody or something is.
> *He's a dentist.   He's an old man.   It's a nice day.*
>
> 4 We use *the* when there is only one of something.
> *The sun is shining.   Who's the president?*

3 Find one more example of each rule in the text in exercise 2.

4 Read the chatroom messages. Choose *a* or *the*. Which rule from the *Learn this!* box applies?

---

gr8place2live.com — Chatroom 1

Sammy I live in ¹a / the beautiful village. It's near ²a / the sea. It's ³a / the great place to live.

Monster Hi Sammy. What's the name of ⁴a / the village?

Sammy Newgate. It's in Wales. Where do you live?

Monster Ashford.

Sammy Is that ⁵a / the town or ⁶a / the village?

Monster It's ⁷a / the small town in ⁸a / the south of England. It's OK here. There's ⁹a / the sports centre and ¹⁰a / the cinema, but ¹¹a / the cinema's only got one screen.

Sammy Cinema! We haven't even got ¹²a / the café!

Type your message here. Press enter to send.

LOOK OUT!

We don't use *the* when we are making generalisations.
What's the weather like? but *I don't like hot weather.*
The lanes near our cottage are very narrow. but *Don't drive fast in narrow lanes.*

---

5 Read the *Look out!* box. Are these sentences generalisations or not? Choose the correct answers.
1 I love **old cottages / the old cottages**.
2 **Villages / The villages** are usually quieter than **towns / the towns**.
3 **Weather / The weather** here was terrible last weekend.
4 **Pedestrians / The pedestrians** can use the footpath, but **cyclists / the cyclists** can't.
5 **Fields / The fields** around this village are full of sheep.
6 Do you think **billboards / the billboards** make **cities / the cities** more attractive?

>>> **GRAMMAR BUILDER 3D: PAGE 108–109** <<<

6 🎧 1.35 **PRONUNCIATION** Listen and repeat the phrases below. How do we pronounce *the* before (a) a consonant sound and (b) a vowel sound?

the cattle   the east   the end   the English   the hedge   the industry   the MP3 player   the scenery   the upper classes

7 **SPEAKING** Work in pairs. Ask and answer questions using the table. Do not use *the* if it is a generalisation.

Do you like	the	big cities?
		weather today?
		scenery in England?
		American films?
		Italian food?
		American President?
		new X-Men film?
		talkative people?
		tracksuits?
		song in Unit 1?
		new Samsung phone?
		ambitious people?

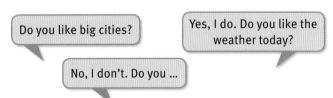

Do you like big cities?

Yes, I do. Do you like the weather today?

No, I don't. Do you ...

WHO WANTS TO BE A FARMER?

Imagine owning a farm where the sun always shines, the crops always grow and the animals are always healthy. Imagine friends visiting for a while to help feed the animals and clean the farmyard. [1]_____ This is the world of FarmVille, an online game that players access through the Facebook website. FarmVille currently has a population of over 82 million – about the same as Germany.

When new players join FarmVille, they receive some 'farm coins' (the special FarmVille currency), some seeds, a plough and a farm with six fields. They plant the seeds and sell the crops to get extra 'farm coins'. [2]_____ Eventually, they can buy more land too and make their farms bigger.

WHY DO PEOPLE ENJOY VIRTUAL FARMING?

[3]_____ Kate Jones is a 25-year-old who lives and works in central London. She grew up in the countryside. She says FarmVille reminds her of her childhood. She's growing wheat and flowers, and she's got some apple trees. She's also keeping chickens and cows. She says that she finds keeping animals relaxing.

Some experts have warned of the dangers of FarmVille and other online games. [4]_____ They also say that even 'free games' can be expensive. FarmVille players can use real money to buy extra 'farm coins' for their farm. You can buy $240 of 'farm coins' for $40 of real money. There are stories of children spending hundreds of dollars on their parents' credit cards to buy virtual money for their online games.

Despite these worries, the population of FarmVille keeps growing as fast as its virtual fruit and vegetables. And while the crops and the animals in FarmVille are imaginary, the money is real. [5]_____

1 SPEAKING Look at the picture opposite. Do you know this game? What other online games can you name?

2 Without looking at the text, guess the answers to these questions.
1 How many people in the world play FarmVille?
2 Can you spend real money playing FarmVille?

3 🎧 1.36 Read the text quickly, ignoring the gaps, and find the answers to exercise 2.

4 VOCABULARY Match the highlighted nouns in the text with the definitions below.
1 the area next to the farm buildings
2 an area of ground
3 the parts of a plant that you put into the ground to grow new plants
4 a plant that is used to make bread
5 plants that farmers grow
6 a machine that farmers use to prepare fields for planting

EXAM STRATEGY

When doing gap-fill exercises, pay attention to words that connect the sentences with the rest of the text. These will often be pronouns (e.g. *they, these, those,* etc.), which relate to the noun. If there are linking words in the text, you have to look for logical relations, such as a response to a question.

5 Read the exam strategy. Underline three examples of demonstratives (e.g. *this, that, these, those*) in sentences A–F below. Then read the text again and try to identify the words and phrases which the demonstratives refer to.

A They use these coins to buy more seeds and also animals for their farm.
B They say that the games are addictive, with players spending up to eight hours a day on the computer.
C Before this, most players were happy to spend no more than an hour a day online.
D Zynga, the company who invented FarmVille, makes an estimated $500,000 a day from its Facebook games.
E For most players it's a relaxing hobby – a change from the pressures of modern city life.
F Now imagine selling those crops and using the money to make your farm bigger and better.

6 Match sentences A–F from exercise 5 with gaps 1–5 in the text. There is one sentence that you do not need.

7 SPEAKING Work in pairs. Ask and answer the questions.
1 How similar is FarmVille to being a real farmer, in your opinion?
2 Why do you think FarmVille is so popular?
3 What other different lifestyles would you like to experience in an online game?

> I think / don't think it's like being a real farmer because …

8 🎧 1.37 Read and listen to the song. Then choose the best summary of the lyrics: a, b or c.
a A man who lives in the city is remembering his happy childhood on a farm and wishing he could go back.
b A man thinks that country life is boring and decides to move to the city and make a lot of money.
c A man moves to the country to escape the pressures of life in the city, but it doesn't make him happy.

Country house

City dweller, successful fella
Thought to himself oops I've got a lot of money
I'm caught in a rat race terminally
I'm a professional cynic but my heart's not in it
I'm paying the price of living life at the limit
Caught up in the century's anxiety
Yes, it preys on him, he's getting thin

He lives in a house, a very big house in the country
Watching afternoon repeats and the food he eats
in the country
He takes all manner of pills and piles up analyst bills
in the country
Ooh, it's like an animal farm, lots of rural charm
In the country, in the country, in the country …
In the country!

Blow, blow me out, I am so sad, I don't know why
Blow, blow me out, I am so sad, I don't know why

Oh, he lives in a house, a very big house
in the country
He's got a fog in his chest so he needs a lot of rest
in the country
He doesn't drink, smoke, laugh, takes herbal baths
in the country
Yes you'll come to no harm on an animal farm
in the country …

I can describe and speculate about a picture.

1 SPEAKING Work in pairs. Match the words below with the photos. You can use the same word for more than one photo.

crowded   empty   enjoyable   indoors   outdoors
relaxing   scary   stressful   sunny   underground

2 🎧 1.38 Listen to Hannah in an oral exam. Which photo from exercise 1 is she talking about: 1, 2 or 3?

3 🎧 1.38 Listen again. Tick the phrases that Hannah uses to describe the photo.

<u>Summarising</u>   This photo shows …
In this photo, we can see …
<u>Locating</u>   on the left / right   in the foreground
in the background   behind the …   in front of the …
next to the …
<u>Speculating</u>   They look (+ adj)   Judging by …   I imagine …

4 SPEAKING Work in pairs. Take turns to say sentences describing the picture of the farmer on page 29. Try to include phrases from exercise 3.

5 🎧 1.39 PRONUNCIATION   Read the speaking strategy. Then listen and repeat Hannah's phrases. Try to copy her intonation.

> ### SPEAKING STRATEGY
>
> When you need time to think during a conversation, say *Let me think*, *Hmm … what else?* or *Let me see*.

6 Look at picture 1. Take turns to ask and answer these questions. Use fillers from exercise 5 if necessary.

1 What are the women drinking?
2 What do you think they're talking about?
3 How many people can you see?
4 What time of day is it, do you think? Why?
5 What country is it, do you think? How do you know?

7 SPEAKING Work in pairs. When you are describing a photo, try to include fillers, and phrases from exercise 3.

Student A: Describe picture 2 to your partner.
Student B: Listen to your partner's description. Then ask: 'How do you think the boy in the foreground is feeling, and why?'
Student A: Answer your partner's question.

Student B: Describe picture 3 to your partner.
Student A: Listen to your partner's description. Then ask: 'How do you think the woman in the red coat is feeling, and why?'
Student B: Answer your partner's question.

1 SPEAKING Work in pairs. Find out what activities your partner enjoys doing on holiday. Ask and answer questions about the activities below and add your own ideas.

Holiday activities buy souvenirs / sunbathe / go skiing snowboarding / shopping / horse-riding / swimming go for a walk / for a bike ride / on a boat trip play cards / tennis / table tennis / volleyball visit a museum / castle / zoo / water park

> Do you enjoy buying souvenirs?

> Yes, I do.

> No, I don't. / Not really. / I quite enjoy it.

2 Read the blog entries by Tessa and Sam. Which activities from exercise 1 are mentioned?

5:18 pm @Tessa321:

There are some fantastic beaches here on the Costa Brava, but the weather this week is terrible. That's really unlucky because it's usually quite good at this time of year. Yesterday, we stayed in the hotel all day and played cards. How boring! Dad lost the game and went to bed early. He was in a bad mood all day today. Tomorrow, we're visiting a huge water park, so it doesn't matter if it's raining. We're flying home on Saturday. Great!

8:14 pm @Sam_Leeds:

We're having a great time here in the Lake District – hot, sunny weather and fantastic scenery. Yesterday, we went for a long bike ride. When we got back, we went swimming in the lake. Joe screamed when he jumped in because the water was freezing. Tomorrow, we're going on a boat trip and then visiting a castle. This holiday is going too fast – I'll be home next week. What a shame!

3 Answer the questions about Tessa and Sam.
1 Where is she/he?
2 What is the weather like?
3 What did she/he do yesterday?
4 What are her/his plans for tomorrow?
5 When is she/he coming home?

4 VOCABULARY Read the *Learn this!* box. Then find extreme adjectives in the blog entries which mean:
1 very good: f_____ and g_____
2 very bad: t_____
3 very big: h_____
4 very cold: f_____

Extreme adjectives
We often use an *extreme adjective* in place of *very* + adjective.
exhausted = very tired   *tiny* = very small
terrified = very scared
We don't use *very* before an extreme adjective.

5 Replace the underlined words with extreme adjectives from exercise 4 and the *Learn this!* box.

We're camping in a very small tent in a very big field. The weather is very cold, especially at night. Last night, I was very scared – there were so many strange noises! It really is a very bad holiday.

WRITING STRATEGY

In informal English, we often use exclamations. An exclamation can be:
an extreme adjective like *Great!* or *Amazing!*
How + adjective – *How exciting!*
What a + (adjective +) noun – *What a (fantastic) view!*

6 Read the writing strategy. Then find three exclamations in the blog entries in exercise 2.

7 You are on a beach holiday with your family. Write a blog entry which includes this information:
• where you are, what the weather is like and whether you are enjoying yourself
• what you did yesterday and what your plans are for tomorrow
• when you are coming home

CHECK YOUR WORK

Have you:
☐ included the information in the task in exercise 7?
☐ used extreme adjectives and/or an exclamation?
☐ checked your spelling and grammar?

Reading

1 `Get ready to READ` Work in pairs. Ask and answer the questions.

1 Why do you think some athletes take drugs?
2 Do you know of any athletes who have been banned from a sporting event for taking drugs?

2 Do the exam task.

READING exam task

Read the text. Choose the best answer, A, B, C or D.

HGH (Human Growth Hormone) could be the favourite drug at the next athletic world championships, and we might never know it. It is a natural substance produced by the human body, and it helps children's bones and muscles to grow. Scientists are allowed to make the drug and it is also legal to take HGH in most countries. HGH is considered a wonder drug for children. It helps many children with growth problems every year.

However, some athletes are now taking the drug. HGH helps add muscle in adults and recent research by the World Anti-Doping Agency shows that HGH may improve a sprinter's time by 5%. Some athletes say that HGH definitely makes them stronger. It also helps them to recover more quickly from injuries.

Although it is banned by most professional sports, HGH is almost impossible to test for. The drug is completely natural and it will only show in tests for around 24 hours after taking it. Testing is usually done only during competitions, but athletes use HGH during training, so it is very difficult to know who has used the drug. This makes it very attractive for some athletes. Scientists are developing a new test which will find the drug in the body for up to two weeks. But it isn't going to be easy. Everybody has different levels of natural HGH in their body.

For this reason, scientists are warning athletes of the possible problems with the drug. Research shows that HGH can give people headaches, pains and – more dangerously – bigger hearts. Finally, high levels of HGH increase the risk of cancer. But is this enough to stop athletes from taking it? Scientists don't think so. Some athletes will do all they can to win, and worry about their health later.

1 Which of these statements is false?
   A HGH is a natural substance.
   B HGH is needed to help bones and muscles grow.
   C HGH is used as medicine for children.
   D HGH is illegally produced in many countries.

2 The second paragraph tells you that
   A some athletes believe HGH can help them do better.
   B HGH is mainly taken by sprinters.
   C research shows that HGH is effective in 5% of athletes.
   D HGH doesn't have any effect on performance.

3 Apart from making them stronger, why is taking HGH attractive for some athletes?
   A Because it can be taken during a competition.
   B Because it is very difficult to detect.
   C Because it is not forbidden to take it.
   D Because it acts within 24 hours.

4 Scientists suggest that
   A some athletes will ignore the dangers of using HGH.
   B there isn't any risk of developing cancer as a result of taking HGH.
   C health problems caused by HGH will stop athletes from taking it.
   D athletes' results are almost equal, so they want HGH to help them be the best.

5 The text is about
   A suggestions for new ways of detecting HGH.
   B HGH as a legal drug for sprinters.
   C the use of HGH in professional sports.
   D HGH as a drug in the treatment of adults.

Speaking

3 `Get ready to SPEAK` Work in pairs. Ask and answer the questions.

1 Which sports are popular with young people in your country?
2 Do you do any sport? Why?/Why not?

4 Do the exam task.

SPEAKING exam task

Answer the questions about the photo. Give reasons for your answers.

1 How are the people feeling? Why?
2 What qualities do you need to be successful at ice skating?
3 Do a lot of young people go ice skating in your country? Why? / Why not?

Listening

5 **Get ready to LISTEN** Work in pairs. Discuss this question. Give reasons for your opinions.

For a student at university, what do you think are the advantages and disadvantages of

a sharing a house or a flat with friends?
b living with your family?

6 Match the words below with the definitions. Use your dictionary to help you.

advertisement detached flat landlord housemate rent upstairs

1 A _____ house is not joined to another house.
2 A _____ is the owner of a house which other people pay to live in.
3 A _____ is somebody who shares a house with you but is not a member of your family.
4 The _____ is the part of the house above the ground floor.
5 An _____ is a notice (usually in a newspaper) that tells people about something (e.g. a job, a service, or something for sale).
6 A _____ is a number of rooms, usually in a large building, where people live.
7 _____ is the money you pay regularly to a landlord.

7 Do the exam task.

LISTENING exam task

🎧 1.40 Read the sentences in the table below. You are going to hear a teenager talking. Decide if the sentences (1–5) are true (T) or false (F). Put X in the appropriate space in the table.

	T	F
1 The speaker and her friend decided to look for another housemate because their house was too big for them.		
2 Melanie was one of the three people who replied to the advert.		
3 The speaker complains that she has to cook every evening.		
4 The girls don't enjoy looking after the garden.		
5 The girls are going to look for a house together next year.		

Speaking

8 **Get ready to SPEAK** How many rooms in a house can you name?

9 Read the speaking exam task in exercise 10. Then complete the sentences with the words below. Which part of the task does each sentence refer to?

cooking food garden lazy reasonable small

1 The bathroom is very _____ .
2 We pay for our own _____ .
3 The house hasn't got a _____ .
4 My housemate is a bit _____ .
5 The rent is quite _____ .
6 I do the _____ and my housemate does the washing up.

10 Do the exam task.

SPEAKING exam task

You and your friend are sharing a rented house. Talk about what it is like and include information about the following points:
- what the house is like
- sharing the costs
- sharing the duties (e.g. cooking, cleaning, shopping)

Use of English

11 **Get ready for USE OF ENGLISH** Work in pairs. How many words can you form from each of the words below? Use a dictionary to help you.

apply success immediate inform accommodate luck responsible difficult prepare reason

apply: applicable, applicant, application, applied

12 Do the exam task.

USE OF ENGLISH exam task

Complete the text with the correct form of the words given.

If your [1]_____ (apply) for a place at university is [2]_____ (success), you'll need somewhere to live. You should [3]_____ (immediate) contact the university and ask for [4]_____ (inform) about their 'halls of residence', which are rooms for students. Most universities don't have enough [5]_____ (accommodate) for all their students. If you are [6]_____ (luck) and the university doesn't offer you a room, it's your [7]_____ (responsible) to find somewhere. Start looking for a room in a shared house or flat. Many students have [8]_____ (difficult) finding somewhere to live very near the university, but if you are [9]_____ (prepare) to travel a few kilometres, you should be able to find a room [10]_____ (reason) quickly.

4A VOCABULARY AND LISTENING At the cinema

I can talk about different types of film.

1 SPEAKING Look at the photos. Do you recognise any of the actors or films?

2 🎧 2.02 VOCABULARY Label the photos with the words below. Which types of film are not illustrated? Listen and check.

Types of film   action film   animated film   comedy   disaster film   documentary film   historical drama   horror film   musical   romantic comedy   science fiction film   thriller   war film   western

3 SPEAKING Work in pairs. What types of film do you like and dislike? Give examples. Use the phrases below.

I'm (not) a big fan of …   I'm (not) really into …
I really (don't) like …   … are OK.
I quite like …   I can't stand …

> I'm really into horror films, like *Wolfman*.

4 🎧 2.03 Listen. Match each film excerpt with a type of film from exercise 2.

5 VOCABULARY Use a dictionary to check the meaning of the adjectives below. Then choose an adjective that best describes the film the people are talking about in sentences 1–7.

Adjectives to describe films   dull   entertaining   funny   gripping   moving   predictable   scary   serious   slow   spectacular   violent

1 I knew exactly what was going to happen at the end.
2 I've never been so bored in my life!
3 The story was fantastic. I couldn't take my eyes off the screen from start to finish.
4 We were all crying when we came out of the cinema.
5 There was too much fighting and blood!
6 There weren't many laughs, but it really made me think.
7 The photography and the special effects were amazing.

⏩ **VOCABULARY BUILDER (PART 1): PAGE 127** ⏪

6 Make notes about a film you really liked and a film you hated. Think about the points below and use the adjectives in exercise 5 to help you.

• the story   • the images / special effects
• the acting   • the music

'Avatar': story – gripping, special effects – spectacular
'Valentine's Day': story – very predictable, acting – bad

7 SPEAKING Work in pairs. Tell your partner about the films. Do you agree with your partner?

> I loved *Avatar*. It's a science fiction film. The story was really gripping, and the special effects were spectacular.

> I couldn't stand *Valentine's Day*. It's a romantic comedy. The story was very predictable. The acting was bad.

⏩ **VOCABULARY BUILDER (PART 2): PAGE 127** ⏪

1 Read the text about Keira Knightley. How many of her films are mentioned?

Keira Knightley rose to fame when she starred in *Pirates of the Caribbean*, the biggest film of 2003. She's one of the most beautiful actresses in Hollywood and also one of the richest, and most critics agree that she is one of the best actresses in the world. She has starred not only in blockbusters like *Pirates*, but also in more serious films, such as *Atonement*, and in funnier films, such as *Love Actually*.

2 Read the text again and underline the comparative and superlative adjectives. Then complete the table.

	Comparative	Superlative
Short adjectives		
rich	richer	1 _____
big	bigger	2 _____
funny	3 _____	the funniest
Long adjectives		
serious	4 _____	the most serious
beautiful	more beautiful	5 _____
Irregular adjectives		
good	better	6 _____
bad	worse	the worst

⟫⟫ **GRAMMAR BUILDER 4B: PAGE 110** ⟪⟪

3 Write sentences comparing the two films in the chart. Use the comparative form of the adjectives below and *than*.

dull entertaining funny long popular scary
short violent

'Star Trek' was longer than 'Up in the Air'.

	Star Trek	Up in the Air
Length	127 minutes	109 minutes
Popularity	✱ ✱ ✱ ✱	✱ ✱ ✱
Violence	✱ ✱ ✱ ✱	✱
Entertainment	✱ ✱ ✱	✱ ✱ ✱ ✱
Laughs	✱ ✱	✱ ✱ ✱ ✱
Fear factor	✱ ✱ ✱	✱

4 Complete the chat room texts. Use the comparative or superlative form of the adjectives in brackets.

Mad about film! Join in the chat …
James Cameron, director of *Avatar*

Profile
Friends
Messages

Log out

sam74
In my opinion, Cameron's ¹_____ (good) director in Hollywood.
filmfreak
²_____ (good) than George Lucas?
sam74
Who?!
filmfreak
He directed Star Wars!
sam74
Oh. I think Cameron's films are ³_____ (entertaining) than Lucas's. But maybe Lucas is ⁴_____ (successful) at the cinema.
mandyb
Avatar was disappointing. It's definitely Cameron's ⁵_____ (predictable) and ⁶_____ (dull) film. Cameron is overrated.
sam74
Are we talking about the same film?!? Avatar is his ⁷_____ (gripping) film yet!
fredstar
I agree with Sam74. Cameron's ⁸_____ (talented) director in Hollywood. Name a ⁹_____ (scary) film than Aliens, a ¹⁰_____ (moving) one than Titanic or a ¹¹_____ (spectacular) one than Avatar!

5 Write the questions. Use superlative adjectives.

1 Who / talented / actor in the world?
   Who's the most talented actor in the world?
2 What / moving / film that you've ever seen?
3 Who / beautiful / actress in the world?
4 What / dull / programme on TV?
5 Who / bad / actor in the world?
6 Who / good-looking / actor in the world?
7 What / scary / film that you've ever seen?
8 What / funny / comedy on TV?

6 **SPEAKING** Work in pairs. Ask and answer the questions in exercise 5.

> In your opinion, who's the most talented actor in the world?

> Brad Pitt. What's the most moving film you've ever seen?

> *Schindler's List.* Who do you think is the most beautiful actress in the world?

I can talk about award ceremonies.

The Oscars

1 SPEAKING Work in pairs. Look at the photos. What can you see? What is happening? Use the words below to help you.

actress   cry   make a speech   outfit   prize   win

2 🎧 2.04 Read the text. Match headings 1–6 with paragraphs A–E. There is one heading that you do not need.

1 Gratitude and tears   4 The most famous winner
2 Dress to impress   5 Deciding the winner
3 Early days   6 A mystery

3 Read the text again. Answer the questions.

1 In the 1930s, how did people know the result before the ceremony?
2 Whose uncle looked like the prize that was awarded to the winners?
3 Who votes for the winners?
4 How much do the female stars usually spend on their outfits for the ceremony?
5 Why are the acceptance speeches often boring?

4 VOCABULARY Match the singular form of the highlighted words in the text with the definitions below.

1 the decision or score at the end of a competition
2 a very formal public event
3 a formal talk that you give in public
4 something that the winner of a competition receives
5 somebody who comes first in a competition

5 🎧 2.05 Listen to a journalist talking about the Razzie Awards. Answer the questions.

1 What are the awards given for?
2 Do most winners come to the awards ceremony?

6 🎧 2.05 Listen again. Are the sentences true or false?

1 The awards ceremony takes place before the Oscars.
2 John Wilson started the Razzies because he hates all Hollywood films.
3 Membership of the Golden Raspberry Award Foundation is free.
4 No winners collected their Razzie Awards before 1988.
5 Sandra Bullock won a Razzie and an Oscar for the same film.

7 SPEAKING Work in pairs. Think of films you have seen recently and discuss this question.

Who would you award (a) Oscars (b) Razzies to in these categories: Best/Worst Film? Best/Worst Actress? Best/Worst Actor?

> I'd award the Worst Film Razzie to … because …

A ☐ The Oscars award ceremony is one of the most famous ceremonies in the world, and is watched live on TV in over 200 countries. The first ceremony happened in Hollywood in 1929, and all of the prizes were for silent films. For the first ten years, the results were given to the newspapers before the ceremony. However, since 1941, the names of the winners have been a secret until the last moment.

B ☐ No one is exactly sure where the name 'Oscars' came from. One story is that in 1931, the director of the Academy thought that the golden award looked like her uncle Oscar – and the name stayed!

C ☐ The Academy of Motion Picture Arts and Sciences has over 6,000 members (actors, directors, producers, etc.). Each year, they vote for the winners in 25 categories. The most important categories are Best Film, Best Director, Best Actress and Best Actor.

D ☐ No one is very interested in what the men wear (they usually come in a dinner jacket or a suit), but the big fashion houses, like Chanel and Dior, try to persuade the most popular female stars to wear their dresses. The stars usually get the dresses for free, and they usually look great. But there are some bad choices too!

E ☐ The speeches that the winners make when they accept their Oscars are often rather boring, as they're usually just a list of people they want to thank (including their mum). The winners often get very emotional – it can sometimes be almost impossible to understand what they're saying!

1 🎧 2.06 **Read and listen to the dialogue between the two casting directors. Are the sentences true or false?**

1 Carrie Oakey is older than Anne Teak.
2 Carrie Oakey hasn't got a very good voice.
3 Sheila Blige isn't very experienced.

Linda	Now we need an actress for the lead role. Anne Teak is certainly attractive enough.
Gideon	Yes, but she's too old to play that role. She's 45.
Linda	That's true. What about Carrie Oakey? She isn't as old as Anne.
Gideon	But her voice isn't good enough, and she hasn't got enough experience. She hasn't acted in many films.
Linda	What about Sheila Blige? She's as experienced as Anne.
Gideon	Yes, she's perfect. Where's my mobile? ... Hello, Sheila? Listen, ...

2 🎧 2.07 **Complete the rules in the *Learn this!* box with *after*, *before* and *between*. Then listen and repeat the examples.**

LEARN THIS!

1 An adjective comes _____ (*not*) as and *as*.
(not) as tall as
2 *too* comes _____ an adjective.
too tall
3 *enough* comes _____ an adjective.
(not) good enough
4 *enough* comes _____ a noun.
(not) enough experience
5 We often use an infinitive with *to* _____ *too* + adjective or adjective + *enough*.
You're old enough to drive.

3 **Write eight sentences comparing yourself with your friends and family. Use *(not) as ... as* and adjectives 1–8.**

I'm not as tall as my sister.

1 tall	4 generous	7 confident
2 patient	5 talkative	8 short
3 clever	6 hard-working	

4 **Write replies to the questions. Use *too* or *not ... enough* and the adjectives in brackets.**

1 'Did you enjoy the new Spielberg film?'
'No. It _____ .' (fast-moving)
2 'Do you like romantic comedies?'
'No, I don't. They _____ .' (predictable)
3 'Was it a dull film?'
'Yes. It _____ .' (slow)
4 'Did your sister see the new Tarantino film?'
'No, she couldn't. She _____ .' (old)
5 'Why don't you watch a DVD with us?'
'I can't, sorry. I _____ to stay awake.' (tired)
6 'Have you got the *Twilight Saga* DVD box set?'
'No, I haven't. It _____ .' (expensive)

5 🎧 2.08 **Complete the conversation. Use *too*, *enough* or *(not) as ... as* and the correct form of the words in brackets. Then listen and check.**

Chloe	Look. *Avatar* is on at the cinema. Fancy seeing it?
Justin	Yeah. Book the tickets online.
Chloe	OK ... Oh, no. It starts in ten minutes. There isn't ¹_____ (time) to get to the cinema.
Justin	What else is there? ... Try *Machete*. It's ²_____ (good) *Avatar*.
Chloe	You have to be eighteen. We aren't ³_____ (old) to see that.
Justin	I'm ⁴_____ (old)! You're not. What about *Warrior*? It isn't ⁵_____ (good) *Avatar* or *Machete*, but we can both see it.
Chloe	OK, hang on. Ah, we're ⁶_____ (late). It's sold out.
Justin	We could hire a DVD.
Chloe	No, the shop's ⁷_____ (far) away. Let's watch TV instead.

⟫ **GRAMMAR BUILDER 4D: PAGE 110** ⟪

6 **SPEAKING** **Work in pairs. Invent reasons why you can't follow the suggestions. Use *too* and *enough*.**

1 Why don't we watch a film on TV?
2 Shall we go to the cinema?
3 Let's go to Los Angeles for our holidays.
4 Why don't you study English at university?
5 Shall we get a burger and chips now?

Why don't we watch a film on TV?

I'm too tired. / I haven't got enough time.

1 SPEAKING Look at the photos. Describe what is happening. Use the words and phrases below to help you.

Photo 1: car   fly   river   upside down
Photo 2: hang   sign   building
Photo 3: fly   kick   in the air

2 Which do you think is the most dangerous stunt? Give reasons.

3 🎧 2.09 Read the text. Match headings 1–6 with paragraphs A–D. There are two headings that you do not need.

1 The golden age of stunts
2 Special effects can't replace stunts
3 Stunts were part of an actor's job
4 A mix of real stunts and computer-generated imaging
5 Actors refuse to do stunts
6 Too many accidents

How did they do that?

A ☐ In the early days of cinema, actors did their own stunts. Stars in silent films, like Charlie Chaplin and Buster Keaton, took great risks to make their films funny. They thought it was part of a comedian's job. Buster Keaton's most famous stunt was in *Steamboat Bill Jr* (1928). The wall of a house falls on Keaton, but he isn't hurt, because he is standing exactly where an open window lands. It was a very dangerous stunt, however, and insurance companies soon started asking for stuntmen and women to take the place of the actors.

B ☐ The stunt industry was at its best in the films of the seventies and eighties. The brave (or mad!) stuntmen and women did more and more amazing things. The James Bond films were famous for stunts. In *The Man with the Golden Gun* (1974), Bumps Willard, as James Bond, drives a car off a bridge and turns it over in the air. At the start of *GoldenEye*, Wayne Michaels bungee-jumps 250 metres from the top of an enormous dam. He said he didn't know if it was possible until he tried! The stunts were often shown in slow motion to make them seem even more fantastic.

C ☐ However, many stunts were extremely dangerous. In the Bond film *Live and Let Die* (1973), stuntman Ross Kananga walks on crocodiles to get across a river. The last crocodile bit his foot! Some stuntmen and stuntwomen even lost their lives doing stunts. In *Top Gun* (1986), the stunt pilot Art Scholl was killed in an air crash. And in the 1995 film *Vampire in Brooklyn*, stuntwoman Sonya Davis died after falling from a high building. Many people criticised the film industry for her death. At the same time, computer-generated imaging (CGI) was developed so that film-makers could create amazing special effects in the film studio which were too dangerous to film on location.

D ☐ Nowadays, most films use both CGI and stunt work. And many actors prefer to do their own stunts. For *The Matrix* (1999), Keanu Reeves trained for six months to do the amazing fight scenes. In the Bond film *Quantum of Solace* (2008), Daniel Craig jumps off buildings onto moving buses. But who is the best stunt actor of all? Film critics say martial arts expert Jackie Chan, who has survived crazy stunts in over 100 films!

2

4 Read the exam strategy and choose the correct answers.

1 In the early days, actors stopped doing their own stunts
   a because stuntmen and women started doing them instead.
   b because they were actors, not comedians.
   c because actors didn't think it was their job.
   d because of the pressure from insurance companies.

2 The stunts in the 1970s and 1980s
   a were only good because they were in slow motion.
   b were mostly in Bond films.
   c were the most impressive of all.
   d were sometimes too dangerous to attempt.

3 In one Bond film, a stuntman
   a refused to do a stunt because it was impossible.
   b tried to do a stunt, but failed.
   c wasn't sure if a particular stunt was possible.
   d thought he might die.

4 CGI stunts were developed
   a to create spectacular but safe stunts in the studio.
   b because people were critical of the film industry.
   c because stuntmen and women refused to risk their lives.
   d because real stunts were too dangerous.

5 Modern actors
   a prefer to use CGI for stunts.
   b often like to perform their own stunts.
   c don't want CGI in their films.
   d don't do stunts on location.

5 **VOCABULARY** Complete the compound nouns and phrases with the words below. Then check your answers in the text.

effects   film   industry   location   woman   motion   scene   studio

1 silent _____ (paragraph A)
2 slow _____ (paragraph B)
3 stunt _____ (paragraph C)
4 film _____ (paragraph C)
5 special _____ (paragraph C)
6 film _____ (paragraph C)
7 on _____ (paragraph C)
8 fight _____ (paragraph D)

6 **SPEAKING** Work in pairs. Do you think actors should perform their own stunts? Why?/Why not? Use the ideas below to help you.

Many stunts are too dangerous ...

Stuntmen and women are specially trained to ...

If stuntmen perform the stunts, you never see the actor's face.

1 🎧 **2.10** Read and listen to the dialogue. Circle the showing that Nancy books on the film guide below.

Assistant	Good evening. How can I help?
Nancy	I'd like to book three tickets for *Eclipse*, please.
Assistant	Which showing?
Nancy	Pardon?
Assistant	Which showing would you like?
Nancy	The seven thirty, please.
Assistant	I'm afraid that showing is sold out.
Nancy	What about the ten thirty showing?
Assistant	Yes, we have tickets for that. Adults or children?
Nancy	Two seventeen-year-olds and a thirteen-year-old.
Assistant	Sorry, did you say one seventeen-year-old?
Nancy	No, two seventeen-year-olds, and a thirteen-year-old.
Assistant	OK. That's two adults and one child. That'll be £21.
Nancy	OK. Here you are.
Assistant	£25. Thank you. And £4 change.

MegaScreen Cinemas Film Guide 22–29 January

Film	Fri–Sat			Tickets
Shrek Forever After Certificate U	16.00	19.00		Adults: £7.50
Robin Hood Certificate PG	18.00	20.30	23.00	Children (under 14), OAPs, Students: £6
Eclipse Certificate 12	16.30	19.30	22.30	Box Office tel: 01548 469644
				Book online at www.msc.co.uk

2 Work in pairs. Practise reading the dialogue, changing the words in blue. Use information from the film guide.

SPEAKING STRATEGY

Don't be afraid to say you don't understand something. Use phrases such as:
Pardon?
Sorry, did you say (two tickets)?
Could you repeat that, please?

3 🎧 **2.11** **PRONUNCIATION** Read the speaking strategy. Then listen and repeat the phrases. Find two of the phrases in the dialogue in exercise 1.

4 🎧 **2.12** Listen to Jeremy booking tickets for a concert. Complete the information for the tickets that he books.

1 Date: _____ February
2 Ticket price: £ _____
3 Number of tickets: _____
4 Total: £ _____
5 Card number: _____
6 Security code: _____
7 Expiry date: _____

5 🎧 **2.12** Put the words in the correct order to make sentences from the dialogue. Listen and check.

1 the / thank / for / Apollo Theatre box office / calling / you
2 I / can / tickets / Jason Mraz / on / book / 3rd February / to see / ?
3 afraid / concert / I'm / that / sold / out / is
4 please / tickets / I'd / three / £35 / at / like
5 would / how / to / you / pay / like / ?
6 have / I / number / can / card / your / please / ?
7 security code / the / on / three-digit / the / back / what's / ?
8 put / I'll / tickets / your / the / in / today / post

6 Work in pairs. Imagine you are booking tickets for a concert or a film. Prepare a dialogue including the information below. Use the expressions in the strategy box.

- name of concert/date and time
- number of tickets (adults or children?)
- tickets available or sold out?/ticket price?
- pay in cash (change?)/pay by credit card (credit card number, security code, expiry date?)
- post the tickets? (name and address)

7 **SPEAKING** Practise your dialogue. Try to memorise it. Then act out your dialogue to the class.

1 SPEAKING Work in pairs. What's the last film you saw in the cinema or on DVD? Did you enjoy it? Why? / Why not? Tell your partner.

2 Read the film review and match four of these headings to the four paragraphs (1–4). There are two extra headings that you do not need.

Characters   Plot summary   Special effects and stunts
Basic information   Overall opinion   Music and songs

A review of *Paul* by Carla Spence

1 Last week, I watched *Paul* on DVD. It's a science fiction film which is also a comedy. The film stars Simon Pegg and Nick Frost, two British actors.

2 It's the story of two friends, Graeme and Clive, who are on holiday in the US. They are science fiction fans and they are visiting all the places that they know about from their science fiction magazines. Near Area 51, they meet an alien called Paul. Paul is running away from the FBI. He asks Graeme and Clive to help him escape and they agree.

3 The characters of Graeme and Clive are interesting because they change during the film. At the start, they're quiet and shy. However, during their adventures they become brave, loyal and strong. The film is really about the relationship between Graeme, Clive and Paul, although there is also a love story.

4 In my opinion, this is a fast-moving and gripping film, although it's also a comedy. The special effects are fantastic. However, the best thing about the film is the acting. Overall, it's a really enjoyable comedy.

3 Read the film review again and decide if these sentences are true or false.

1 The main actors in the film are British.
2 'Paul' is both the name of the film and the name of a character.
3 There's no love story in the film.
4 Carla didn't really enjoy the film.

4 Complete these phrases from the review in exercise 2.
1 The film _____ Simon Pegg and ...
2 It's the _____ of two friends ...
3 The film is really _____ the relationship between ...
4 In my _____ , this is a fast-moving and gripping film
5 _____ , it's a really enjoyable comedy.

5 Write five sentences about the film you talked about in exercise 1. Use phrases from exercise 4.

The film stars Johnny Depp.

6 Read the writing strategy. Find two examples of *however* and two examples of *although* in the review in exercise 2.

> **WRITING STRATEGY**
>
> We use *however* to express contrast between two sentences. We usually put a comma after it.
> *It isn't a very long film. However, the plot is complicated.*
> We use *although* to express contrast between two pieces of information in the same sentence.
> *Although it's a children's film, the ending is quite sad.*

7 Complete the sentences with *however* or *although*. Add commas where necessary.

1 The film wasn't very funny, _____ it was supposed to be a comedy.
2 _____ it was slow, the film was quite gripping.
3 *Jaws* is one of Spielberg's first films. _____ it's one of his best.
4 _____ there are some good scenes in the film, overall I didn't enjoy it.
5 The story was good. _____ I didn't like the music.
6 I really enjoyed the film. _____ my best friend hated it.
7 The special effects were very unconvincing, _____ they spent millions of dollars on them.
8 I found the plot really exciting, _____ I guessed the ending.

8 Write a film review of a film you saw recently. Include this information:
- basic facts (name of film, actors, genre, etc.)
- what the story is about
- what you thought of one or two aspects (characters, special effects, music, dialogue, etc.)
- your overall opinion of the film

> **CHECK YOUR WORK**
>
> **Have you:**
> ☐ followed the task in exercise 8?
> ☐ used *however* and *although* to express contrast?
> ☐ checked your spelling and grammar?

Unit 3

1 Complete the missing words.

1 A p_____ is where you walk, at the side of the road.
2 A b_____ is a large building where farmers keep animals.
3 A b_____ is a very large board in the street, with an advertisement.
4 A c_____ is a small house in the country.
5 A p_____ c_____ is a place to cross the road safely.
6 A s_____ is a very small, narrow river.

Mark: ___ /6

2 Put the words in order to make directions.

1 go / on / straight
2 the / to / of / lane / walk / end / the
3 into / turn / lane / the / right
4 along / road / this / go
5 first / the / take / right
6 your / go / gate / the / on / left / through

Mark: ___ /6

3 Choose the correct words.

There are ¹**a lot of / a little** shops in the town centre, and ²**a few / a little** cafés. There isn't ³**much / many** pollution because there aren't ⁴**some / any** cars. There are ⁵**some / any** modern buildings, but not ⁶**much / many** old ones.

Mark: ___ /6

4 Complete the sentences with *a/an*, *the* or – (nothing).

1 I don't like _____ traffic.
2 I can see _____ sea from my house.
3 My mum's _____ actress.
4 I live in a village. _____ village is very quiet.
5 There's _____ telegraph pole outside our house.
6 Newcastle is in _____ north of England.

Mark: ___ /6

5 Complete the phrases for describing photos with the words below.

imagine in looks of on shows

1 This photo _____ ...
2 _____ the foreground
3 _____ the left
4 I'd _____ ...
5 in front _____ the ...
6 It _____ like ...

Mark: ___ /6

Total: ___ /30

Unit 4

6 Complete the sentences with the types of film below.

action films comedies historical dramas musicals
romantic comedies science fiction films

1 _____ are films with a lot of songs and music.
2 _____ are funny films with lots of jokes.
3 _____ are films about people in the past.
4 _____ are love stories that are also funny.
5 _____ often have exciting car chases and fights.
6 _____ often show aliens and the future.

Mark: ___ /6

7 Complete the adjectives that describe films.

1 sp _ ct _ c _ l _ r
2 _ nt _ rt _ _ n _ ng
3 s _ r _ _ _ s
4 pr _ d _ ct _ bl _
5 m _ v _ ng
6 v _ _ l _ nt

Mark: ___ /6

8 Complete the sentences. Use the comparative or superlative form of the adjectives in brackets.

1 That's _____ comedy I've ever seen! (funny)
2 The book is usually _____ than the film. (good)
3 What's _____ film you've ever seen? (moving)
4 Who is _____ , Rihanna or Madonna? (beautiful)
5 Britney Spears is a _____ actress than Madonna. (bad)
6 Who is _____ actor in the world? (good-looking)
7 The USA has got _____ film industry in the world. (big)
8 Horror films are _____ than war films. (scary)

Mark: ___ /8

9 Rewrite the sentences using the words in brackets.

My dad isn't as impatient as my mum. (more ... than)
My dad is more patient than my mum.

1 She's too young to go into a bar. (enough)
2 It's funny. His other films were funny too. (as ... as)
3 I need more money to buy that DVD. (haven't / enough)
4 Towns are noisier than villages. (not as / quiet)
5 You aren't tall enough to reach that shelf. (too / short)

Mark: ___ /5

10 Complete the dialogue with the words below.

afraid book help showing sorry

Assistant   Good evening. How can I ¹_____ ?
Sam   I'd like to ²_____ tickets for the 7.30 ³_____ of *Avatar*, please.
Assistant   I'm ⁴_____ it's sold out.
Sam   ⁵_____ , did you say it's sold out?
Assistant   Yes, but we have tickets for 9.30.

Mark: ___ /5

Total: ___ /30

Lead-in

1 What is the biggest town or city you know? Do you enjoy being in a big city? Why?/Why not?

Reading

2 Imagine you are visiting Leeds for a weekend. Read the text and find the names of the places in the photos.

LOVE LEEDS ❤!

1 Sports lovers

Sports fans are spoilt for choice in Leeds. Watch Leeds United play football at the Elland Road Stadium, or see the Leeds Rhinos play rugby. International cricket matches take place regularly at Headingley, while at Wetherby Racecourse, under-16s can watch top-quality horse racing for free.

2 History lovers

Visitors to Leeds are surrounded by history. For example, Harewood House is a wonderful historic building with beautiful gardens. It is still the family home of the Earl of Harewood, although it is also open to visitors between April and November. And history comes to life at the Royal Armouries Museum, where they put on shows of medieval combat in full costume!

3 Culture lovers

Leeds is famous for its live music and has one of the best venues in the UK: the O2 Academy. Many top bands perform here. Recent acts include Lily Allen, Kaiser Chiefs, Elbow and Duffy. For fans of dance, there is the Northern Ballet Theatre, one of the most important classical dance companies in Britain. And every year, Leeds is home to the biggest film festival in the UK outside London. Sixteen different cinemas around the city show more than 300 new films.

4 Food lovers

In Leeds, every meal offers the chance of a new experience. Choose from over 200 flavours of milkshake at Shaky Jakes, or book a table for dinner on the *Black Prince*, a riverboat, and explore the waters of the Aire Valley while you eat! Whether you are looking for a fancy ten-course meal, an authentic Indian curry, or traditional fish and chips, Leeds has it all.

3 Are the sentences true or false?

1 You can watch rugby at the Elland Road Stadium.
2 Children do not have to pay to watch horse racing at Wetherby Racecourse.
3 You can visit Harewood House all year round.
4 Lily Allen performed at the O2 Academy in Leeds.
5 The Leeds Film Festival is the biggest in the UK.
6 You can have your drinks on a boat at Shaky Jakes.
7 Restaurants in Leeds offer a wide range of British and ethnic food.

Listening

4 🎧 2.13 Listen to Anna, Dani and Jack. How does Anna feel at the end of the scene? Choose the best adjective.

angry   bored   embarrassed   excited   happy   shocked

5 🎧 2.13 Listen again. Complete the sentences with the correct name: *Anna*, *Jack* or *Dani*.

1 _____ gives Anna the programme for the film festival.
2 _____ has a car and can drive them all to Leeds.
3 _____ chooses the film.
4 _____ chooses a CD to listen to in the car.
5 _____ thinks the animated film might be OK.
6 _____ wants to leave immediately.
7 _____ says sorry to the others.

Speaking

6 Work in pairs. Ask and answer the questions.

1 What is your favourite kind of film? Are there any kinds of film you dislike?
2 What was the last film you saw?
3 Did you enjoy it? Why?/Why not?
4 Did you watch it on TV, DVD or at the cinema?

Writing

7 Write a message for an Internet discussion board about films. Using your ideas from exercise 6 to help you, write about a film you like and explain:

• what the film is called and which actors are in it.
• what kind of film it is (thriller, horror film, etc.).
• what the film is about.
• why you like the film.

THIS UNIT INCLUDES

Vocabulary ▪ shops ▪ verbs: shopping and money ▪ special occasions
Grammar ▪ present perfect ▪ *been* and *gone* ▪ present perfect and past simple
▪ *How long ...?* ▪ *for* and *since*
Speaking ▪ giving and receiving gifts ▪ buying clothes
Writing ▪ a formal letter

5A VOCABULARY AND LISTENING At the shops

I can identify different shops and what they sell.

1 SPEAKING Look at the photos. Imagine you have got €250 to spend in one shop only. Choose a shop and explain why you rejected the other two options.

2 VOCABULARY Work in pairs. Where would you buy these things? Match each item (1–12) with a shop from the list below.

1 apples	5 a magazine	9 a ring
2 bread	6 medicine	10 sausages
3 a DVD	7 paint	11 a tree
4 a flat or a house	8 a pencil	12 a fridge

<u>Shops</u> baker's butcher's chemist's DIY store
electrical store entertainment store
estate agent's garden centre greengrocer's
jeweller's newsagent's stationer's

3 🎧 2.14 PRONUNCIATION Listen, repeat and check.

4 Work in pairs. Think of one or two things you can buy at each shop in the list below.

bookshop card shop clothes shop computer shop
mobile phone store sports shop toy shop

⟫⟫ **VOCABULARY BUILDER (PART 1): PAGE 128** ⟪⟪

5 🎧 2.15 Listen to three dialogues and answer these three questions about each customer.
1 Which shop from exercise 2 is the customer in?
2 What does the customer want to buy?
3 Has the shop got what the customer wants?

6 🎧 2.15 Listen again. Which sentence do you hear: a or b?

Dialogue 1:	1 a Can I get a refund?	☐
	b Can I get my money back?	☐
	2 a I'll buy it.	☐
	b I'll have it.	☐
Dialogue 2:	3 a It's a present.	☐
	b It's a gift.	☐
	4 a I'll look in another shop.	☐
	b I'll try somewhere else.	☐
Dialogue 3:	5 a What's the price?	☐
	b How much is it?	☐
	6 a Is there anything else?	☐
	b Is that all for today?	☐

7 SPEAKING Play a memory game in class. Each student adds one shop and one item.

I went to the baker's for some bread.

I went to the baker's for some bread and the entertainment store for a CD.

I went to the baker's for some bread, the entertainment store for a CD and the jeweller's for a watch.

⟫⟫ **VOCABULARY BUILDER (PART 2): PAGE 128** ⟪⟪

5B GRAMMAR Present perfect

I can talk about recent events.

1 Read the email. Has Alice bought a present for:

a her mum? **b** herself? **c** Kayla? **d** Joe?

> ✉ **Inbox**
>
> Hi Kayla
> We've been in Manchester since 9.30 this morning. We've been to every shoe shop in the city and Mum has tried on a million pairs of shoes, but she hasn't bought any.
> I've been here in this café for an hour. Mum has gone to the clothes shop opposite. She hasn't stopped shopping since we got here, but I've had enough!
> I've bought a present for you – it's a surprise!
> Lots of love
> Alice
> PS Has Joe asked for my email address?

2 Read the email again. Complete the examples in the table.

Present perfect
affirmative
We've ¹_____ in Manchester since 9.30 this morning. Mum ²_____ tried on a million pairs of shoes.
negative
She hasn't ³_____ any.
interrogative
⁴_____ Joe _____ for my email address?

3 Read the *Learn this!* box. Underline more examples of the present perfect in the email. Which use do they show?

> **LEARN THIS!**
>
> We use the **present perfect**
> **1** to talk about recent events and to give news.
>   *Have you heard? Sally's passed her driving test.*
> **2** with *for* or *since* to say how long a situation has existed.
>   *I've had this watch since Christmas.*

4 🎧 2.16 Complete the phone conversation. Use the present perfect form of the verbs in brackets. You can check the forms on page 113. Then listen and check.

Mum Hi Alice. ¹_____ (you / leave) the café?
Alice No, I'm still here.
Mum I ²_____ (finish) in the shop now.
Alice ³_____ (you / buy) anything?
Mum I ⁴_____ (find) a few little things. I ⁵_____ (not spend) much money. Are you bored?
Alice No, I'm fine. I ⁶_____ (send) a few emails.
Mum Let's have lunch. I ⁷_____ (not eat) since six o'clock this morning.
Alice I ⁸_____ (have) lunch. Sorry, I couldn't wait!

>>> GRAMMAR BUILDER 5B (EXS 1–2): PAGE 112 <<<

5 In Alice's email, find examples of (a) *been to*, (b) *gone to* and (c) *been* as the past participle of *be*.

> **LOOK OUT!** *gone* and *been*
> The verb *go* has two past participles: *gone* and *been*.
> We use *gone* when somebody has gone away and not returned.
> *David isn't here. He's gone to the shops.*
> We use *been* when somebody has gone and returned.
> *The fridge is full of food. Mum has been to the shops.*
> **Note:** *been* is also the past participle of *be*.

6 Read the *Learn this!* box. Complete the sentences with *for* or *since*. Write similar sentences about yourself.

1 I haven't seen my best friend _____ six months.
2 I've been at this school _____ 2011.
3 I've been in this room _____ half an hour.
4 I haven't eaten _____ 7.30 this morning.
5 I've known my best friend _____ 2008.
6 I've lived in this town _____ ten years.

> **LEARN THIS!**
>
> **1** We use **How long ... ?** to ask about the length of time of a current situation.
>   *How long have you been here?*
> **2** We use **for** when the answer is a period of time.
>   *I've been here for 45 minutes.*
> **3** We use **since** when the answer is a point in time.
>   *I've been here since 2.30.*

>>> GRAMMAR BUILDER 5B (EXS 3–5): PAGE 112 <<<

7 SPEAKING Work in pairs. Ask and answer questions with *How long ... ?* and *for* or *since*. Use the phrases below.

have a mobile phone? have those shoes?
be at this school? know me?

> How long have you had a mobile phone?

> Since 2009. / For three years.

I can talk about a famous shopping and entertainment district.

The one and only ...
Covent Garden!

A | **Flowers, fruit and vegetables**

In the 17th century, Covent Garden was the biggest and most important flower, fruit and vegetable market in Britain. It was also one of the first markets to start selling pineapples and for this reason, the pineapple became the market's logo. Today, there is no longer a fruit and vegetable market at Covent Garden, but you can still see pineapples as part of the architecture.

B | **Eating and drinking**

Around 1700, workers at the market often went to a pub called the Lamb and Flag to drink beer or gin after work. (It wasn't safe to drink water!) They sometimes saw illegal boxing matches there, and for that reason, the pub's nickname was the 'Bucket of Blood'! The pub is still open today. The oldest restaurant in London, Rules, is in Covent Garden. It has been open since 1798 and serves traditional English food, including pies and puddings.

C | **Entertainment and shopping**

Covent Garden is the only venue in London where buskers and other street performers are allowed to work. A lot of people want to perform there, so there are auditions and only the best artists can perform. Bon Jovi once busked there in front of a very surprised audience! In fact, if you want to spot a celebrity, Covent Garden is a good place to start. Singer Lily Allen owns a clothes shop there, and if you can't afford the outfits, you can hire them just for a night out!

1 **SPEAKING** Look at the photos of the tourist area Covent Garden in London. What do you know about this place? What can you guess from the photos?

2 🎧 2.17 Read the text. Match the photos (1–3) with the paragraphs (A–C).

3 Read the text again. Answer the questions.
1 Why did the pineapple become the logo of Covent Garden?
2 Why did workers at Covent Garden not drink water?
3 What was the nickname of the Lamb and Flag pub? Why?
4 When did the oldest restaurant in London open?
5 How many places are there in London where people are allowed to perform in the streets?
6 What can you do if the outfits in Lily Allen's shop are too expensive for you to buy?

4 **VOCABULARY** Find these words in paragraph C of the text. Match them with the definitions below.

artist   audience   audition   busk   busker   venue

1 _____ : to play a musical instrument and/or sing in public for money; _____ : somebody who does this
2 _____ : a group of people watching entertainment together
3 _____ : a performance in front of judges, to see if you are good enough to perform
4 _____ : a place for performances
5 _____ : an entertainer or performer of some kind

5 🎧 2.18 Listen to five announcements. What is their main purpose? Choose a, b or c.
a to advertise something   c to give a warning
b to give advice

6 🎧 2.18 Listen again. Are the sentences true or false? Correct the false sentences.

Announcement 1
You have to send your competition entry by email.

Announcement 2
You must contact the organisers immediately if you want to take part in the auditions.

Announcement 3
If you hire two items from Lucy in Disguise during the sale, you only pay for one of them.

Announcement 4
All rooms at the Tavistock Hotel cost between £150 and £200 a night.

Announcement 5
There is at least one performance of *The Lion King* at the Lyceum Theatre every day of the week.

7 **SPEAKING** Work in pairs. Ask and answer the questions.
1 Imagine you are spending an afternoon in Covent Garden. What activities would you like to do?
2 Is there a similar place in your town? What can you do there?

1 🎧 2.19 **Read and listen to the dialogue. Are the sentences true or false?**

1 Both Joe and Eva have been to London.
2 Both Joe and Eva have bought something from Harrods.

Joe Have you ever shopped at Harrods?
Eva Yes, I have. I went there with my dad last year. It's great. Have you been there?
Joe No, I haven't.
Eva We went shopping in Covent Garden too.
Joe Lucky you! I've never visited London. But I've shopped at Harrods online.
Eva Really? What did you buy?
Joe I bought some tea for my grandma. It was really expensive, but she loved it.

2 **Read the dialogue again. Which tense are each of the verbs in blue: present perfect or past simple?**

3 **Read the *Learn this!* box. Why are some verbs in the dialogue in the past simple and some in the present perfect?**

> **LEARN THIS!**
>
> 1 We use the **present perfect** to talk about an experience at any time in the past. The exact time of the experience isn't important.
> *I've seen the latest Megan Fox film.*
> *Have you ever been to Spain?*
> 2 We use the **past simple** to talk about a specific occasion in the past.
> *I saw the latest Jim Carrey film last night.*
> *Did you go to Spain last summer?*

4 **Choose the correct tenses.**

1 **I've bought / I bought** this coat yesterday. Do you like it?
2 Oh no. Where's my phone? **I've lost / I lost** it!
3 Shakira writes good songs, but **she's written / she wrote** a few bad ones too!
4 It was my birthday last month and my parents **have given / gave** me a digital camera.
5 I love skiing, but I **haven't tried / didn't try** snowboarding.
6 Zac Efron is her favourite actor. **She's seen / She saw** all his films.

LOOK OUT! Present perfect and past simple
We often use the present perfect to ask and answer questions about an experience, and then the past simple to give more information about a specific occasion.
'Have you ever been windsurfing?'
'Yes, I have. I went windsurfing on holiday last summer.'

5 **Read the *Look out!* box. Then complete each dialogue with the present perfect + *ever*, and the past simple. Use the verbs in brackets.**

1 A <u>Have you ever written</u> a letter to a famous person? (write)
  B Yes, I have. I <u>wrote</u> to Fergie from the Black Eyed Peas last year, but she didn't reply.
2 A _____ a piece of jewellery in the street? (find)
  B Yes, I have. I once _____ a ring on the pavement.
3 A _____ a Ben Stiller film? (see)
  B Yes, I have. I _____ *Zoolander* a few weeks ago.
4 A _____ sheep's milk? (drink)
  B Yes, I have. I _____ some in Greece last year.
5 A _____ an important event or arrangement? (forget)
  B Yes, I have. I _____ my English exam last year.
6 A _____ in a show? (take part)
  B Yes, I have. I _____ in the school play last year.

⟫⟫⟫ **GRAMMAR BUILDER 5D: PAGE 112** ⟪⟪⟪

6 **Complete the questions with the past participle of the verbs below.**

buy forget leave meet pay take part write

Have you ever …
1 <u>taken part</u> in an online auction?
2 _____ to download a song?
3 _____ a present and then kept it for yourself?
4 _____ a British person?
5 _____ to do your homework?
6 _____ a letter of complaint to a shop?
7 _____ a shop without paying for something?

7 **SPEAKING** **Work in pairs. Ask and answer the questions. If you answer yes, give more information using the past simple.**

> Have you ever taken part in an online auction?

> Yes, I have. I bought a computer game on eBay last month. What about you? Have you ever taken part in an online auction?

1 SPEAKING Do you know what eBay is? Have you or a family member ever used it? Do you know any other auction sites?

2 🎧 2.20 Read the three texts. Are the sentences true or false?

A Ian Usher's auction on eBay didn't attract much attention.

B The people of Albert were pleased when the town was sold.

C The police know who put the money in the box.

EXAM STRATEGY

If the text contains a word you do not know, try to guess its meaning from the context (surrounding words). Ask yourself: what part of speech is it? What does the rest of the sentence mean?

3 Read the exam strategy and look at the highlighted words in the text. What part of speech is each word? Choose from: singular noun, plural noun or verb.

4 VOCABULARY Now look at the rest of the sentence around the highlighted words. Use the context to help you to match the words with the definitions below.

1 _____ are offers of money at an auction.
2 _____ means using announcements and/or pictures to make people want to buy things.
3 If something is for _____ , you can buy it.
4 _____ are paper money.
5 To _____ something means to buy it.
6 _____ are things that you have bought.
7 A _____ is a good price for something.

5 Read the text again. Choose the correct answers.

1 Ian Usher wanted to sell everything so he could
  a move to Australia.
  b become an actor.
  c make a fresh start in life.
  d make new friends.

2 Mr Usher thought the money he received was
  a much more than he expected.
  b not enough to achieve his ambitions.
  c not acceptable.
  d not as much as he expected.

3 The town of Albert is
  a in San Antonio.
  b in Gillespie County.
  c about 100 km outside Texas.
  d about 100 km outside Gillespie County.

4 The real reason for selling the town on eBay was
  a the seller wanted to be in the news.
  b nobody lived in the town.
  c the seller wanted to be an estate agent.
  d the seller wanted to move to Italy.

A Life for Sale

A

Ian Usher, a British man living in Australia, was unhappy with his life. He decided that he wanted a new start – but how? Then he had an idea. He put his whole life up for sale on the online auction site eBay. The sale included his three-bedroom house and all its contents, his car and his jet ski. It even included his job and introductions to his friends. The auction began and attracted 1.75 million visits in the first few hours. Eventually, the bids reached nearly 400,000 Australian dollars (£192,000). Mr Usher was disappointed with the price, but he accepted it. He moved out of his home, and started his new life. He used the money from his sale to achieve his 100 top ambitions – all in 100 weeks! These included swimming with sharks off the coast of Japan, riding an ostrich in South Africa, and getting a part in a Hollywood movie.

A town called Albert

B

In 2007, an unusual item was put up for sale on eBay: a town called Albert. The town is in Gillespie County in Texas, about 100 km away from the city of San Antonio. There's a school there, a dance hall and a bar. There are also peach and pecan orchards. In the end, a buyer from Italy paid about $3 million for the town. We don't know why he or she wanted to purchase it. What do the people who live in Albert think of the sale? The answer is: nothing. Nobody has lived in the town for years! The main aim of the sale was to create lots of free advertising for the seller – in this case, an estate agent.

5 When the boy opened the box,
  a he knew why it contained the money.
  b the goods weren't in it.
  c his parents took it from him.
  d some of the things he ordered were missing.

6 The boy can apply to keep the money if
  a he promises not to use it for crime.
  b he can find out where it came from.
  c the government decides that he needs it.
  d nobody can find out where it came from.

c What a bargain!

When a British 16-year-old paid £95 on eBay for a second-hand PlayStation 2 console and two games, he wasn't sure if it was a bargain. But when the goods arrived and he opened the box, the console was there but the games weren't. Instead, there was €65,400 in banknotes! The boy, who has not given his name, was amazed. He told his parents, and they gave the money to the police, who began an investigation. So far, they haven't found out who the cash belongs to or how it got into the box. So what happens to the money? That depends. If the police discover that the money came from crime, it belongs to the government. But if nobody can prove where it's from, the boy and his family can apply to keep it!

6 SPEAKING Work in pairs. Do you agree or disagree with the opinions below? Discuss your ideas. Then share them with the class.

1 It's dangerous to buy things online because you can't see what you're getting.

2 There are some things that you shouldn't be allowed to sell on online auction sites.

3 Selling things online is the easiest way to make money without working.

I can complain in a shop.

1 Describe the picture below. Then ask and answer the questions in pairs.

1 What do you think the customer is saying?
2 What do you think the assistant is saying?
3 Have you ever taken anything back to a shop? Why?

2 🎧 2.21 Read and listen to the dialogue. Answer the questions.

1 Why is Kylie complaining?
2 Is her complaint successful?

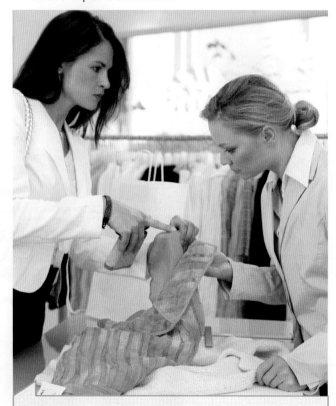

Assistant	Can I help you?
Kylie	Yes. There's a problem with this top.
Assistant	Oh, OK. When did you buy it?
Kylie	Last weekend.
Assistant	And what's wrong with it?
Kylie	The zip has come off.
Assistant	Oh dear!
Kylie	I've only worn it once!
Assistant	Hmm. I see.
Kylie	I've got the receipt. Can I have my money back?
Assistant	Well, OK.
Kylie	Thank you.

3 🎧 2.22 **PRONUNCIATION** Listen and repeat four of Kylie's sentences from the dialogue. Try to copy the intonation.

4 **VOCABULARY** Complete the first column of the chart with the items below.

a DVD a jacket a television

Item	Possible problems
1 _____	The zip / A button has come off. There's a hole in it.
2 _____	It's scratched. / It sticks. / It jumps.
3 _____	The picture/sound isn't right. The screen is scratched.

5 **SPEAKING** Work in pairs. Practise reading the dialogue in exercise 2, changing the words in blue. Use different items and problems from the chart in exercise 4.

6 🎧 2.23 Listen to two customers complaining. Complete the chart.

	Shop	Item	Problem
Dialogue 1			wrong colour
Dialogue 2			stopped working

7 🎧 2.23 Complete the sentences (1–6) with the words below. Then listen to the dialogues again and check your answers.

back enough exchange speak receipt refunds

1 I want to _____ it.
2 I haven't got the _____ .
3 Can I _____ to the manager, please?
4 I want my money _____ .
5 We don't give _____ .
6 That's not good _____ .

SPEAKING STRATEGY

Useful phrases and expressions for conversation can be found in the Functions Bank at the back of the Workbook.

8 Read the speaking strategy. Then work in pairs and prepare a dialogue following the instructions below.

Student A: You are a shop assistant.
Student B: You are a customer making a complaint.
• What has the customer bought?
• When did they buy it?
• What is wrong with it?
• Outcome: refund/exchange/repair?

9 **SPEAKING** Act out your dialogue to the class.

1 Read the letters. Why did Oliver Brown and Tracey Swift write to Talkback Phones and Jewellery Online?

8 Cedar Avenue
Cambridge CM13 7TY
14th January 2012

Customer Services Department
Talkback Phones
London E19 7PP

Dear Sir or Madam,

A I am writing to report a fault with the phone that I bought from your shop in Cambridge on 28th December.

B It works fine when I make calls, but when I try to take photos, it does not work. The photos are all very dark and you can't see any of the people in them.

C I am returning the phone to you with this letter. I would be grateful if you could repair the fault or send me a new phone. As you will understand, not having a phone is extremely annoying, so I would appreciate it if you could deal with this matter immediately.

I look forward to hearing from you.

Yours faithfully

Oliver Brown

Oliver Brown

---

2 Clanfield Rd
Bradford BD12 4FG
3rd February 2012

Keith Black
Jewellery Online
Manchester M5 5HJ

Dear Mr Black,

A I am writing to complain about a ring that I bought last week from your website, Jewellery Online. It is the first time I have bought jewellery from your company and I must say, it has not been a positive experience.

B On your website, the picture clearly showed a gold ring with a red stone. But when it arrived, it was silver with a green stone. This is simply not acceptable.

C I am enclosing the ring and a copy of the receipt for your reference. Could you please refund my money as soon as possible? I am not interested in exchanging the ring because I have already found what I want on another website.

I look forward to hearing from you.

Yours sincerely

Tracey Swift

Tracey Swift

2 Work in pairs. Student A: Look at the first letter only and answer questions 1–6. Student B: Look at the second letter only and answer questions 1–6.

1 What did the writer buy?
2 Where did he/she buy it?
3 When did he/she buy it?
4 What is the problem with it?
5 Does he/she send it back?
6 What does he/she want the company to do?

3 SPEAKING Find out about your partner's letter. Ask and answer the questions from exercise 2.

4 Read the writing strategy. Then circle examples of rules 1–4 in the letters.

WRITING STRATEGY

A formal letter
1 After writing your address, add the date in full.
2 If you do not know the name of the recipient, start with *Dear Sir or Madam*, and finish with the expression *Yours faithfully*.
3 If you know the recipient's name, start the letter with the expression *Dear Mr/Mrs X*, and finish with the expression *Yours sincerely*.
4 Write your full name.
5 Use expressions common for formal letters.
6 Do not use short forms.

5 Translate these phrases into your own language.

1 *I am writing to …*
2 *I am returning … with this letter.*
3 *I would be grateful if you could …*
4 *Could you please …*
5 *I look forward to hearing from you.*
6 *I am enclosing … for your reference.*
7 *I would appreciate it if you could …*

6 Imagine you have bought something faulty. Write a formal letter of complaint (120–150 words) to the shop or website. Follow rules 2–6 in exercise 4 and this writing plan:

• **Introduction:** Say what the item is, and where and when you bought it.
• **Main body:** Explain in detail what the problem is.
• **Conclusion:** Tell the company you are returning the item. Ask them to repair it, exchange it or refund your money.

CHECK YOUR WORK

Have you:
- [ ] included the information in the task in exercise 6?
- [ ] followed the formal letter rules 2–6 in exercise 4?
- [ ] written 120–150 words?
- [ ] checked your spelling and grammar?

Listening

1 **Get ready to LISTEN** Work in pairs. Ask and answer the questions.

1 Do you like ballet? Why?/Why not?
2 What other sorts of performances do you enjoy watching?

2 Do the exam task.

LISTENING exam task

🎧 2.24 **You will hear an interview with a dancer called Fernando Dias. Choose the best answer, A, B or C.**

1 Fernando was born in
A Florida.
B Cuba.
C Birmingham.

2 When did he decide to become a dancer?
A When he was a teenager.
B When he saw his uncle dancing.
C When he was still a child.

3 Which of these statements about Carlos Acosta is false?
A He came from a large family.
B He went to a ballet school.
C He didn't like playing football.

4 Carlos's story inspired Fernando because
A they both had similar childhoods.
B Carlos had a successful career even though he was born poor.
C Fernando's father was also worried about his son's future.

5 What does Fernando believe about talent?
A To be successful, talent must be combined with hard work.
B Talented people will be successful.
C To be successful, you have to start your career as early as possible.

Use of English

3 Do the exam task.

USE OF ENGLISH exam task

Rewrite the sentences, keeping the meaning the same. Use two to five words including the word in brackets.

1 This pizza is very hot. I can't eat it. (too)
This pizza _____ eat.
2 No boy in the class is as tall as John. (tallest)
John _____ the class.
3 Liam doesn't drive as well as Peter. (driver)
Peter is _____ Liam.
4 Kate is more intelligent than Jasmine. (as)
Jasmine _____ as Kate.

5 The last time I saw Fred was two days ago. (for)
I _____ two days.
6 Antonio came to London in 2009. (been)
Antonio _____ since 2009.

Speaking

4 **Get ready to SPEAK** Match the words with the photos. You can match some words with both photos.

microphone   stage   costume   guitar   old-fashioned
audience   voice   singer   modern   classical   musician

5 Work in pairs. Think of some similarities and some differences between the photos. Use these phrases to help you.

Both photos show …
In the first photo I can see … , but in the second photo …

6 Do the exam task.

SPEAKING exam task

Compare and contrast the two photos. Answer the questions about the photos.

1 How are the performances different?
2 What sort of audience do you think would listen to these types of music?
3 Which of the two would you prefer to go to? Why?

Reading

7 **Get ready to READ** Match the activities with the types of holidays. Some activities match more than one holiday.

beach holiday	trekking
spa holiday	sunbathing
activity holiday	swimming
walking holiday	paragliding
city holiday	sightseeing
	windsurfing
	relaxing in a sauna

8 Which sort of holiday would you like best? Why?

9 Do the exam task.

READING exam task

Read the holiday adverts. Match the sentences (1–8) with the holiday adverts (A–E). Write A, B, C, D and E in the table. Each letter can be used more than once.

A Relax on a remote tropical island! Come to the Maldives in the Indian Ocean. Enjoy windsurfing on the crystal-clear water. Eat under the palm trees while looking at the beautiful blue ocean. Travel in January or February for under £1,000 per person.

B Try a summer holiday in the mountains. If you enjoy walking, how about trekking in the French Alps? A guided walking holiday is £595 per person per week for groups of four, stopping at a different typical French hostel every night. If you don't need a guide, it's £495.

C Why not book a typical family beach holiday this summer? Book bed and breakfast accommodation with a sea view in Sunnyside Hotel, Hope Cove, Devon. Family rooms cost £120 a night. Hope Cove is a fishing village with cafés, shops and two beautiful sandy beaches. The kids will love it!

D Take a short holiday in March in beautiful County Kerry in Ireland. Three nights in a double room in the luxury Killarney Hotel on Muckross Lake costs just £700, including dinner. And if the weather is bad, you can relax in the hotel's indoor swimming pool and sauna. Come on – treat yourself!

E Come to The House, a multi-activity centre for 15–17 year-olds on the Norfolk coast. You can take part in activities like rock climbing and paragliding, and there are dance lessons with parties and music in the evenings. Learn something new and have fun!

1	This place offers an alternative for rainy days.	
2	This is a holiday for people of similar ages.	
3	People with children will enjoy this place.	
4	People who don't like staying in one place will like this holiday.	
5	This is a holiday for people who like exotic surroundings.	
6	This place offers a wide range of activities for teenagers.	
7	This deal is for people who don't have time for a long holiday.	
8	On this holiday, you will need to pay for dinner in a restaurant.	

Speaking

10 **Get ready to SPEAK** Work in pairs. Ask and answer the questions.
1 Do you like shopping? Why?/Why not?
2 What sorts of thing do people complain about in shops and restaurants?
3 Have you ever complained in a shop or restaurant, or have you seen someone else complaining? What was the complaint about?

11 2.25 Read the speaking exam task in exercise 13 and then listen to a student completing the task. Does she get a refund? Why?/Why not?

12 2.25 Listen again. Find one mistake in the student's responses. What is the correct response?

13 Now do the exam task.

SPEAKING exam task

There is a problem with a pair of jeans you bought while on holiday and you have taken them back to the shop. During a conversation with a salesperson, include information about the following points:
• what you bought and when you bought the item
• what the problem is
• your previous experience with a similar item
• what you expect the shop to do

6 How techie are you?

THIS UNIT INCLUDES
Vocabulary ▪ electronic devices ▪ phrasal verbs ▪ websites: verb + noun phrases ▪ adverbs ▪ social activities ▪ household appliances
Grammar ▪ *will* and *going to* ▪ zero conditional ▪ *may, might* and *could*
Speaking ▪ making predictions ▪ making invitations
Writing ▪ a message (operating instructions)

6A VOCABULARY AND LISTENING Electronic devices

I can describe electronic devices.

1 SPEAKING Work in pairs. List the three electronic devices that you use most regularly.

2 VOCABULARY Label the photos with words from the list below. Which devices are not illustrated?

Electronic devices camcorder digital photo frame digital radio ebook reader games console HD TV hard disk recorder MP3 player notebook satnav satellite TV smartphone tablet PC

3 🎧 2.26 **PRONUNCIATION** Listen, repeat and check.

4 VOCABULARY Complete the sentences with the words below.

ebook reader hard disk recorder HD TV notebook satellite TV smartphone

1 I can carry hundreds of books around with me on my _____ and I don't need a bag!
2 We can record over 100 hours of television programmes on our _____ .
3 We've got _____ at home. There's a choice of more than 100 channels!
4 My dad takes his _____ with him on the train so that he can work.
5 I can do anything on my _____ – play music, record videos, send emails – and make phone calls of course!
6 The picture on our new _____ is amazingly clear.

⟫⟫⟫ **VOCABULARY BUILDER (PART 1): PAGE 129** ⟪⟪⟪

EXAM STRATEGY

Listen for the key words that will help you understand what is being said. Before listening to the recording, think about which words you would expect to hear.

5 Read the exam strategy. Which of the phrases below might appear in adverts for devices a–e?

charge the battery download a book find the way make a call pick up email play music record/rewind/pause a programme store photos surf the Net watch films

a tablet PC   c MP3 player   e satnav
b hard disk recorder   d ebook reader

6 🎧 2.27 Listen to four radio advertisements. Match each advertisement (1–4) with a device (a–e) from exercise 5. There is one device that you do not need.

1 _____   2 _____   3 _____   4 _____

7 🎧 2.27 Listen again for the phrases in exercise 5. Were your predictions correct?

8 SPEAKING Work in pairs. Imagine you have won two of the devices from exercise 2 in a competition. Which would you choose? Why?

9 Tell the class what you think. Vote for the three most popular devices.

⟫⟫⟫ **VOCABULARY BUILDER (PART 2): PAGE 129** ⟪⟪⟪

1 SPEAKING Describe what is happening in the picture in exercise 2. Use the words below to help you.

go windsurfing   jetty   film (v)   stand   watch

2 🎧 2.28 Declan, Maya and Tom are on holiday. Read and listen to the dialogue and choose *will* or *going to*.

Maya   Look! Tom's windsurfing. ¹**Are you going to / Will you** have a go too?
Declan No, I'm going to stay on dry land. Let's film Tom, shall we?
Maya   How? We didn't bring the camcorder.
Declan Didn't we? Oh, I know. ²**I'm going to / I'll** use my smartphone. It's got a video camera. ... Oh no, it needs recharging.
Maya   Here, ³**I'm going to / I'll** lend you mine.
Declan OK, thanks. ... Wow, Tom's good isn't he?
Maya   Yes. Don't go too near the edge of the jetty, Declan.
Declan It's all right. ⁴**I'm not going to / I won't** fall in! Wow, I'm getting some great film!
Maya   Watch out! ⁵**You're going to / You'll** walk off — Declan, are you OK?
Declan Yes, I'm OK!

3 Read the *Learn this!* box. Match the uses of *will* and *going to* with examples 1–5 in the dialogue.

> **LEARN THIS!**
>
> We use ***will*** for
> 1 predictions, especially after *I (don't) think* ... .
>   *I think she'll pass all her exams.*
> 2 offers and promises.
>   *I'll lend you my umbrella.*
>   *I won't come home late.*
> 3 decisions that you make while you are speaking.
>   *She isn't answering her mobile. I'll text her.*
>
> We use ***going to*** for
> 4 predictions, especially when they're based on what we can see.
>   *Look at that black cloud. It's going to rain!*
> 5 intentions.
>   *I'm going to work hard next term.*

>>> **GRAMMAR BUILDER 6B: PAGE 114** <<<

4 Complete the speech bubbles. Use *will* or *going to*.

I don't think I want to jump.

Come on. I ¹_____ help you.

Quick! Run! He ²_____ fall!

I don't think I ³_____ play tennis today.

Why has John got those flowers?

He ⁴_____ say sorry to his girlfriend.

5 🎧 2.29 **PRONUNCIATION** Listen and repeat the answers to exercise 4. How is the word *to* pronounced in *going to*?

LOOK OUT!
We can use *probably* and *definitely* to talk about how certain our intentions are.
I'm definitely going to buy a new tablet PC.
We'll probably get satellite TV.
I probably won't go online this evening.

6 Make notes about your own future. Write down:
- two things you're definitely going to do this evening.
- two things you're definitely going to do in the next month.
- two things you probably won't do in the summer holiday.
- two things you'll probably do after you leave school.

7 SPEAKING Work in pairs. Tell your partner your intentions and predictions from exercise 6. Are any of them the same?

1 SPEAKING Work in pairs. Discuss these questions.

1 How many social networking sites can you name?
2 What do people use them for?

2 🎧 2.30 Read the text. Answer the questions.

1 How often does Bethan go on Facebook?
2 What activities does she do on Facebook?
3 What made her realise that she might have a problem?
4 How did her friends react when she left Facebook?
5 What aspects of her life improved after she left Facebook?
6 In her opinion, what are the advantages of Facebook?

3 VOCABULARY Complete the phrases in the chart with the words below. Then find them in the text.

create   deactivate   log on   post   update   upload

Websites: verb + noun phrases			
1 _____ to a website	4 _____ a message
2 _____ a photo	5 _____ an account
3 _____ a profile	6 _____ an account

4 🎧 2.31 Listen to a radio programme about social networking. What is Professor Brown's opinion: 1, 2 or 3?

1 Lots of people are addicted to social networking sites, but it's just a harmless hobby.
2 Some people spend too much time on social networking sites, but it isn't a serious problem.
3 Some people are addicted to social networking sites, but that's no different from being addicted to any other hobby.

5 🎧 2.31 Listen again. Are the sentences true or false? Correct the false sentences.

1 Professor Brown thinks that people who spend 30–40 hours a week on social networking sites have a serious addiction.
2 Professor Brown thinks that Facebook is no more addictive than hobbies like collecting stamps.
3 The interviewer believes that the online world is also the 'real world'.
4 Professor Brown thinks that addiction to social networking sites isn't a serious problem.
5 The professor thinks that people should go online at night rather than during the day.

6 SPEAKING Work in pairs. Discuss these questions.

1 How often do you visit social networking sites?
2 How long do you usually stay on them?
3 Do you think teenagers spend too much time on social networking sites? Give reasons.

| NewsToday.com | HOME | FOREIGN | SPORT | WEATHER |

Electronic obsessions

Over 25 million people in the UK use Facebook. That's 45% of the population! And on average, each user spends over six hours a month on Facebook. Is Facebook a dangerous obsession or just harmless fun? Seventeen-year-old Bethan has written on her blog about what it was like to stop using Facebook …

Facebook and Me
by Bethan

1st May
I think I am a Facebook addict. I log on to Facebook every day to chat to my friends – real friends and loads of online friends. Sometimes I have ten conversations going at the same time. I upload photos and update my Facebook profile all the time. But recently I've started to feel worried if I am offline for more than a few hours. And then last weekend I forgot to meet a real friend because I was online! I've realised I could have a problem. So I've decided to give it up a for a while …

11th May
I found it really hard. Facebook and my friends demanded to know why I had left. I spent the first few evenings wondering what everyone was chatting about on Facebook. I even phoned a couple of friends to find out. The fourth night wasn't quite so bad. I actually concentrated on my homework better and I had more time to watch my TV programmes. And I spoke to my friends during the day at school. At the end of the first week, I reactivated my account. I think Facebook is fun and it's useful for posting messages to friends and sharing photos. But I'll try not to spend so much time on it in future.

....

Nathan, London:
I created a Facebook account because my friends all use it. But I think it's boring.

....

Dan, Brighton:
Wow, you've really made me think. I'm going to deactivate my account and see how I do.

1 Read the text. What three things do lie detectors measure?

ARE YOU LYING?

Lie detectors detect small changes in a person's body when they aren't telling the truth. If you tell a lie, you feel stressed. And if you are stressed, your heart starts to beat faster. The lie detector measures your heart rate while you are answering questions. It also checks your breathing. You breathe slowly if you are relaxed, but if you tell a lie, you breathe more quickly. Finally, it measures the sweat on your fingers. If you lie, you sweat more!

2 Study the verbs in the zero conditional sentences in blue in the text. Then complete the first rule in the *Learn this!* box.

> **LEARN THIS!**
>
> **Zero conditional**
> 1 We use the _____ tense in the *if* clause and we usually use the _____ tense in the main clause.
> 2 The *if* clause can come before or after the main clause. If it comes after, we don't use a comma.
> *You breathe slowly if you are relaxed.*

≫≫ **GRAMMAR BUILDER 6D: PAGE 114** ≪≪

3 SPEAKING Work in pairs. Can you complete the facts? Use the zero conditional and the verbs below.

get   get   get   heat   melt   water

1 If you leave butter in the sun, …
2 Plants die if …
3 If you mix green, red and blue light, …
4 If you mix green, red and blue paint, …
5 Metal turns red and then white if …
6 If you subtract 12345 from 23456, …

4 Complete the sentences with information that is true for you. Use the zero conditional.

1 My parents get angry if …
2 If I don't feel very well, …
3 I do better in exams if …
4 If I stay out very late, …
5 I get annoyed if …
6 If I feel sad, …

5 SPEAKING Work in pairs. Compare your sentences from exercise 4. Are any of them the same?

may, might and *could*

6 Read the text and underline all the examples of *may*, *might* and *could*. Which two are negative?

Imagine a boy is talking to a girl he secretly loves. But how does she feel about him?

She may love him too, or she may not even like him. How can he find out? Ask her? That could be embarrassing for both of them and she might not give a true answer. No, this boy needs the Romance Reader app. Load the app onto your phone and press 'start'. Then, when you are chatting to the person you are interested in, the Romance Reader listens and tells you if he or she likes you. It might be the start of a big romance …

7 Read and complete the rules in the *Learn this!* box.

> **LEARN THIS!**
>
> 1 To talk about possibility in the present or future, we can use *may*, *might* or *could* followed by the infinitive without *to*.
> *They may/might/could be at home now.* (present)
> *He may/might/could go out this evening.* (future)
> 2 We use *might not* or _____ *not* for the negative. We don't use *could not*.

8 Complete the sentences. Use *may*, *might* or *could* and the verbs below.

be   get   not give   refuse   sell   use

1 If it's a war film, it _____ quite violent.
2 If the stunt is too dangerous, she _____ to do it.
3 If you write down your PIN number, someone _____ it.
4 I _____ a burger from the take-away.
5 If you lose your receipt, they _____ a refund.
6 They _____ garden furniture at the garden centre.

≫≫ **GRAMMAR BUILDER 6D: PAGE 114** ≪≪

9 SPEAKING Work in pairs. Tell your partner:

• something you may do if the weather's nice on Sunday.
• something you might not want to do this evening.
• somewhere you could go on Saturday evening.
• something you could wear to a party.
• somebody you might see in the next couple of days.
• a subject you could study at college or university.
• somewhere you might go on holiday.

1 Translate the proverb. What does it mean?
"Necessity is the mother of invention."

2 🎧 2.32 Read the texts quickly and match them with the pictures.

Crazy ways of getting around – past, present and future

Ever since the horse and buggy, people have been inventing new ways of travelling – some more effective than others. Here are three of them ...

1 Past The C5

'Imagine a vehicle that can drive you five miles for a penny. A vehicle that needs no petrol, just a battery.' This might sound like an amazingly good idea now, but back in 1985, when Clive Sinclair invented the C5, people weren't so sure.
'It will be the answer to our inner-city traffic problems,' explained the marketing executives. 'You won't need a driving licence. Anyone can drive it, whether you are 14 or 40.' The problem was, the C5 didn't work well in the British climate and could be dangerous on wet roads.

2 Present The Segway

Its inventor, Dean Kamen, confidently predicted that the Segway 'will be to the car what the car was to the horse and buggy'. Despite sales predictions of 40,000 a year when it appeared in 2001, sales have been disappointingly low. But the Segway might not be a total failure.

The police in some European countries use them (though probably not in high-speed car chases), and they are popular in theme parks, warehouses and some airports. You aren't allowed to use them on public roads in many European countries, though that might change and sales could then increase dramatically.

3 Future The Uno

Canadian teenager Ben Gulak has recently won an award for the best new invention of the future – the Uno. He has already appeared on American television to demonstrate his unique electric vehicle. It looks exactly like a motor scooter except the wheels are beside each other. A computerised system keeps the vehicle carefully balanced. You can easily ride it – it has absolutely no controls. There is only an on-off switch. To move it, you move your body. To go forward, you simply lean forward. To stop it, you lean back. You lean left or right to go round a corner. 'People really seem to like it,' says Gulak. With the right business help, the Uno might become a common sight on our roads in the future.

3 Read the exam strategy. Then read the text. Are the sentences true or false?

1 In 1985 people welcomed the idea of an environmentally friendly car.
2 The C5 failed partly because it was dangerous in bad weather.
3 Dean Kamen predicted that Segways would be more popular than cars.
4 They've sold more Segways than they expected.
5 Ben Gulak has placed advertisements for the Uno on US TV.
6 The driver doesn't have to operate any controls on the Uno.

4 **VOCABULARY** Find twelve adverbs ending in *-ly* in the texts.

5 Read the *Learn this!* box. Which adverbs are used with adjectives in the texts?

LEARN THIS!

We can use adverbs before adjectives and other adverbs.
These shoes were amazingly cheap.
The car was travelling incredibly slowly.

6 Look at the inventions in the pictures and read these questions. Make notes. Use the words below each photo to help you.

1 How do you think each invention works?
2 Which invention do you think is the most or least useful? Why? Try to use adverbs if you can.
3 What is a fair price for each invention, in your opinion?

7 **SPEAKING** Work in pairs. Ask and answer the questions in exercise 6.

How do you think the first invention works?

You attach the toilet paper holder to your head, and unroll the paper. Then you use it to …

Which invention do you think is the most useful and why?

I think the … is most useful because it's really …

What is a fair price for the first invention, in your opinion?

I think a fair price is €15.

2
Nouns rake   sausage   barbecue   fire
Verbs hold   stick   cook

1
Nouns toilet paper   holder
Verbs attach   blow your nose   unroll

3
Nouns fan   noodles   chopsticks
Verbs attach   blow   not burn   cool

1 🎧 2.33 **Read and listen to the dialogues. What are Olivia and Ryan's intentions?**

Olivia	I'm having some friends over tomorrow night to watch a DVD. Would you like to come?
Katie	I'd love to, thanks. Shall I eat before I come?
Olivia	No, we're going to eat while we watch the film.
Katie	Shall I bring some food, then?
Olivia	You don't need to bring anything. I'm going to make hotdogs and popcorn!
Katie	Cool. I love popcorn. What time shall I come?
Olivia	About eight o'clock, but I'll text you.
Katie	OK. See you tomorrow.

Ryan	I'm meeting some friends for a meal in town tomorrow. Fancy joining us?
George	What time?
Ryan	One o'clock.
George	Sorry, I can't make it. I have to look after my little brother while my parents are at work.
Ryan	Shame. Are you going to be busy all day?
George	Yes, I am.
Ryan	Well, maybe we'll call round and see you after lunch.
George	Sounds good. See you then.

2 **Read the dialogues again. Answer the questions.**

1 Does Katie accept the invitation?
2 What does Katie offer to bring?
3 What is Ryan doing tomorrow?
4 Why can't George accept the invitation?
5 When might Ryan go and see George?

3 **Read the *Learn this!* box and find three examples of *shall* in the first dialogue in exercise 1.**

> **LEARN THIS!**
>
> We can use *shall* for suggestions and offers, and to ask for instructions.
> *Shall we go now?*
> *Shall I help you with that bag?*
> *What film shall we see?*

4 🎧 2.34 **Listen to five conversations in which people make invitations. Match each conversation with an activity from the list below.**

Social activities   go for a bike ride   go shopping go skateboarding   go to the cinema / a rock concert have a barbecue   have a party   have lunch in a café meet friends   play basketball   play computer games watch a football match

1. have lunch in a café

5 🎧 2.34 **Listen again. Do the speakers say yes or no?**

6 **VOCABULARY** **Complete the phrases in the *Learn this!* box with the words below.**

cool   definitely   don't   fancy   glad   like   make sorry   sounds   time

> **LEARN THIS!**
>
> **Invitations**
> **1 Making**
>   Would you ¹_____ to come?
>   ²_____ joining us?
>   Why ³_____ you come along?
> **2 Accepting**
>   I'd love to, thanks.
>   Yes. ⁴_____ good.
>   Thanks. I'll ⁵_____ be there.
>   **Reacting**
>   ⁶_____ ! See you there.
>   ⁷_____ you can make it.
> **3 Declining**
>   I'm ⁸_____ , I can't.
>   I'd love to, but I can't.
>   Sorry, but I can't ⁹_____ it.
>   **Reacting**
>   Shame.
>   Sorry you can't make it.
>   Another ¹⁰_____ , maybe.

7 🎧 2.35 **PRONUNCIATION** **Listen, repeat and check. Try to copy the intonation.**

8 **SPEAKING** **Work in pairs. Imagine you have just met a friend. Prepare two short dialogues, following the instructions below. Use phrases from the *Learn this!* boxes and the model dialogues.**

Dialogue 1: Make and accept an invitation.
          Organise the time and meeting place.
Dialogue 2: Make and decline an invitation.
          Give a reason for not accepting.

9 **SPEAKING** **Act out your dialogues to the class.**

I can write a message giving operating instructions.

Emily,
I've gone out for the day. Dad is still in bed. There's cereal in the cupboard or bread if you want toast. If you want a coffee, plug in the coffee machine by the kettle. If we run out of milk, can you ask Dad to go and buy some?
See you later
Mum X

Fred,
Hope you had a good day at school. I'm working late this evening, so I won't get back until just after six. There's cottage pie in the fridge. You can heat it up in the microwave. Can you please load the dishwasher when you've finished?
Love, Dad

Elaine,
I've gone home to my parents for the weekend. I just can't stand the mess in the flat. Can you please wash up the plates and mugs you've used and clear up the mess in the living room? It's your turn! The vacuum cleaner is in my room, next to the wardrobe. Back Sunday evening.
Suzie

Mike,
I couldn't make breakfast this morning because the cooker isn't working. Can you call the electrician? I've gone to the gym. My class finishes at 5. Don't forget to drop Jenny off at her ballet class. I'll pick her up on the way home. Back about 6.
Tania X

1 **Read the messages. Who:**

1 didn't have breakfast?
2 has gone out for the day?
3 has made a mess?
4 has to load the dishwasher?
5 is fed up with her flatmate?
6 is going to bring her daughter home?
7 might have to buy some milk?
8 will arrive home just after six?

2 **VOCABULARY** Check the meaning of the household appliances below. Which ones (a) have you got at home? (b) do you use?

Household appliances   coffee machine   cooker   dishwasher   freezer   fridge   iron   kettle   microwave   toaster   vacuum cleaner   washing machine

3 Find seven of the appliances in the messages.

4 **The sentences below all contain phrasal verbs. Find them in the messages and complete them.**

1 Plug _____ the coffee machine by the kettle.
2 If we run _____ of milk, can you ask Dad to go and buy some?
3 I won't get _____ until just after six.
4 You can heat it _____ in the microwave.
5 Can you please wash _____ the plates … and clear _____ the mess in the living room?
6 Don't forget to drop Jenny _____ at her ballet class.
7 I'll pick her _____ on the way home.

5 **Read the *Learn this!* box. Then find examples of *can* for requests in the notes.**

> **LEARN THIS!**
> We can use *can* for requests.
> *Can you buy some milk, please?*
> We also use *can* for permission.
> *Can I go out this evening?*

6 **Complete the questions with *Can I* or *Can you*.**

1 _____ borrow your laptop?
2 _____ unload the dishwasher for me?
3 _____ have another piece of cake, please?
4 _____ give Mary a lift to the station?
5 _____ use your mobile, please?

7 **Imagine that you live in a flat and are going away for the weekend. Write a message to your flatmate. Include the following information:**

- Tell him/her where you've gone.
- Remind him/her to do something that involves a household appliance.
- Ask him/her to buy some food/drink.
- Say when you'll be home.

CHECK YOUR WORK

Have you:
- [ ] included the information in the task in exercise 7?
- [ ] used some phrasal verbs?
- [ ] checked your spelling and grammar?

Unit 5

1 Complete the names of the shops.

1 You can buy medicine at the c_____ .
2 You can buy meat at the b_____ .
3 You can buy magazines at the n_____ .
4 You can buy fruit at the g_____ .
5 You can buy pencils and paper at the s_____ .
6 You can buy plants and flowers at the g_____ .

Mark: ___ /6

2 Complete the sentences with the words below.

all   buy   gift   price   refund   somewhere

1 Can I get a _____ ?   4 I'll try _____ else.
2 I'll _____ it.   5 It's a _____ .
3 What's the _____ ?   6 Is that _____ for today?

Mark: ___ /6

3 Complete the email. Use the present perfect form of the verbs below.

be   not be   buy   rain   spend   not visit

Hi Sam,
We ¹_____ here in Scotland since Saturday. The weather
²_____ very good – it ³_____ every day! We ⁴_____ Loch
Ness. I think we're going there tomorrow. Mark ⁵_____ a lot
of souvenirs. I think he ⁶_____ all his money!
See you soon
Jemma

Mark: ___ /6

4 Complete the conversation. Use the present perfect or past simple form of the verbs in brackets.

Kim   ¹_____ you _____ (enjoy) Tania's party?
Ned   Yes, I ²_____ (meet) a really nice girl. She ³_____
      (give) me her phone number.
Kim   ⁴_____ you _____ (call) her yet?
Ned   No, but I ⁵_____ (text) her last night. We're going to
      see the latest *X-Men* film this evening. ⁶_____ you
      _____ (see) it?
Kim   No, but I want to.

Mark: ___ /6

5 Put the lines of the dialogue in the correct order.

a [ ] Yes. I'd like to exchange this jacket, please.
b [ ] It doesn't fit.
c [ ] Can I help you?
d [ ] Yes. It's in the bag.
e [ ] Have you got the receipt?
f [ ] What's the problem with it?

Mark: ___ /6

Total: ___ /30

Unit 6

6 Match 1–6 with a–f to make electronic devices.

1 hard disk   a player
2 HD   b PC
3 games   c nav
4 tablet   d TV
5 MP3   e console
6 sat   f recorder

Mark: ___ /6

7 Complete the phrases with the verbs below.

charge   download   make   pick up   rewind   surf

1 _____ a call   4 _____ a program
2 _____ a book   5 _____ the battery
3 _____ the Net   6 _____ emails

Mark: ___ /6

8 Complete the sentences. Use *will* or *going to*.

1 A It's looking very dark outside.
  B Yes, it _____ rain.
2 A It's a bit cold in this room.
  B OK. I _____ close the window.
3 A Can you come out this evening?
  B I _____ know until I ask my parents.
4 A Are you doing anything on Saturday morning?
  B No. I _____ stay in bed all morning!
5 A The white shirt is €15 and the blue shirt is €20.
  B I _____ have the blue one, please.
6 A Have you got any plans for the summer?
  B No. We _____ do anything this year.

Mark: ___ /6

9 Complete the sentences with the words below.

be   don't hand in   if   might   might not   goes out

1 _____ you heat water to 100°C, it boils.
2 She gets angry if you _____ your homework on time.
3 If I press this button, the light _____ .
4 Liverpool aren't playing very well. They _____ win.
5 Wear a hat, scarf and gloves. It _____ snow.
6 Sandra isn't at home. She could _____ in town.

Mark: ___ /6

10 Write the missing words to complete the dialogue.

Tim   Jake and I are watching a DVD at my place this
      evening. ¹_____ joining us?
Mia   Cool! I'd ²_____ to. ³_____ I eat before I come?
Tim   You ⁴_____ need to. Mum's going to make pizzas.
Mia   Great. ⁵_____ time shall I come?
Tim   About seven.
Mia   Sounds ⁶_____ . See you then.

Mark: ___ /6

Total: ___ /30

Lead-in

1 Look at the photos. Would you like to go shopping in these places? Why?/Why not?

Speaking

2 Work in pairs. Student A: Describe photo 1 to your partner. Student B: Describe photo 2 to your partner.

3 Work in pairs. Ask and answer the questions.
1 Do you think shopping is a good hobby to have? Why?/Why not?
2 What do you enjoy buying most? What do you dislike buying?

Reading

4 Read Anna's email to her English penfriend, Libby, ignoring the gaps. What does she ask for advice about?

✉ **Inbox**

Dear Libby

How are you? I've phoned your house a couple of times this week but you weren't in. ¹_____ It's deleted some of my contacts. Can you email me your mobile number again?

I've been here for five months and I still haven't had a chance to visit you. Can you believe it? Now it's summer and hundreds of people have arrived at the holiday camp. ²_____ Why don't you come and see me here instead? There's plenty of room in my caravan!

The job is going really well and I've met some nice people here. There's one guy who's really sweet. He's called Jack. I really like him, but I don't think he feels the same way about me. Anyway, I think he's going out with Dani, the girl from the gym. ³_____ Never mind. Actually, I do mind!

I went shopping in Leeds yesterday. What a disaster! ⁴_____ And when I tried to change the jacket I bought last week, the shop refused because I didn't have my receipt. I'm going to do all my shopping online from now on!

What can I do about Jack? Nothing, I guess. What do you think? ⁵_____ Advice, please!

Love
Anna

---

5 Read the email again. Match the gaps (1–5) with sentences A–F below. There is one sentence that you do not need.

A I tried on fifty pairs of jeans, but I didn't like any of them.
B It's really difficult for me to take a weekend off.
C That's why so many people come here for their holidays every year.
D I haven't asked, but they seem very close.
E Come on, you've known me for years.
F I've had a few problems with my new smartphone recently.

Listening

6 🎧 2.36 Listen to the dialogue. What has Anna asked Jack to fix? Does he fix it?

7 🎧 2.36 Listen again. Choose the correct answer.
1 Jack says that he knows
   a nothing about phones.
   b everything about phones.
   c a little about phones.
2 One of the problems with Anna's phone is that
   a she can't make phone calls.
   b she can't receive emails.
   c she can't send emails.
3 Jack asks for
   a a black coffee.
   b coffee with milk and sugar.
   c coffee with milk.
4 What's Jack going to do later?
   a have dinner and go to the gym
   b go to the gym and then have dinner
   c have dinner and watch TV
5 What happens when Jack sees Libby's email?
   a He finishes his coffee quickly.
   b He invites Anna to the cinema.
   c He leaves quickly.

Writing

8 Imagine you are on a shopping trip in a big city. Write a blog entry in English explaining:
- where you are and why you are there.
- whether you're having a good or a bad time, and why.
- which shops you have visited.
- what you have bought and how much you have spent.

THIS UNIT INCLUDES

Vocabulary ■ gestures ■ phrasal verbs ■ special occasions ■ events and places to visit
Grammar ■ *must*, *mustn't* and *needn't* ■ first conditional
Speaking ■ in a tourist office
Writing ■ an invitation and a reply

7A VOCABULARY AND LISTENING Body language

I can describe how people greet each other in different countries.

1 VOCABULARY Match the pictures with the gestures below. Which can be used as greetings?

Gestures (1) beckon bow hug kiss nod point wave wink

2 Complete the expressions with the parts of the body below. Some expressions use the same parts of the body.

arms back hands head legs shoulders thumbs

Gestures (2) give a _____ up
fold your _____
cross your _____ / _____
hold _____
shake _____
shake your _____
pat somebody on the _____ / _____
shrug your _____

3 🎧 2.37 PRONUNCIATION Listen and repeat all the gestures in exercises 1 and 2. Mime the gestures as you say them.

▶▶▶ VOCABULARY BUILDER (PART 1): PAGE 130 ◀◀◀

4 🎧 2.38 Listen to three people talking about customs in their countries. Match the two halves of the sentences.

1 Akiko thinks that Japanese people are
2 Marco thinks that Italian people are
3 Abdullah thinks that Saudi Arabian people are

a warm and talkative.
b formal and respectful.
c polite and modest.

5 🎧 2.38 Choose the correct words. Listen again and check.

1 In Japan, when you meet a woman, you should **bow** / **kiss her on the cheek**.
2 It is **OK** / **not OK** to beckon someone with your fingers in Japan.
3 Italians usually shake hands **every time they meet** / **when they meet for the first time**.
4 When Italians kiss, they usually start on the **right** / **left** cheek.
5 In Italy, men sometimes greet each other with **a hug** / **a pat on the back**.
6 In Saudi Arabia, men shake hands when they meet, **but not** / **and sometimes** when they say goodbye.
7 Saudi male friends **sometimes** / **always** kiss more than once when they meet.

6 SPEAKING Work in pairs. Answer the questions.

1 How do you greet people you see every day?
2 How do you greet friends and family that you haven't seen for a few weeks?
3 How do you greet (a) an adult (b) a girl of your own age (c) a boy of your own age, when you meet them for the first time?

▶▶▶ VOCABULARY BUILDER (PART 2): PAGE 130 ◀◀◀

1 🎧 2.39 Read and listen to the text. Choose the correct verbs.

> **Table manners around the world:**
>
> # PERU 🇵🇪
>
> You **must / needn't** worry because most of the table manners in Peru are the same as in Europe, but …
>
> - you **needn't / mustn't** put your hands under the table. Keep them on the table.
> - you **must / mustn't** wait until everyone has a drink before drinking.
> - you **must / mustn't** say 'buen provecho' when you leave or join the table. It means 'Enjoy your meal'!

2 Look at your answers to exercise 1. Then complete the rules in the *Learn this!* box with *must, mustn't* or *needn't*.

> **LEARN THIS!**
>
> 1 We use _____ to express necessity (something that is very important to do).
> 2 We use _____ to express lack of necessity (something that isn't necessary).
> 3 We use _____ to express prohibition (something that is very important not to do).

>>> GRAMMAR BUILDER 7B: PAGE 116 <<<

3 Read the advice for job interviews. Rewrite the sentences using *must, mustn't* or *needn't*.

1 It's necessary for you to shake hands with the interviewer.
   You must shake hands with the interviewer.
2 Don't wear casual clothes to an interview.
3 It's necessary for you to arrive on time.
4 It isn't necessary for you to give very long answers.
5 Don't fold your arms.
6 It's necessary for you to look the interviewer in the eye.
7 Don't leave your mobile phone switched on.

4 Write sentences about your school using *must, mustn't* and *needn't*. Use phrases from the list below.

copy your friend's homework   run in the corridor
switch off your mobile phone in class   study English
stand up when the teacher comes in   wear a uniform

At our school we mustn't …

5 SPEAKING Work in pairs. How many more sentences can you make about rules in your school?

6 Complete the facts about customs around the world with *must, mustn't* or *needn't*.

1 In Britain, if you are invited for a meal at somebody's home, you _____ take a gift. It's very rude not to bring anything.
2 In many parts of Asia, you _____ touch or pat somebody on the head – it is considered impolite.
3 If you receive an invitation with RSVP on it, you _____ reply.
4 In Saudi Arabia, you _____ use a knife and fork to eat – you can use your fingers if you prefer.
5 In many countries, you _____ use your finger to beckon somebody – it is very rude.
6 In most cultures, you _____ speak with food in your mouth. Swallow your food before you start talking.
7 Generally, you _____ use formal language in emails to friends. But in business emails, you _____ use colloquial language.

7 Write notes about how to be polite when you go to somebody's house for a meal in your country. Use the ideas below to help you.

arrive exactly on time   belch at the table   bring a gift
eat everything that you are given   eat quietly
eat with your fingers   eat with a knife and fork
keep your elbows off the table   sit up straight

You must …   You mustn't …   You needn't …

8 SPEAKING Work in pairs. Compare your ideas.

> You must arrive exactly on time.

> You mustn't belch at the table.

1 **VOCABULARY** Which of these special occasions do you and your family celebrate? When do you give or receive gifts?

<u>Special occasions</u> All Saints' Day birthdays Christmas
Easter Father's Day Halloween Mother's Day
name days New Year's Eve St Nicholas's Day
Twelfth Night Valentine's Day wedding anniversaries

2 **SPEAKING** Describe the photo. Which special occasion does it illustrate? What are the people doing?

3 🎧 2.40 Read the text. Match the opinions below with the people. Write the names. There is one opinion that you do not need.

1 Christmas starts far too early. _____
2 Christmas isn't important to people nowadays. _____
3 It's good that Christmas is commercial. _____
4 Christmas is all about money. _____
5 It's different now, but still good fun. _____
6 People can choose how to celebrate it. _____

4 **SPEAKING** Which opinions do you agree with? Give reasons.

5 🎧 3.02 Listen to four people talking about gifts. Match the people with the question (a–d) they are answering.

1 Craig _____   3 Harry _____
2 Vicky _____   4 Beth _____

a What's the best gift you've ever given?
b What's the worst gift you've ever given?
c What's the best gift you've ever received?
d What's the worst gift you've ever received?

6 🎧 3.02 Listen again. Complete the chart with the words and phrases below.

birthday a book Christmas a costume
Mother's Day perfume tickets for a show
wedding anniversary

	Occasion	Gift
Craig	1 _____	2 _____
Vicky	3 _____	4 _____
Harry	5 _____	6 _____
Beth	7 _____	8 _____

7 **SPEAKING** Work in pairs. Ask and answer questions a–d in exercise 5.

8 Tell the class about your partner.

> The best gift Philip has ever given is …

Has Christmas become too commercial?

Tell us what you think!

Joanna, Glasgow, Scotland
For most people in Britain nowadays, gift-giving, parties and entertainment are more important at Christmas than religion. You can see adverts for Christmas presents on TV and in shops in October, and people feel under pressure to spend lots of money. Some shops are even open on Christmas Day and most people don't go to church. Christmas has lost its true meaning.

Mandy, Oxford, England
You never hear a child complain that Christmas starts too early! Yes, it may be very commercial, but you can give Christmas whatever meaning you like. I think it's up to each individual or family to decide when to begin the celebrations and how much money to spend on presents, cards, food, etc.

Liz, Bangor, Wales
It is true that for many Britons, Christmas doesn't have the same religious meaning as it did in the past. But does that really matter? Families still get together and everyone still has a great time, especially the children.

Thomas, Belfast, Northern Ireland
My dad owns a small gift and toy shop. He makes more money in November and December than in all the other months of the year together. Christmas needs to start as early as possible for him. He needs time to attract customers and get them to spend money. It's also good for the customers because they can spread the cost of Christmas over two or three months.

Nathan, Plymouth, England
Christmas starts much too soon in the UK. Shops should wait until after Halloween and Bonfire Night before they put up decorations and start selling Christmas puddings. I'm bored with Christmas by 25th December! And then as soon as Christmas is over, shops start selling Easter gifts – even before the New Year!

1 How many British superstitions do you know? Match the beginnings and endings of these superstitions.

BRITISH SUPERSTITIONS

1 If you open an umbrella indoors,
2 If you see two magpies,
3 If the sky is red in the evening,
4 Something bad will happen to you
5 You'll have a male visitor

a if you walk under a ladder.
b it'll bring bad luck.
c if you drop a knife (and a female visitor if it's a fork).
d you'll be lucky.
e the weather will be good the next day.

2 🎧 3.03 Listen and check. Are any of the superstitions the same in your country?

3 Study the sentences in exercise 1. Then complete the information in the *Learn this!* box with *after*, *present simple*, and *'will' + verb*.

LEARN THIS!

1 We use the **first conditional** to predict the result of an action. We use the _____ to describe the action and _____ to describe the result.
If you walk under a ladder, it'll bring bad luck.

↑ action   ↑ result

2 The *if* clause can come before or after the main clause. If it comes _____ , we don't use a comma.
You'll have good luck if you carry a rabbit's paw in your pocket.

⟫⟫ **GRAMMAR BUILDER 7D: PAGE 116** ⟪⟪

4 Complete the sentences about superstitions. Use the present simple or *will* form of the verbs in brackets.

1 Turkey If you get out of the bed on the right side, your day _____ (start) well.
2 China If you _____ (not eat) meat on the first day of the Chinese year, you'll have a long and happy life.
3 France If an unmarried girl steps on a cat's tail, she _____ (not find) a husband in the next year.
4 Ireland If you _____ (put) a pair of shoes on a table, it'll bring bad luck.
5 Korea If you give your boyfriend or girlfriend a pair of shoes, he or she _____ (leave) you.
6 Russia If you _____ (look) in a broken mirror, you'll have bad luck.

5 🎧 3.04 PRONUNCIATION Listen and repeat the sentences in exercise 4. How are the words *will* and *won't* pronounced?

6 Complete the text. Use the correct form of the verbs in brackets.

Superstitions around the world

Different countries have different superstitions. For example, in Britain and Japan, if a black cat ¹_____ (walk) in front of you, you ²_____ (have) good luck. But in the USA and many other countries it's the opposite: if a black cat ³_____ (cross) your path, it ⁴_____ (bring) you bad luck. However, many superstitions are almost the same the world over. For example, if you ⁵_____ (break) a mirror, you ⁶_____ (be) unlucky for seven years, but if you ⁷_____ (touch) wood, it ⁸_____ (prevent) bad luck.

There are also superstitions about numbers. If you ⁹_____ (look) at the seats on some aeroplanes, you ¹⁰_____ (not find) the number 13. In Japan the number 4 is unlucky because it is pronounced the same as the word for 'death'. However, dates where the numbers are the same (for example 12/12/12) are very lucky. If a Japanese couple ¹¹_____ (decide) to get married, they ¹²_____ (try) to have the wedding on such a date.

7 SPEAKING Work in pairs. Ask and answer the questions.
What will you do if:
• the weather is fine at the weekend?
• you wake up in the middle of the night?
• you don't feel well on Monday morning?
• you forget your best friend's birthday?
• you can't do your homework?
• there's nothing good on TV this evening?

What will you do if the weather is fine at the weekend?

I'll go to the beach.

READING Don't get fooled again

I can understand an article about a cultural tradition.

1 Look at the pictures and the labels. What can you see? What is strange about them?

April Fool!

Do you celebrate April Fool's Day? On 1 April, people in Britain like to play jokes on each other. If someone can trick another person before midday, then they can call them an 'April Fool'. The tradition probably began in France in the 16th century when the calendars changed and ten days disappeared from the year 1582. **1**

This annual tradition is repeated in different countries and cultures around the world, but not always on the same date, and with different kinds of joke:

- In France, the tradition is called 'poisson d'avril' or 'April fish'. You have to try to pin a paper fish on another person's back without the person noticing.

- In Spanish-speaking countries, people play tricks on 28 December, the Day of the Holy Innocents, to celebrate childhood.

- The Portuguese celebrate April Fool's Day on the Sunday and Monday before Lent. The custom there is to throw flour at each other.

- In Belgium, children have to try to lock their parents or teachers out of the house or school. **2**

TV stations, radio stations and businesses around the world try to trick people with false stories. Some stories have become famous. On 1 April 1998, Burger King advertised its new 'hamburger for left-handed people'. Many people went into restaurants to buy them. **3** In Cologne, Germany, a radio station asked people not to run faster than 10 km/h in the city park, so that they wouldn't upset the squirrels.

On British television, the BBC has played tricks on people for decades. In 1957, a news programme reported that people grew spaghetti in Italy. It showed a film of people picking long strings of spaghetti from trees. **4** More recently, a BBC nature documentary reported that there were penguins in Antarctica that could fly. It showed a film of the birds flying to the Amazon rainforest to enjoy some sunshine. **5**

Record spaghetti crop in Italy

APRIL

1	2	3	4	5	6
7	8	9	10	11	12
13	14	15	16	17	18
19	20	21	22	23	2
25	26	27	28	29	3

Big Ben has a new digital clock face

Amazing discovery in Antarctica

2 🎧 3.05 Read the text. In your opinion, which is the funniest April Fool's trick mentioned in the text?

EXAM STRATEGY

- Read the text to make sure you know what it is about.
- Try to predict what kind of information is missing.
- Read the sentences and look for words that are connected with the topic of a specific paragraph.
- Pay attention to the sentences before and after the gap.

3 Read the exam strategy. Then read sentences a–f and match them with gaps 1–5 in the text. There is one sentence that you do not need.

a And many right-handed people complained!
b Many people forgot the new dates and other people made fun of them.
c It didn't fool many people, but it became one of the most popular videos on the Internet.
d The aim is to trick the other person.
e Then they ask for treats before opening the door!
f Millions of viewers were fooled and some phoned the BBC to ask where they could buy a spaghetti tree.

4 Read the text again. Answer the questions.

1 When and where did April Fool's Day probably start?
2 What do people in (a) France (b) Portugal and (c) Belgium do on April Fool's Day?
3 What was Burger King's 'new invention'?
4 What did the BBC say about spaghetti?
5 According to the nature documentary, where do the 'flying penguins' go for the winter?

5 VOCABULARY Match the highlighted words in the text with the definitions below.

1 pages showing the days, weeks and months of a year
2 ten years
3 the day and month
4 happening every year
5 12 o'clock in the middle of the day
6 100 years

6 VOCABULARY Work in pairs. In your own language, explain the meaning of these words and phrases to your partner.

1 to fool somebody
2 to make fun of somebody
3 to play a joke on somebody
4 to trick somebody
5 a practical joke

7 Work in groups. Find out about an April Fool's Day joke in your country.

1 Who played the joke?
2 What did they do?
3 Did it work?
4 How did the other person/people react?

8 PROJECT In your groups, prepare a presentation about the joke you found out about in exercise 7. You can illustrate it with pictures. Then give your presentation to the class.

9 🎧 3.06 Listen to the song. Complete gaps 1–12 with the words below. Use some words more than once. Does the singer think superstitions are a good thing or a bad thing? How do you know?

baby   devil   face   luck   problem   song   things   wall

10 🎧 3.06 Write these words from the song in full, correct English. Then listen again and check.

'bout   lookin'   ain't   goin'   wanna   yeah   nothin'

SUPERSTITION

Very superstitious, writing's on the [1]_____ ,
Very superstitious, ladder's 'bout to fall,
Thirteen-month-old [2]_____ , broke the lookin' glass
Seven years of bad [3]_____ , the good things in your past.

When you believe in [4]_____ , that you don't understand,
Then you suffer,
Superstition ain't the way.

Very superstitious, wash your [5]_____ and hands,
Rid me of the [6]_____ , do all that you can,
Keep me in a daydream, keep me goin' strong,
You don't wanna save me, sad is my [7]_____ .

When you believe in [8]_____ that you don't understand,
Then you suffer,
Superstition ain't the way, yeah, yeah.

Very superstitious, nothin' more to say,
Very superstitious, the [9]_____ 's on his way,
Thirteen-month-old [10]_____ , broke the lookin' glass,
Seven years of bad [11]_____ , good things in your past.

When you believe in [12]_____ that you don't understand,
Then you suffer,
Superstition ain't the way, no, no, no.

1 **SPEAKING** Look at the photo and answer the questions.

1 Where are the people?

2 What do you think they are saying?

2 🎧 3.07 Read and listen to the dialogue. How many things does the information officer suggest?

Information Officer Good morning. Can I help you?

Lucy Yes, we're visiting Bath for a couple of days and we were wondering what to see.

IO I can certainly help you with that. Here's a leaflet. I think you should visit the Roman Baths. They're 2,000 years old.

Lucy Are they nearby?

IO Yes, just 100 metres from here.

Lucy What else can you recommend?

IO If you take an open-top bus tour of the city, you'll see all the major sights.

Lucy That sounds fun. Are there any festivals or carnivals on at the moment?

IO No, I'm afraid not. What else are you interested in?

Lucy We'd like to do some shopping.

IO You ought to go to SouthGate, the main shopping centre.

Lucy OK. Thanks. Where do we catch the sightseeing bus?

IO The bus stop is marked here on the map. You needn't buy a ticket in advance. You can just get on.

Lucy Great. Thanks very much.

3 **VOCABULARY** Divide the words below into two groups: *Events* and *Places to visit*.

Events and places to visit   art gallery   carnival   castle cathedral   church   concert   festival   market   museum old town   opera house   palace   park   restaurant shopping district

4 🎧 3.08 Listen to the dialogue. Which places from exercise 3 do the people talk about?

5 🎧 3.08 Listen again. Tick the sentences that the people say (one sentence in each pair).

1 a Can you give us some information about the city? ☐

   b We'd like some information about the city. ☐

2 a What do you recommend we see? ☐

   b What sights do you recommend seeing? ☐

3 a How much does it cost to get into the castle? ☐

   b What are the castle opening hours? ☐

4 a Have you got a leaflet with information? ☐

   b This leaflet here has all the information. ☐

5 a Can you show me where that is on the map? ☐

   b Have you got a map of the city? ☐

6 a Is there a taxi rank nearby? ☐

   b Where can we get a taxi from? ☐

6 Read the *Learn this!* box. Underline examples of *should* and *ought to* in the dialogue in exercise 2.

> **LEARN THIS!**
>
> 1 We use *should* and *ought to* for suggestions, advice and opinions.
>
> 2 We often use *I think* or *I don't think* with *should* and *ought to*.
>   *I think you ought to get a taxi.*
>   *I don't think you should walk from here.*

>>> **GRAMMAR BUILDER 7F: PAGE 117** <<<

7 Give advice to someone visiting your town, region or country for two days. Use *should* and *ought to*.

8 Work in pairs. Prepare a dialogue in an information office.

Student A: You are a tourist in your country. Decide what kind of tourist attractions you want to visit. Ask the information officer for recommendations. Ask questions (where the places are, cost, opening hours, etc.).

Student B: You are a tourist information officer. Recommend two or three places and say why the tourist should visit them. Answer the tourist's requests for further information.

9 **SPEAKING** Act out your dialogue to the class.

7G WRITING Invitations

I can write a note replying to an invitation.

1 Read the notes. Are they (a) making, (b) accepting or (c) declining an invitation?

Hi Marcus,
Thanks very much for the invite to your fancy dress party on New Year's Eve. I'm really into fancy dress. Is there a theme? Or can we come as anyone? (or anything?!) I'll be there for sure! It's gonna be awesome!
Imogen X
PS Shall I bring any food, e.g. crisps?

Hi Jane,
Thanks for inviting me to your party, but I can't make it – sorry! It's too bad, because I love a good party! I messed up – I've arranged to go and see my cousins that night – I haven't seen them for ages. Sorry!!! Anyway, hope you have a great party!
Louis

Dear Liam,
It's my birthday next Saturday and I'm going to have some mates round for a sleepover. We're gonna get in loads of pizzas and watch DVDs. Fancy joining us?
Sam
PS RSVP Tel. 643492

Hi Julie,
Can you come to the beach for a BBQ on Sunday? It should be fab. There'll be loads of burgers, chicken and stuff, so you needn't bring any food. It'll start at 3 p.m. Let me know asap.
Hannah

2 Underline the expressions used in each note to make, accept and decline invitations.

3 Read the notes again. Answer the questions.
1 When is Marcus's party?
2 What is Imogen's opinion of fancy dress parties?
3 How is Sam going to celebrate his birthday?
4 What is Louis going to do on the evening of Jane's party?
5 What does Hannah invite Julie to do?
6 Does Hannah want Julie to bring anything?

WRITING STRATEGY

In informal invitations or messages (e.g. to relatives or friends) you can use short forms and colloquial expressions. Do not use them in formal texts.

4 Read the writing strategy. What do abbreviations 1–6 mean? Use the phrases below.

barbecue   as soon as possible   for example
I also want to say   Please reply   telephone number

1 e.g. _____   4 RSVP _____
2 Tel. _____   5 BBQ _____
3 PS _____   6 asap _____

5 Match the highlighted colloquial expressions in the notes with the definitions below.

1 come   4 invitation   7 other things
2 fabulous 5 a long time   8 really good
3 buy   6 certainly   9 made a mistake

6 Complete the colloquial expressions with the words below. Then match them with the meanings (a–d).

chill out   cash   guys   place

1 I'm a bit short of _____ .
2 We're just gonna _____ .
3 Can you come over to my _____ ?
4 Are you _____ doing anything tomorrow?

a We're just going to relax.
b I haven't got much money.
c Are you busy tomorrow?
d Can you come to my house?

7 Imagine you are having a party to celebrate finishing your exams. Write a note inviting a friend to the party. Try to include some colloquial expressions.
• Explain the reason for the party.
• Say when and where the party is going to be held.
• Say what the entertainment plans are (e.g. fancy dress, films, food).
• Ask the friend if he/she can come.

8 Swap notes with a partner. Now write a note either accepting or declining the invitation.
• Thank the person for the invitation.
• Accept or decline the invitation.
• If yes, ask a question about the party.
• If no, say why you can't go.

CHECK YOUR WORK

Have you:
- included the information in the task in exercise 7?
- used some colloquial expressions and abbreviations?
- checked your spelling and grammar?

Reading

1 **Get ready to READ** Work in pairs. Ask and answer the questions.

1 How many famous scientists can you name from
  a your country?
  b other countries?
2 What did they discover or invent?

2 Do the exam task.

READING exam task

Read the text. Match headings 1–6 with paragraphs A–D. There are two extra headings that you do not need.

1 A questioning mind
2 A brilliant student
3 Fame achieved
4 An unpromising start
5 No job and no qualifications
6 Part-time scientist

A ☐ Every so often, a genius comes along. Albert Einstein completely changed our ideas of space and time. He is called the 'father of modern physics'. But what does a genius look like as a child? Einstein was born in Germany. He wasn't impressive as a child. He was very slow to start talking and his parents were worried about him. At school, his teachers weren't impressed either. He found school boring and was badly behaved! He left at the age of 15 without passing his final exams.

B ☐ However, Einstein was very curious about the world. His father and uncle had an engineering company, and he was always asking questions about electricity and machines. When he was small, his father gave him a compass. Einstein was fascinated because the needle always pointed north. He wanted to find out about the universe, but the answers to many of his questions weren't taught in schools. So he read lots of books on his own.

C ☐ Einstein finished his education in Switzerland. He wanted to work in a university, but no one thought he was good enough. When he was 23, he got a job in a government office in Switzerland. His job was to look at people's inventions and give them a patent for their ideas. The work was easy for him and he had time to think. He spent a lot of time writing about the laws of physics and the universe. He sent his papers to scientific magazines. The science world was amazed to read them. No one had ever heard of this young office worker.

D ☐ Between 1901 and 1954, Einstein published more than 300 scientific works. When he was 30, he was finally offered a job at Zurich University. $E = mc^2$ is his famous theory about energy. The idea was so advanced that no one could actually prove it worked until much later. In 1919 one of Einstein's theories about light was proved to be correct and he finally became famous. In 1921 he won the Nobel Prize for Physics. He was very happy about this. But he told everybody, 'I have no special talents. I am only passionately curious.'

Speaking

3 Match items in columns A and B to make ten smartphone functions. Which of these functions has your phone got?

A	B	A	B
MP3	book	text	access
address	calendar	email	recording
appointment	keyboard	video	messaging
web	browser	digital	dialling
onscreen	player	voice	camera

4 **Get ready to SPEAK** 🎧 3.09 Listen and complete the instructions for sending a text message. Use the words below.

button   icon   key in   pressing   scroll down
select   touch   turn on

¹_____ the phone by ²_____ this button. To send a message, ³_____ the 'Messages' ⁴_____ , then ⁵_____ the list of contacts and ⁶_____ the one you want. Then ⁷_____ your message and touch the 'send' ⁸_____ .

5 Do the exam task.

SPEAKING exam task

You are talking to a friend about a mobile phone you have recently bought. She would like to buy a similar phone. Include information about the following points:

• the phone's look and size
• the phone's functions
• how to use one of the functions
• something about the phone that you are unhappy with

Listening

6 **Get ready to LISTEN** Work in pairs. Ask and answer the questions.

1 What is your favourite dish or meal?
2 What ingredients do you need to cook it?

7 Do the exam task.

LISTENING exam task

🎧 3.10 Listen to five chefs talking. Match the sentences (A–F) with each speaker (1–5). There is one extra sentence that you do not need.

1	2	3	4	5

A This dish is no longer very popular.
B This dish has no meat or fish in it.
C This dish wasn't eaten in this chef's home.
D This dish has got meat and one vegetable in it.
E This dish has fried vegetables in it.
F This dish is still very popular.

Use of English

8 Do the exam task.

USE OF ENGLISH exam task

Complete the text. Use one word only in each gap.

¹_____ 2005, the city of Las Vegas celebrated ²_____ 100ᵗʰ birthday. There was an enormous party, and, ³_____ course, a birthday cake. But this wasn't ⁴_____ ordinary cake – it was ⁵_____ world's largest birthday cake! A thousand people worked ⁶_____ three days ⁷_____ make it. They baked 30,000 small cakes and stuck them together ⁸_____ icing. The cake was 31 m long, 15 m wide, 50 cm high and weighed more ⁹_____ 50 tonnes! It was big ¹⁰_____ to feed half ¹¹_____ million people – that's one piece of cake each for every person ¹²_____ Las Vegas!

Speaking

9 **Get ready to SPEAK** Work in pairs. Ask and answer the questions.

1 Do you often eat in restaurants? Why?/Why not?
2 What is your favourite type of restaurant? Why?

10 Look at the pictures in the speaking exam task in exercise 13. Describe the restaurants using the adjectives below.

cheap   crowded   elegant   expensive   formal   friendly   healthy   informal   noisy   quiet   relaxed

> The restaurant in photo 1 looks noisy.

> The restaurant in photo 2 might be quite expensive.

11 🎧 3.11 Listen to a student answering a question in the exam task. Which restaurant does she decide to go to?

12 🎧 3.11 Listen again. Tick the expressions that she uses to make and justify her choice.

I'd rather …	I'd like / I wouldn't like (to) …
I'd prefer to …	It looks … It seems …
I prefer …	I'm not very keen on …

13 Do the exam task.

SPEAKING exam task

Compare and contrast the photos. Which restaurant would you prefer to eat at with your friends? Give reasons. Include information about the following points:

- the food
- the cost
- the atmosphere
- the service

THIS UNIT INCLUDES

Vocabulary ■ natural disasters ■ word formation: noun suffixes *-ion*, *-ation* and *-ness*
Grammar ■ second conditional ■ *I wish ...*
Speaking ■ discussing natural disasters ■ stimulus-based discussion
Writing ■ an essay

8A VOCABULARY AND LISTENING Planet Earth

I can talk about natural disasters.

1 SPEAKING Look at the photos. Have you seen any of these events in real life? Have you seen them on TV?

2 VOCABULARY Match the photos with six of the words below.

<u>Natural disasters</u> avalanche disease drought
earthquake famine flood forest fire hurricane
landslide tornado tsunami volcanic eruption

3 🎧 3.12 PRONUNCIATION Listen and repeat all the words. Check your answers to exercise 2.

▶▶▶ **VOCABULARY BUILDER (PART 1): PAGE 131** ◀◀◀

4 Which of the natural disasters involve:
1 water (in any form) or no water?
2 wind?
3 very hot temperatures?
4 rocks or earth moving?

5 🎧 3.13 Listen to ten people talking. Decide which natural disaster from exercise 2 each person is speaking about.

6 🎧 3.14 Complete the news report with the words below. Listen and check.

damaged destroyed injured lasted left lost
reached rescued sent ~~struck~~

Tipton Bay Hurricane

The hurricane ¹ *struck* the town of Tipton Bay on the south coast at 4 p.m. on Saturday afternoon and ² _____ for twelve hours. Winds ³ _____ speeds of 200 km/h. Luckily, people ⁴ _____ their homes before the hurricane arrived, and nobody ⁵ _____ their life. However, flying metal and glass ⁶ _____ about twenty people. Emergency services ⁷ _____ over 50 people from boats near the coast, and charities quickly ⁸ _____ food and tents to help people without homes. The hurricane seriously ⁹ _____ hundreds of buildings and ¹⁰ _____ crops in the fields around the town.

7 Work in small groups. Read the notes about a tornado and write a short news report like the one in exercise 6.

> Tornado
> when – last night, 03.00 for 30 minutes
> where – city of Tulsa, Oklahoma, USA
> winds – 250 km/h
> damage – homes, cars, shops, crops near the city
> people – 25 injured
> emergency services – rescued people from a train; sent medical supplies

8 SPEAKING Present your news report to the class. Include phrases from exercise 6.

> The tornado struck at three o'clock in the morning and lasted about half an hour. It struck the city of ...

▶▶▶ **VOCABULARY BUILDER (PART 2): PAGE 131** ◀◀◀

1 Read the text. What is the connection between actress Olivia Wilde and solar power?

POWER UP!

If you went to hospital and there were no electricity, you would be amazed. You'd probably feel scared, too! But in some of the world's poorest countries, hospitals often have no power. Doctors sometimes perform operations by candle light! If they had electric lights, these operations would be easier and safer.

Power Up Gambia is a charity that provides solar energy for hospitals and health clinics in The Gambia, West Africa. Its most famous supporter is Olivia Wilde, star of the American TV show *House*.

'If I were a superhero, I'd want electrical power in my fingers,' Olivia once said. Perhaps supporting Power Up Gambia is the next best thing.

2 Read the *Learn this!* box. Find three second conditional sentences in the text in exercise 1. Circle the *if* clauses and underline the main clauses.

>>> GRAMMAR BUILDER 8B: PAGE 118 <<<

3 Match 1–5 with a–e to make second conditional sentences. Complete them with the correct form of the verbs in brackets.
1 If we _____ (use) our cars less,
2 If everybody _____ (take) showers instead of baths,
3 Some islands _____ (be) underwater
4 I _____ (walk) to school
5 If shoppers _____ (pay) for plastic bags,

a they _____ (use) less water.
b they _____ (reuse) them more.
c if sea levels _____ (rise).
d the air _____ (be) cleaner.
e if I _____ (live) closer.

4 Complete the text. Use the correct form of the verbs below.

be   be   not be   build   cycle   do   improve   not think   travel   use

Green light for bikes!

'I believe our country [1]_____ a better place to live if the government [2]_____ more to help cyclists. At the moment, cycling on busy roads is dangerous. If the government [3]_____ more cycle paths, the roads [4]_____ safer. More people [5]_____ to school or work if they [6]_____ it was dangerous. If more people [7]_____ by bike, the roads [8]_____ so busy. Cycling is also a good form of exercise. If people [9]_____ bikes more, their health [10]_____ .'

5 What would you do in these situations? Make notes.
1 If you could have any job in the world ...
2 If you saw a ghost ...
3 If you found an expensive watch in the street ...
4 If you didn't have to go to school ...
5 If you won a million dollars ...
6 If you saw your friend stealing from a shop ...

6 Write questions for the situations in exercise 5.
1. What would you do if you could have any job in the world?
2. If you saw a ghost, what would you do?

7 **SPEAKING** Work in pairs. Ask and answer the questions in exercise 6. Use your notes from exercise 5.

> What would you do if you could have any job in the world?

> I'd be an astronaut!

8 Tell the class about your partner.

> If Simon saw a ghost, he would take a photo of it.

1 Look at the photo and the title of the text. Why do you think the family might be proud of their dustbin?

2 🎧 3.16 Read the text quickly and check your ideas.

PROUD OF THEIR DUSTBIN!

The dustbin is full to the top with crisp packets and coloured plastic. In fact, it's so full that it's difficult to put the lid on. But the Strauss family, who own this dirty, old dustbin full of rubbish, are very proud of it. Why? Because it contains all the family's rubbish for a whole year!

Two years ago, Richard and Rachelle Strauss and their daughter Verona read an article about plastic bags and how they cause pollution and harm sea creatures. They decided to stop using plastic bags completely. Now, when they buy food, they reuse their own bags each time. They recycle as much as they can – glass bottles, plastic bottles, paper, cardboard, cans – and they simply don't buy things if they can't recycle the packaging. (They buy their toothpaste in aluminium tubes just because aluminium can be recycled.) And they never throw food away – they eat their leftovers or use them to make compost.

At the moment, it's impossible to recycle plastic crisp packets and sweet wrappers – and Verona loves crisps. If she bought a packet of crisps a day, she'd have to throw away lots of plastic. So she buys the biggest packets she can find – and each packet lasts for a week!

The family are keeping a record of their lifestyle on their website. They hope that other people will read it and reduce their waste. If everyone recycled a bit more, it would make a huge difference.

3 Read the text again. Answer the questions.

1 Why is it difficult to put the lid on the Strauss family's dustbin?
2 Why did they stop using plastic bags?
3 Why do they take their own bags to the shop?
4 Why do they buy toothpaste in aluminium tubes?
5 Why does Verona buy one big packet of crisps every week?
6 Why does the family have a website?

4 **VOCABULARY** Complete the phrases from the text with the verbs below.

cause   eat   harm   make   make   recycle   reduce   reuse

1 _____ pollution	5 _____ left-overs
2 _____ sea creatures	6 _____ compost
3 _____ bags	7 _____ waste
4 _____ packaging	8 _____ a difference

5 🎧 3.17 Listen to four teenagers talking about recycling. Match each person with the best summary of their opinion. There is one summary that you do not need.

1 Ava _____   3 Charlotte _____
2 James _____   4 Archie _____

a I'm better at recycling than the other people in my family.
b My family takes recycling very seriously and tries to reduce the amount of rubbish we produce.
c If there were more recycling bins in my town, I would do a lot more recycling – but I never see any.
d I'm aware of recycling, but I don't think it's very important and I don't really do it.
e I don't recycle everything, but I try to recycle when I can – and that's better than doing nothing.

6 🎧 3.17 Read the speaking strategy. Then listen again and tick the phrases you hear.

SPEAKING STRATEGY

To express your opinion you can use the following phrases: *In my view … In my opinion … The way I see it … What I think is … .*

7 **SPEAKING** Work in pairs. Ask and answer the questions. Use phrases from the strategy box and from exercise 4.

1 What sort of things do you recycle at home?
2 How can people reuse or repair things instead of replacing them?
3 Is there anything else you can do to help the environment?

1 Look at the pictures and answer the questions.

I wish I didn't live near a factory.

Keep Clear DANG

1 Does she live near a factory? Is she happy about it?

I wish I knew somebody here.

2 Does he know anyone at the party? Is he happy about it?

2 Which tense do we use after *wish*? Read the *Learn this!* box. Choose the correct tense to complete rule 1.

1 We use *wish* + the **present / past / future** tense to say that we want something to change.
I wish people recycled more.
Do you wish you lived in another country?
2 We normally use *were* instead of *was* after *I*, *he*, *she* and *it*.
I wish it weren't so cold today.

▶▶▶ **GRAMMAR BUILDER 8D: PAGE 118** ◀◀◀

3 Complete these wishes with the correct form of the verbs in brackets. Which wishes do you agree with?

1 I wish Ferraris _didn't cost_ so much. (not cost)
2 I wish the climate here _____ warmer. (be)
3 I wish we _____ study English at school. (not have to)
4 I wish I _____ travel into space. (can)
5 I wish a day _____ more than 24 hours. (have)
6 I wish I _____ on a boat. (live)
7 I wish animals _____ speak. (can)
8 I wish weekends _____ three days long. (be)

4 Complete the sentences. Then match them with the thought bubbles (1–4).

a I wish I _____ my bus ticket.
b I wish these bags _____ so heavy.
c I wish I _____ an umbrella.
d I wish I _____ still in bed.

5 Complete the sentences with *I wish* and a suitable verb.

1 _I wish I didn't have_ so much homework.
2 _____ enough money for that jacket.
3 _____ better at maths.
4 _____ Spanish really well.
5 _____ football as well as Messi.
6 _____ as rich as Bill Gates.
7 _____ in a bigger flat.
8 _____ an English exam tomorrow.

6 Write one wish for each verb below.

be   can   have   know   live   play   speak
I wish I were five years older.

7 **SPEAKING** Work in pairs. Compare your wishes with your partner.

I wish I were five years older. What about you?

I wish I were better at basketball.

1 Read the exam strategy. Then look at the pictures and predict what the text will be about. Choose a, b, c or d.

a what would happen if a huge volcano erupted

b what life would be like if we lived on another planet

c what would happen to the Earth if a huge asteroid collided with it

d what would happen to us if there were a nuclear war

EXAM STRATEGY

If the text is accompanied by an illustration, look at it before you start reading. This will help you to better understand the content of the text.

2 Look at the text quickly. Check your answer to exercise 1.

3 🎧 3.18 Read the text. Match headings A–E with sections 1–4 of the text. There is one heading that you do not need.

A What would happen?

B Where do the asteroids come from?

C What can we do about it?

D Science fiction or science fact?

E Why hasn't it happened already?

4 Read the text again. Are the sentences true or false?

1 Most asteroids come from outside the solar system.

2 Asteroids can be as big as mountains.

3 A large asteroid wouldn't cause much damage if it landed in the ocean.

4 If an asteroid landed in a very remote area, it could still be a disaster.

5 All of the dinosaurs disappeared because a huge asteroid landed in Siberia.

6 It is possible for an asteroid to change the weather.

7 Scientists don't know exactly how to make an asteroid change direction.

5 **VOCABULARY** Find the highlighted verbs in the text that belong to the same word family as the words below.

1 death

2 failure

3 collision

4 destruction

5 explosion

6 **SPEAKING** Read the text again. Then cover the text, and say what would happen if a large asteroid landed (a) in a big city, (b) in the ocean, or (c) in a remote area. Use words from exercise 5 to help you.

COLLISION COURSE

1

It is 2036. An enormous asteroid is going to collide with Earth. If it isn't stopped, it will crash into the Pacific Ocean, creating a devastating tsunami. What happens next?

And no, that isn't a question about the plot of a science fiction film. It's a question about a very real danger. There are millions of asteroids in our solar system, and if a large one collided with the Earth, it would be a disaster.

2

If a large asteroid crashed into the Earth tomorrow, what would happen? If it landed in a large city, millions of people would die instantly. The impact would cause massive destruction – imagine colliding with a rock as big as a mountain that is travelling at 20 km/s! If the asteroid landed in the ocean, there would be a giant tsunami. Thousands of cities around the world would flood. If the asteroid landed in a very remote area of land, there would be fewer deaths at first. However, the explosion would send a huge cloud of dust into the Earth's atmosphere. This dark cloud would block the light and heat from the sun. Crops wouldn't grow and it would be impossible to feed people.

3

The short answer is: it has happened already.
About 65 million years ago, most life on Earth
disappeared – including all of the dinosaurs.
We now believe that this was because of a huge
asteroid which changed the Earth's weather.
The asteroid was at least 10 km in diameter
and landed in Mexico, leaving a hole more than
180 km across.

On the morning of 30 June, 1908, a much smaller
asteroid (about 90 metres across) exploded in the
sky above central Siberia. Nobody lived nearby,
so there were no deaths – although the explosion
was so powerful that it destroyed an enormous
area of forest and knocked a man off his chair
112 km away!

4

Scientists believe that there are two main options:
we could blow up the asteroid with nuclear
weapons or we could make it change direction.
Both options have their disadvantages. If we
blew up the asteroid, it could break into smaller
pieces. Each piece could then be a danger!
There are several ideas about how to make an
asteroid change direction, but nobody knows
which would work best – and it's impossible to
test the technology. And if we failed, we probably
wouldn't get another chance.

1 **SPEAKING** Have you ever taken part in a fund-raising event? If so, what did you do and what was the money for?

2 **VOCABULARY** Look at the two photos. Complete phrases a–f with the verbs below, then match three phrases with each photo.

collect   dress up   get   sponsor   take part   wave

a _____ fit
b _____ as an animal
c _____ at passers-by
d _____ a runner
e _____ money
f _____ in a sponsored run

3 🎧 3.19 Read the task below. Then listen to Peter doing the task. How many different reasons does he give for preferring the first method?

You are raising money to buy sports equipment for your school. Look at the photos. Which fund-raising method will you choose, and why? Why are you rejecting the other option?

4 🎧 3.19 Listen again. Tick the phrases that Peter uses – one from each group (A–D).

A Making a choice
I'd (much) rather …
I'd prefer to …
I think … would be better
I'd choose …

B Rejecting options
I don't think … would be as good
I wouldn't choose …
I'm rejecting … because ¦ …

C Giving reasons
This is because …
The main reason for this is that …

D Adding extra reasons
What's more, …
There's also the fact that …

5 Read the exam strategy. Write sentences about the fund-raising methods in exercise 2 using *would* and the prompts below.

1 only need a few volunteers
  The second method would only need a few volunteers.
2 be good for everybody's health
3 be easy to organise
4 need a lot of space
5 make young children happy
6 be embarrassing

6 Read the task below. Look at the two photos. Think about which method you would choose, and write down three reasons.

You are raising money to help victims of a flood. Look at the photos below. Which method will you choose, and why? Why are you rejecting the other option?

7 **SPEAKING** Work in pairs. Do the task from exercise 6. Remember to give reasons for your choice, and for rejecting the other option. Use phrases from exercise 4.

1 SPEAKING Read the list of possible problems. Which ones are problems where you live?

air pollution   crime   homelessness   lack of facilities
litter   noise   traffic   unemployment

2 Read the essay task and Amy's essay. Which of her ideas do you like best? Why?

> If you were the mayor of your town or village, what would you do to improve the quality of life there? Talk about three specific problems. Write an essay of 120–150 words.

Essay   by Amy

1   My town is a great place to live, but there are a few problems here too. Firstly, there are quite a lot of homeless people in the town centre. Secondly, the air quality in the town is not good. And thirdly, there is a lot of litter on the streets.

2   If I were mayor, I would build special hostels so people didn't have to sleep on the streets. To reduce air pollution, I would encourage people to cycle or walk to work by banning people from driving cars in the city centre. To make the streets cleaner, I would provide more rubbish bins in the town centre. I would also make it illegal to drop litter in the street.

3   In my opinion, this would make a big difference to life in my town. But if I could only do one thing, I would ban cars from the town centre because air pollution affects everybody's health.

3 Which three problems from exercise 1 does Amy write about? How many solutions does she suggest for each one?

1st problem: _____ – _____ solution(s)
2nd problem: _____ – _____ solution(s)
3rd problem: _____ – _____ solution(s)

WRITING STRATEGY

Writing an essay
1   Include a short introduction. The introduction should explain what the rest of the essay is about.
2   Write a longer paragraph for the main body of the essay. Include all the necessary information in a logical order.
3   Include a short conclusion. This should emphasise your personal opinion and/or the most important point in your essay.

4 Read the writing strategy. In which paragraph (1–3) of her essay does Amy:

a   talk about making the streets cleaner?
b   say how she would help homeless people?
c   talk about methods of transport?
d   explain why one problem is the most serious?
e   mention all three problems?

5 Tick the phrases that Amy uses in her essay.

1   do something about …
2   (try to) reduce …
3   (try to) improve …
4   ban … / ban people from + -ing
5   provide (more) …
6   make it illegal to …
7   pass a law against + -ing
8   encourage people to …
9   make it easier for people to …
10   force people to …

6 Order the words to make sentences which include phrases from exercise 5.

1   do / about / should / we / unemployment / something
2   reduce / would / I / traffic / to / try
3   let's / to use / make / easier / it / public transport / people / for
4   noisy motorbikes / pass / against / law / a / I'd
5   to use / buses / force / we / should / people
6   facilities / improve / here / the / try / should / to / we

7 Work in pairs. Plan your own answer to the essay task in exercise 2. Choose three problems from exercise 1 or include your own ideas. Think of possible solutions.

problem   solution(s)

1 _____   _____
            _____

2 _____   _____
            _____

3 _____   _____
            _____

8 Write an essay using your notes from exercise 7. Remember to include all the points in your plan.

CHECK YOUR WORK

Have you:
☐   included the information from your plan in exercise 7?
☐   divided your essay into paragraphs, including an introduction and a conclusion?
☐   included expressions from exercise 5?
☐   written 120–150 words?
☐   checked your spelling and grammar?

Unit 7

1 Match the gestures (1–6) with the parts of the body you use when you make them.

eye finger hand head mouth shoulders

1 beckon	3 wink	5 wave
2 shrug	4 nod	6 kiss

Mark: ____ /6

2 Match the special occasions below with the months.

All Saints' Day Christmas Easter Halloween
Twelfth Night Valentine's Day

1 Jan _____	3 Mar/Apr _____	5 Nov _____
2 Feb _____	4 Oct _____	6 Dec _____

Mark: ____ /6

3 Complete the sentences with *must*, *mustn't* or *needn't*.

1 It's freezing outside. You _____ wear your coat!
2 You _____ cook dinner for me. I can eat later.
3 She _____ bring any money. The tickets are free.
4 You _____ laugh at him. It's very rude!
5 You _____ always wash your hands before dinner.
6 You can borrow my laptop any time. You _____ ask.

Mark: ____ /6

4 Complete the sentences. Use the present simple or *will* form of the verbs in brackets.

1 If you _____ (not invite) Eva, she _____ (be) angry.
2 You _____ (not fail) your exam if you _____ (work) hard.
3 If it _____ (rain), we _____ (go) to the cinema.
4 If Dad _____ (see) this mess, he _____ (not be) very happy!
5 They _____ (not win) the match if they _____ (not start) playing better.
6 If I _____ (pass) my exams, I _____ (study) law.

Mark: ____ /6

5 Choose the correct words to complete the dialogue.

Guide	Good morning. [1]**Can / Will / Do** I help you?
Ben	Yes. What do you recommend seeing in Cambridge?
Guide	Well, what are you interested [2]**at / in / to** ?
Ben	We'd like to [3]**have / go / do** some shopping.
Guide	There are some lovely shops in the town centre.
Ben	OK. What [4]**else / also / too** can you recommend?
Guide	You [5]**should / will / ought** go to the food festival. It's very interesting.
Ben	Great! Thanks very [6]**many / much / lot** .

Mark: ____ /6

Total: ____ /30

Unit 8

6 Complete the missing words.

1 A d_____ is an illness you often get from other people.
2 A t_____ is a storm with wind which moves in a circle.
3 A d_____ is a long period of no rain.
4 A t_____ is a big wave which can come after an earthquake.
5 An a_____ is when a lot of snow moves quickly down a mountain.
6 A h_____ is a storm with very strong winds.

Mark: ____ /6

7 Match the verbs and nouns to make phrases.

1 raise		a	unwanted clothes
2 display		b	a raffle
3 hold		c	money
4 donate		d	a poster
5 sell		e	a prize
6 win		f	tickets

Mark: ____ /6

8 Complete the second conditional sentences. Use the correct form of the verbs below.

be die find learn live play

1 If I was seventeen, I _____ to drive.
2 I _____ badminton if there was a sports centre nearby.
3 She wouldn't be rude to you if you _____ nicer to her.
4 If I _____ £50, I'd give it to charity.
5 I'd go swimming every day if I _____ by the beach.
6 If a tsunami hit New York, thousands of people _____ .

Mark: ____ /6

9 Complete the wishes. Use the correct form of the verb in brackets.

1 I wish it _____ so cold today. (not be)
2 I wish I _____ a laptop. (have)
3 I wish I _____ better English. (speak)
4 I wish money _____ on trees. (grow)
5 I wish I _____ to do homework. (not have)
6 I wish you _____ more patient! (be)

Mark: ____ /6

10 Match the two halves of the sentences.

1 I'd rather		a	would be better.
2 I think a talent show		b	wouldn't raise much money.
3 I wouldn't choose		c	that it's hard to organise.
4 What's more, it		d	do a sponsored run.
5 There's also the fact		e	to collect money in town.
6 I'd prefer		f	that kind of event.

Mark: ____ /6

Total: ____ /30

Lead-in

1 Imagine you could start a charity to help one group of people in your own country or abroad. Which group would you choose and why? What would you call the charity?

Reading

2 Read the text. Explain the significance of these dates and numbers.

1985   1988   1997   27 million   600 million

RED NOSE DAY

In 1985 there was a terrible famine in the African country of Sudan. Richard Curtis, a British comedy writer, and his friend Alexander Mendis saw the news reports and wanted to make a difference. They began a charity called Comic Relief, with the help of charity worker Jane Tewson.

In 1988, the charity had the idea of selling red plastic noses to raise money. It was a huge success, and selling red noses became a regular part of the charity's fundraising efforts. They also encouraged people around Britain to organise sponsored events – the funnier the better. The money helped projects all over Africa and in the UK too.

In 1997, BBC television supported Comic Relief with a whole afternoon and evening of special TV programmes, calling it Red Nose Day.

People around Britain organised fundraising events around the same time and sent their money to Red Nose Day. In total, the event raised over £27 million for charity.

Since it began, Comic Relief has raised more than £600 million, thanks to the generosity of the British public and the help of the celebrities who take part. The charity produces books, CDs and other items to help raise money. In 2001, JK Rowling wrote two books for Comic Relief based on her famous *Harry Potter* novels, and all the money from the sales went to the charity.

3 Choose the correct answer.

1 Curtis and Mendis started Comic Relief because
  a they knew a lot of people in TV.
  b Jane Tewson asked them to.
  c it was easy for them to raise money.
  d they wanted to help people in Sudan.

2 They sold red plastic noses to raise money for people
  a in Africa and the UK.
  b in poor countries around the world.
  c all around Britain.
  d in Africa and Latin America.

3 What was different about Red Nose Day in 1997?
  a Some famous people took part.
  b Red Nose Day was on TV.
  c The BBC organised fundraising events.
  d People bought red noses.

4 The author JK Rowling helped Comic Relief by
  a donating money she made from *Harry Potter*.
  b making a Harry Potter CD.
  c wearing a red nose on TV.
  d writing two special books for the charity.

Listening

4 🎧 3.20 Listen to Anna, Dani and Jack discussing Red Nose Day. Who suggests these fundraising events?

  a a sponsored run
  b a quiz night
  c a talent show

5 🎧 3.20 Listen again. Are the sentences true or false?

1 Jack and Dani are already discussing Red Nose Day when Anna arrives.
2 Anna thinks a sponsored run is a great idea.
3 Dani really likes quizzes.
4 The talent show won't just be for singers.
5 They decide to do two of the three ideas for events.
6 Red Nose Day is over a month away.

Speaking

6 Work in pairs. Discuss the three ideas for fundraising events from the listening and decide which is the best idea. Why are you rejecting the other two ideas?

Writing

7 Imagine you have organised a fundraising event for Red Nose Day. Write an invitation to your friends.

  • Explain the type of fundraising event.
  • Give the time and place of the event.
  • Say what the plans are (food? fancy dress? etc.).
  • Ask your friends to reply.

THIS UNIT INCLUDES
Vocabulary ▪ crimes and criminals ▪ word formation: noun suffixes -*er*, -*ist* and -*ian*
▪ colloquial expressions
Grammar ▪ past perfect ▪ reported speech
Speaking ▪ asking and replying to personal questions ▪ reporting a theft
▪ giving opinions
Writing ▪ an email

9A VOCABULARY AND LISTENING Crimes and criminals

I can describe different crimes.

1 SPEAKING Match six of the news headlines on the website with the photos. Can you name the crimes in the photos?

NewsToday.com | HOME | FOREIGN | SPORT | WEATHER

TOP CRIME STORIES

1 → Murderer escapes from Dartmoor Prison

2 → Drug dealer caught and jailed for six years

3 → Police investigate shop manager over theft of £10,000

4 → Country house burgled – valuable electrical goods stolen

5 → Police arrest shoplifter for tenth time

6 → Joyriders steal cars and set fire to them

7 → Gang robs bank in broad daylight

8 → Yobs vandalise public toilet

9 → Arsonists set fire to old house

10 → Muggings on the increase in London

2 🎧 3.21 Complete the chart with words from the headlines. Then listen and check.

Crime	Criminal	Verb
arson	1_____	set fire to (a building, etc.)
burglary	burglar	2_____ a house
drug dealing	3_____	deal drugs
joyriding	4_____	go joyriding
5_____	mugger	mug someone
shoplifting	6_____	shoplift
robbery	robber	7_____ someone / a bank, shop, etc.
8_____	thief	steal something
vandalism	vandal	9_____ something
murder	10_____	murder someone

3 Are any of these crimes a problem where you live?

▶▶▶ VOCABULARY BUILDER (PART 1): PAGE 132 ◀◀◀

4 🎧 3.22 Listen to six news reports. What are the crimes? Choose from the crimes in exercise 2.

LOOK OUT! *rob* and *steal*
You rob a place or a person.
Gangsters robbed a bank on Saturday.
You steal something from a person or a place.
Someone has stolen my calculator.

---

5 🎧 3.22 Read the *Look out!* box. Then choose the correct verb in the sentences. Listen again and check.

1 A gang of criminals **robbed** / **stole** a bank in central Paris yesterday.

2 The police have **questioned** / **asked** a number of teenagers.

3 Police suspect that somebody deliberately **put** / **set** fire to the hall.

4 Somebody **broke** / **burgled** into Highfield School on Saturday night.

5 A woman **stole** / **robbed** jewellery worth £1,000 from a shop in the town centre.

6 Police **escaped** / **arrested** a 45-year-old man yesterday in connection with her death.

6 SPEAKING Work in pairs. Decide which three of the crimes in exercise 2 are the most serious, and why. Tell the class which crimes you have chosen.

> We think ... is the most serious crime because ...

> We don't think ... is as serious as ... because ...

▶▶▶ VOCABULARY BUILDER (PART 2): PAGE 132 ◀◀◀

9B GRAMMAR Past perfect

I can describe an event using different past tenses.

1 Read the text. What did the man steal?

Last weekend, a very large man walked out of a shopping centre in Moscow with a cash machine on his shoulders that weighed 90 kilograms.
He **had entered** the shopping centre and **had pulled** the cash machine out of the wall! Fortunately, a shop assistant **had seen** the crime and called the police. They arrested the man later as he was trying to put the cash machine into his car. The man later told the police that he **had trained** as a sumo wrestler!

2 Look at the verbs in blue in the text. Did these events happen *before* or *after* the man walked out of the shopping centre?

3 Complete rule 2 in the *Learn this!* box with *before*, *after* or *at the same time as*.

> **LEARN THIS!**
>
> **1** We form the **past perfect** with *had* or *hadn't* + past participle.
> *When I got home, the thieves had stolen my motorbike.*
>
> ```
> past                        now        future
> ◄──────✕──────────✕─────────↓──────────►
>        ↑          ↑
>   The thieves    I got home.
>   stole
>   my motorbike.
> ```
>
> **2** We use the **past perfect** to talk about an event that happened _____ another event in the past.
> *He remembered that he hadn't locked the doors.*
> *Had they already finished eating when he arrived?*

4 Complete the sentences. Use the past perfect form of the verbs in brackets. (For sentences 5 and 6, look again at the *Look out!* box on page 45.)

1 After the thief _____ (steal) the painting, he sold it online.
2 The police arrived after the shoplifter _____ (run away).
3 The police caught the vandals after they _____ (smash) a shop window.
4 After the police _____ (catch) him, he confessed to the crime.
5 The house was empty when the burglars broke in because we _____ (go) to the shops.
6 After the teenagers _____ (go) joyriding, they burned the car.

⟫⟫⟫ **GRAMMAR BUILDER 9B: PAGE 120** ⟪⟪⟪

5 Complete the text. Use the past perfect form of the verbs in brackets.

Last Saturday morning, a giant chocolate rabbit disappeared from a sweet shop window.
The shop owner wondered who [1]_____ (steal) it, as he [2]_____ (not see) the thief pass by. Later on, he watched the shop's security film and found out that a three-year-old girl [3]_____ (take) the 60-centimetre-tall rabbit! The child [4]_____ (pull) the large chocolate animal out onto the street and [5]_____ (hide) it in her pushchair.
Her mother [6]_____ (not notice) this. She was confused when she later found the rabbit, but she only realised what [7]_____ (happen) when she saw a photo of herself in the newspaper!

6 Complete the sentences. Use the past perfect and your own ideas.

1 I was worried that I had lost my keys.
2 I couldn't believe that …
3 I was embarrassed because …
4 I was disappointed because …
5 I was pleased because …
6 I suddenly remembered that …

7 Imagine one bad thing that happened yesterday, and write it down. Look at the examples to help you.

The dog chewed my trainers.
My brother broke my iPod.
My mum burned my dinner.

8 SPEAKING Play a memory game in class. Each student adds an idea from exercise 7. Remember to use the past perfect.

> When I got home yesterday, the dog had chewed my trainer.

> When I got home yesterday, the dog had chewed my trainer, and my brother had broken my iPod.

> When I got home yesterday …

1 SPEAKING What do you know about Robin Hood? Have you seen any films about him?

2 🎧 3.23 Read the text quickly, ignoring the gaps, and find:
1 the century in which Robin Hood probably lived.
2 the name of the king at that time.
3 the name of the forest where Robin Hood lived.

3 Read the text again and match sentences a–e with gaps 1–4. There is one sentence that you do not need.
a Richard's brother John ruled England while he was away.
b But it is the heroic figure in the legend that we remember.
c However, he was also a great fighter.
d In fact, stories about the adventures of Robin Hood have existed for over six hundred years.
e They also robbed rich people who were travelling through the forest and gave the money to poor people.

4 VOCABULARY Match the highlighted words in the text with the definitions below.
1 a very large group of soldiers
2 facts that show that something is true
3 fought (to do something); had great difficulty (doing something)
4 a person who leads a country, and has power
5 people who have committed crimes, and are hiding
6 something that is very unfair/wrong

5 🎧 3.24 Read the exam strategy. Listen to three people talking about whether it is ever OK to steal. Are the sentences true or false?
1 Kevin thinks it's OK to steal in some circumstances.
2 Kevin thinks it's better to steal from a shop than a big organisation.
3 Jill's friend thinks it's OK to steal.
4 Jill thinks it's never OK to steal.
5 A shop assistant once gave Andy the wrong change.
6 Andy feels bad about underpaying in the restaurant.

6 SPEAKING Work in pairs. Do you think it's ever OK to steal? Give reasons and examples.

The Legend of Robin Hood

Robin Hood is one of the most popular and interesting figures in English folklore, and his story is quite well known across the world. **1** [ ] There have been several films made about him, including three in Hollywood. But who was he, and did he actually exist?

In the thirteenth century, the story goes, there was a brave young man in Nottingham who fought against injustice with his band of outlaws. At that time, King Richard and his army were fighting in foreign lands. **2** [ ] John was a mean and cruel ruler, and so was his friend – the terrible Sheriff of Nottingham. The Sheriff demanded money from all the people who lived in the area of Nottingham. The poor had to pay large amounts, and struggled to survive and feed their families.

In the legend, Robin Hood was angry at the injustice and decided to fight against it. He and his band of outlaws lived in Sherwood Forest, an enormous wood near Nottingham that belonged to the King. They hunted the King's deer for food. **3** [ ] The forest was considered a dangerous place, but to Robin and his band, it was a place of safety, away from the Sheriff's men.

There is some evidence that a man called Robin Hood actually lived during the thirteenth century, but it is unlikely that he was quite such a good man. **4** [ ] Today, Sherwood Forest is a tourist attraction. Nearly a million people every year go to the Visitor Centre there to learn about Britain's most famous outlaw. And even if he wasn't quite such a great man, it's a great story!

1 Read the text. Did Mark steal the bag? Did the police officer believe him?

Mark was sitting at the bus stop when a young man ran up and put a bag on the bench next to him. He told Mark that he could have the bag, and then ran off. Mark was confused. He was just looking inside the bag when a police officer arrived and told Mark that she was arresting him. She said that Mark had stolen the bag. Mark replied that he was innocent, but the officer said that criminals always pretended they hadn't done anything wrong.

2 Read the quotations and underline the parts of the text in exercise 1 where they are reported.

1 'You can have this bag.'
2 'I'm arresting you.'
3 'You stole the bag.'
4 'I'm innocent!'
5 'Criminals always pretend they haven't done anything wrong!'

3 Compare the quotations in exercise 2 with the underlined text in exercise 1. How do the verbs and pronouns change?

4 Read the rules in the *Learn this!* box and choose the correct options: a or b.

> **LEARN THIS!**
>
> When you change **direct speech** to **reported speech**,
> 1 verbs in the present simple usually change to
>   a the future.   b the past simple.
> 2 verbs in the present continuous usually change to
>   a the present simple. b the past continuous.
> 3 verbs in the past simple usually change to
>   a the past perfect.   b the present perfect.
> 4 *can*
>   a changes to *could*. b doesn't change.
> 5 pronouns
>   a always change.   b sometimes change, depending on the context.

⨠⨠⨠ **GRAMMAR BUILDER 9D: PAGE 120–121** ⨞⨞⨞

5 Rewrite what Freya says using reported speech.

1 I'm bored.
  Freya said that she was bored.
2 I don't want to watch a film.
3 I'm going to ring Lesley.
4 I can't find my mobile!
5 I can borrow my mum's phone.
6 My mum doesn't have Lesley's number on her phone.
7 I'm going to Lesley's house.

6 Rewrite the quotations in reported speech. Change the pronouns if necessary.

1 'I stole a CD from the music shop,' he said.
  He said that he had stolen a CD from the music shop.
2 'I want to catch the shoplifter,' the security guard said.
3 'The police arrested a vandal,' she said.
4 'It's difficult to catch drug dealers,' said the police inspector.
5 'We are questioning two teenagers about the burglary,' the police officer said.
6 'I sometimes go joyriding with my friends,' he said.
7 'The police are looking for the bank robbers,' she said.
8 'A boy in my class vandalised a park bench,' my brother said.

7 Write two true sentences and one false sentence. Use the present simple, present continuous, past simple or *can*.

1. I never have breakfast.
2. I'm going to a barbecue on Saturday.
3. I can touch my nose with my tongue.

8 SPEAKING Work in pairs. Read the sentences to your partner. Your partner reports them to another pair of students. They say whether the sentences are true or false.

> I never have breakfast.

> James said that he never had breakfast.

I can understand texts about modern crimes.

1 SPEAKING Look at the photos and the titles of the four texts (A–D). What do you think the crimes have in common?

2 🎧 3.25 Read texts A–D quickly and match them with the words and phrases (1–4).
1 credit or debit card fraud
2 a computer virus
3 spam
4 identity theft

3 Read the texts again. Match two sentences about the 'high-tech criminals' with each text. Write *A*, *B*, *C* or *D*.
1 He worked with other criminals. _____
2 The identity of the criminal is a mystery. _____
3 He ran an advertising company. _____
4 He sent junk emails which weren't illegal. _____
5 He tried to steal money from thousands of people. _____
6 He didn't actually commit a crime. _____
7 He/She stole a lot of money from one person. _____
8 He damaged computers in many countries. _____

Cyber Crime

A ☐ Copy cat

A man was jailed for four years last week for copying thousands of debit cards. Theogones de Montford was the leader of a gang of criminals who added a special hidden machine to cash machines at petrol stations. The tiny machine copied the information from the debit cards that people put into the machines. The gang then made copies of the cards and used them to buy things in shops and on the Internet. They also put the cards into cash machines and took money from people's bank accounts. De Montford had copied 35,000 cards and had stolen over £720,000!

B ☐ Are you who you say you are?

Sam Jenkins was astonished when she discovered that her bank account was empty. Just two weeks before, there had been £15,000 in it. The bank told her that she had moved the money herself to a new account with another bank. A month before, Sam had received an email which asked her to give personal information such as bank account details, passwords and PIN numbers. She thought the email was from her bank, but it wasn't –

the person who sent it used the information to steal Sam's identity and open a new bank account. They then moved Sam's money into the new account, took the money out, and closed the account. Sam still doesn't know who sent the fake email.

C ☐ Email my love to you

'I love you' was an email message that people were delighted to receive. It was sent to thousands of people on the morning of 4 May 2000. But it contained a virus! When they opened the email, the virus went to everyone in their address book. It quickly spread around the world, and caused terrible damage to hundreds of computer systems. Most large organisations, including the British government, had to close their email systems to get rid of it. A Filipino computer programmer had written the virus. The police arrested him, but at that time it wasn't a crime to write computer viruses, so they had to let him go.

D ☐ Click on the link

Sanford Wallace is called the 'Spam King'. During the 1990s, he had a company called Cyber Promotions, which helped other companies to advertise their products by email. He did this by sending about 30

million 'junk emails' every day. Many people were very angry when they received enormous numbers of email advertisements, but Wallace hadn't done anything illegal. Then, in 2009, Wallace sent emails to 14 million Facebook users. The emails directed them to other websites that paid Wallace for each visit. That was illegal and he was told by the courts to pay Facebook $711 million.

4 VOCABULARY Complete these nouns from the texts.

1 _____ machine (text A)
2 _____ account (text A)
3 _____ information (text B)
4 _____ word (text B)
5 _____ number (text B)
6 _____ programmer (text C)
7 _____ email (text D)

5 Complete the sentences with nouns from exercise 4.

1 I get so annoyed with all this _____ . I never want anything that they're advertising.

2 It's essential to remember your _____ when you want to get cash out from a _____ .

3 You mustn't tell anyone your _____ . They could use it to steal _____ from you.

4 My sister is an amazing _____ . She can even make computer games!

5 I've just opened a new _____ for the money from my new job.

6 SPEAKING Work in pairs. Ask and answer the questions.

1 Have you ever received junk email? Does it annoy you?
2 Why do you think people create computer viruses?
  a They are vandals.
  b They want people to notice and admire them.
  c It is a challenge – they want to see if it's possible.
  d They are bored and have nothing better to do.
  e Another reason (say what it is).

> I think people create computer viruses because …

3 In your opinion, should people who create computer viruses go to prison? Why? / Why not?

> I think they should … because …

> I don't think they should … because …

4 In your opinion, which of the 'crimes' in the texts is the worst? Give reasons.

1 SPEAKING Describe the picture. What is happening? What do you think the people are saying?

Officer	Good afternoon. What can I do for you?
Sally	I'd like to report a theft, please. Someone has stolen my rucksack.
Officer	May I just ask you some questions? Where did you last have the rucksack?
Sally	I think I left it in a shop in the high street.
Officer	And when was that?
Sally	About half an hour ago.
Officer	And you've been back to the shop to see if it's there?
Sally	Yes, I went straight back, but it wasn't there.
Officer	OK, I'll just take some details. Could you describe the rucksack, please?
Sally	Yes, it's yellow. It's made of canvas.
Officer	And what was in the rucksack?
Sally	Some books, some keys and some make-up.
Officer	OK. Was there any ID in the rucksack?
Sally	I'm not sure.
Officer	That's fine. If you could just fill in this form, please …

2 🎧 3.26 Read and listen to the dialogue. Is the situation formal or informal?

3 SPEAKING Work in pairs. Practise reading the dialogue, changing the words in blue. Use information from the chart.

Item stolen	Where / when?	Colour	Material	Contents
wallet	café, an hour ago	brown	plastic	£10 in cash, credit card
school bag	bus stop, just now	black	leather	schoolbooks, mobile, calculator
sports bag	*you decide*	*you decide*	canvas	*you decide*

4 In Britain, we use 'please' a lot when we make polite requests. Complete these requests with the words below. Which ones are used in the dialogue in exercise 1?

ask   could   if   may   mind

Polite requests
Would you ¹_____ [+ -*ing* form], please?
²_____ you … , please?
³_____ you could just …
Could I ⁴_____ you to … , please?
⁵_____ I just ask you some questions?

5 🎧 3.27 Listen to a conversation in a police station. Choose the correct answers.

1 Michael thinks that somebody stole his wallet
  a in the tourist information office.
  b in a café.
  c in the park.
2 The police officer advises Michael to
  a go back to the café.
  b contact the credit card companies.
  c contact the travel insurance company.
3 Michael wants the police officer to
  a find the phone number of his bank.
  b look for a man he saw in the tourist information office.
  c contact his bank for him.

6 🎧 3.27 Listen again and tick the questions that the police officer asks.

1 a What can I do for you? ☐
  b How can I help you? ☐
2 a Would you mind telling me your name, please? ☐
  b Could you tell me your name, please? ☐
3 a Could I ask what was in the wallet? ☐
  b If you could just tell me what was in the wallet. ☐
4 a Would you mind describing the wallet, please? ☐
  b Could I ask you to describe the wallet, please? ☐

7 Work in pairs. Prepare a dialogue in a police station. Use the language in exercises 4, 5 and 6 to help you.

Student A: You are the victim of a theft.
• Decide what has been stolen and where you last had it.
• Decide what it looks like and, if appropriate, what was in it.
• Report the crime at the police station.

Student B: You are a police officer.
• Ask questions about what has been stolen, where and when.
• If necessary, give advice to Student A.

8 SPEAKING Act out your dialogue to the class.

WRITING An email

I can write an email describing a crime.

1 **SPEAKING** Read the email quickly. Choose the correct answers. Give reasons.

1 Millie is Lisa's **friend / sister / teacher**.
2 The message is **formal / informal**.

✉ **Inbox**

Hi Lisa,

I've just got back. I must tell you what I saw on the way home!

I was walking down Fore Street when a guy suddenly shot out of a department store. A security guard was chasing him and shouting 'Stop him! Stop that man!' He'd obviously nicked something.

But a bunch of teenagers at the end of the road had heard all the yelling. One of them stuck his foot out. The man tripped and fell over. Then the rest of the teenagers sat on him! LOL! Then the security guard arrived and held the thief until the police arrived. Apparently, he'd stolen some very expensive watches.

It was awesome – just like in a film! I reckon the teenage boys will get a reward.

BFN Millie x

PS What are you up to this evening?

2 Read the email again and put the events in the order that they happened.

a ☐ Millie arrived home.
b ☐ A man stole some watches from a department store.
c ☐ The police arrived.
d ☐ The man ran out of the department store, chased by a security guard.
e ☐ The teenagers sat on the man.
f ☐ The man fell over.
g ☐ A teenager tripped up the man.

3 We often use colloquial expressions and abbreviations in emails. Find expressions and abbreviations in Millie's email that mean the same as the phrases below.

1 a man _____
2 ran very fast _____
3 stolen _____
4 group _____
5 shouting _____
6 laugh out loud _____
7 think _____
8 bye for now _____
9 What are you doing? _____

4 Read the writing strategy and identify the three types of information in Millie's email.

WRITING STRATEGY

When reporting an event, the information should be given in the following order:

1 Context. Describe the place of the event. Use the *past continuous* to describe the background, e.g. what the people were doing or wearing or what the weather was like
2 The description of the event. Use the *past simple* as well as the *past perfect* and *past continuous*.
3 The summary. Write a short summary or describe your reaction to the event.

5 Imagine you witnessed a crime. Plan an email to a friend describing the crime. Make notes using the questions below.

• What was the crime? (shoplifting/vandalism/mugging?)
• Who were the criminals? (how many? age? description?)
• What did they do? (steal/damage something? mug someone?)
• What happened? (called police? shouted for help? they ran away?)
• Did the police catch the criminals? (chased the criminals? arrested them? they escaped?)

6 Write the email (120–150 words).

CHECK YOUR WORK

Have you:
☐ included the information from your plan in exercise 5?
☐ set the scene, described the events and used informal language?
☐ written 120–150 words?
☐ checked your spelling and grammar?

Listening

1 <u>Get ready to LISTEN</u> Describe the photo. Use the words below to help you.

dangerous   degrees Celsius   endangered species
hunt   ice   melt   polar bear   seal   swim
temperature   the Arctic

2 Do the exam task.

LISTENING exam task

🎧 3.28 You will hear part of a radio documentary about polar bears. Decide if the sentences (1–7) are true (T) or false (F). Put **X** in the appropriate space in the table.

		T	F
1	Polar bears live in more than one country.		
2	They have to live on sea-ice.		
3	Polar bears mainly eat whales.		
4	The main threat to polar bears is hunters.		
5	The amount of ice has just started to decrease.		
6	Polar bears die in the sea because they can't swim very well.		
7	There are only 2,000 polar bears now in the Arctic.		

Speaking

3 <u>Get ready to SPEAK</u> Do you know the names of any organisations which campaign for environmental protection, endangered species or animal rights? What do they do to help?

4 Complete the questions with the words below. Then, in pairs, ask and answer the questions.

charity   leaflets   march   petition   politician

Have you or anyone you know ever:
- donated money to a _____ ? Which one?
- sent an email or a letter to a _____ ?
- given out _____ ?
- been on a protest _____ ?
- signed or organised a _____ ?

5 Do the exam task.

SPEAKING exam task

You are talking to a friend about a charity event you are both organising. Include information about the following points:

- Which charity will you support?
- What kind of event will you organise?
- How will you advertise the event?
- How much money do you want to raise?

Use of English

6 Do the exam task.

USE OF ENGLISH exam task

Complete the sentences with the correct form of the words in brackets.

1 There was a huge _____ eruption at Mount St Helens in 1980. (volcano)
2 You can save _____ by turning off lights. (electric)
3 We must stop _____ our rivers and lakes. (pollution)
4 There are some _____ bins in the car park. (recycle)
5 _____ campaigners advise people to use tap water, not bottled water. (environment)
6 The _____ of the rain forest will lead to an increase in global warming. (destroy)
7 Each year, _____ 200 billion bottles of water are consumed globally. (approximate)

Reading

7 `Get ready to READ` Complete the sentences with the words below.

art collector   forgery   original   painting   style

1 I've got a poster of Van Gogh's *Sunflowers* in my room. The _____ painting is in a museum in Amsterdam.
2 This isn't a genuine Picasso. It's a _____ .
3 My uncle is an _____ . He's got about 100 paintings.
4 In our art lesson we tried to paint in the _____ of Monet.
5 What a beautiful _____ ! Who's it by?

8 Do the exam task.

EXAM STRATEGY

Read the text for general understanding, ignoring the gaps. When choosing the missing sentences for the gaps, remember that the sentences must fit the context, make sense and be grammatically correct.

READING exam task

Read the text. Complete each gap (1–6) with a sentence (A–G). There is one sentence that you do not need to use.

Real or fake?

John Myatt is an artist. He may not be the greatest artist in the world, but he is possibly the world's greatest forger. He is able to paint pictures in the style of famous artists like Monet and Matisse.

¹_____ This unusual skill got Myatt into a lot of trouble in the 1990s. For many years he taught art at a secondary school, but then he got divorced and he gave up his job to spend more time with his children. In order to make some money he started painting pictures in the style of famous artists and selling them. ²_____ He was honest about his work – he wrote his name on the back, and he sold them for £150 each.

However, one of his customers, John Drewe, started to resell Myatt's paintings as genuine, original works. Drewe had sold one of Myatt's paintings for £25,000. He contacted Myatt and suggested that they go into business together. Myatt agreed. He continued to paint and Drewe sold his paintings to art collectors around the world. ³_____

The amazing thing is that Myatt painted his pictures with decorator's paint. ⁴_____ But it soon came to an end. Drewe was divorced too, and his ex-wife found out about the forgeries. She went to the police and they arrested Drewe and Myatt. At their trial Drewe was sent to prison for six years and Myatt for less than one year.

⁵_____ When he came out he started to produce pictures in the style of famous artists again. But he put his name on the back, as he'd done before he met Drewe. Myatt is now famous and instead of charging £150 for a painting, he can charge £40–50,000. ⁶_____

A That's more than Drewe gave him for his 'genuine' paintings!
B It wasn't illegal.
C Then he decided to stop copying famous paintings.
D Myatt only spent four months in prison for good behaviour.
E They are so good that experts can't tell that they are not originals.
F It was the same paint that people use to paint houses!
G Between 1986 and 1994 they sold about 200 paintings and made over a million pounds.

Speaking

9 `Get ready to SPEAK` Match the words below with the photos in the speaking exam task. Which other words might you need to describe them?

queue   clothes   food   free   guard   happy   prison
prisoner   punish   uniform   canteen

10 Do the exam task.

SPEAKING exam task

Choose one of the photos and discuss these points:
• who the people are
• where they are
• what is happening in the photo

Compare and contrast the photos. Answer the questions.

1 How are life in prison and normal life different?
2 How are the people in the photos feeling?

THIS UNIT INCLUDES
Vocabulary ▪ publications ▪ books and text ▪ words related to literature
Grammar ▪ the passive (present and past simple)
▪ the passive (present perfect and future)
Speaking ▪ talking about reading habits ▪ arranging to meet
Writing ▪ an informal letter

10A VOCABULARY AND LISTENING Publications

I can identify and talk about different publications.

1 SPEAKING What was the last book you read? Did you enjoy it? Who wrote it? Tell your partner.

2 VOCABULARY Divide the list of publications below into two groups: *fiction* and *non-fiction*.

Publications atlas autobiography biography comic cookbook dictionary encyclopaedia grammar book guidebook magazine manual newspaper novel play short story textbook thesaurus

3 🎧 3.29 PRONUNCIATION Listen, repeat and check. Underline the stress in each word.

4 VOCABULARY Which publication from exercise 2 would you read if you wanted to:

1 read the story of a person's life, written by that person?
2 read the story of a person's life, written by someone else?
3 find out which countries are next to Egypt?
4 learn how your new HD TV works?
5 look up a word you don't understand?
6 read something written for the theatre?
7 read stories with lots of pictures and not many words?
8 find information about rainforests?
9 read the latest gossip about pop stars?
10 read a long fictional work?
11 read about what is happening in the world?
12 find out what to do and see when you're on holiday?
13 find out how to cook a nice meal?
14 prepare for a maths exam?
15 find different words with the same meaning?
16 learn the rules of the English language?
17 read a short fictional work?

>>> **VOCABULARY BUILDER (PART 1): PAGE 133** <<<

5 SPEAKING Work in pairs. Do you recognise any of these characters? What books are they from?

6 Match the books from exercise 5 with five of the authors below. Do you know any other books by these authors?

Jane Austen   Arthur Conan Doyle   Charles Dickens
JRR Tolkien   Lewis Carroll   Stephenie Meyer   JK Rowling

7 🎧 3.30 Listen to Matt and Rachel doing a questionnaire. Complete the sentences with *Matt* or *Rachel*.

1 _____ reads a lot of comics.
2 _____ reads a lot of magazines.
3 _____ finds films more exciting than books.
4 _____ thinks fame is more important than money.
5 _____ has written a science-fiction short story.

8 🎧 3.30 Listen again. Complete the questions.

1 _____ books a year do you read?
2 Would you rather read a novel or _____ of that novel?
3 If you were an author, would you prefer to be _____ but famous, or _____ but unknown?
4 Have you ever written a short story for _____ ?

9 SPEAKING Work in pairs. Ask and answer the questions from exercise 8.

>>> **VOCABULARY BUILDER (PART 2): PAGE 133** <<<

1 Read the facts. Which do you think is the most surprising?

Did you know ... ?

- More than 32 million books are kept in the Library of Congress in Washington, D.C.
- Every book that is published in the UK is sent to the British Library free of charge.
- 57 books are bought every second by shoppers in the USA.
- Before 1450, books weren't printed – they were copied by hand.
- The first Harry Potter manuscript was offered to twelve publishers – and they all said no!
- The novel *Gadsby: Champion of Youth* was written in 1939 by Ernest Vincent Wright without using the letter 'e'.
- A copy of *Alice's Adventures in Wonderland* was sold for $1.5 million in New York.

2 Find three examples of the passive in blue in the text. Complete the rules in the *Learn this!* box.

> **LEARN THIS!**
> 1 The **passive** is formed with the correct form of the verb _____ and the past participle.
> 2 We use the _____ simple for the **present passive** and the _____ simple for the **past passive**.
> 3 If we want to say who performed the action, we use *by*.

3 Underline five more examples of the passive in exercise 1. Are they present simple passive or past simple passive?

⟫ GRAMMAR BUILDER 10B: PAGE 122 ⟪

4 Complete the sentences in the chart. Use the present or past simple passive form of the verbs in brackets. Then match four of the sentences with pictures a–d.

Publishing – past and present	
50 years ago	**Today**
Manuscripts [1]_____ (write) by hand or on a typewriter.	Manuscripts [2]_____ (type) on a computer.
The finished manuscript [3]_____ (send) to the publisher by post.	The finished manuscript [4]_____ (email) to the publisher.
Pictures [5]_____ (draw) on paper.	Most pictures [6]_____ (create) on a computer.
Metal plates [7]_____ (make) by the printers.	Some books [8]_____ (print) directly from a computer.
Books [9]_____ (sell) only in bookshops.	More books [10]_____ (buy) online than from bookshops.

5 🎧 3.31 Listen and check.

6 Complete the questions. Use the correct passive form of the verbs in brackets.

a __Was__ the Duke of Edinburgh Award scheme s̲t̲a̲r̲t̲e̲d̲ by the Queen's husband? (start)

b _____ teenage surfer Bethany Hamilton _____ by a shark? (attack)

c _____ fox-hunting _____ in the UK in 2004? (ban)

d _____ FarmVille _____ by 82 million people around the world? (play)

e _____ the first *Pirates of the Caribbean* film _____ in 2010? (make)

f _____ Facebook _____ by more than 60% of people in the UK? (use)

g _____ April Fool's Day _____ in France? (celebrate)

h _____ the Earth _____ by an enormous asteroid about 65 million years ago? (hit)

i _____ England _____ by King John during the fifteenth century? (rule)

7 SPEAKING Work in pairs. Ask and answer the questions in exercise 6. You can find the answers in these lessons:

a	1C	c	3C	e	4B	g	7E	i	9C
b	2E	d	3E	f	6C	h	8E		

1 In pairs, use the words below to make the titles of five plays by William Shakespeare. Have you seen any of them on TV, or in the cinema or theatre?

and and Caesar Cleopatra Antony Hamlet Juliet
Julius Lear King Romeo

2 Read the text. What do these numbers refer to?

1 eight   4 thirty-seven
2 fifteen   5 a hundred and fifty-four
3 eighteen   6 fifty-two

1. *Shakespeare was one of eight children.*

William Shakespeare

William Shakespeare is probably the most famous playwright in history. He was born on 23 April 1564 in Stratford-upon-Avon in England. He was one of eight brothers and sisters. His father, John Shakespeare, was a successful businessman. William went to school in Stratford and learnt Latin and Greek, but he didn't go to university. At the age of fifteen he went straight to work in his father's business.

When he was eighteen, he met and fell in love with Anne Hathaway. She was eight years older than him. They got married in November 1582, and six months later their daughter Susanna was born. In 1585 they had twins, Hamnet and Judith. Little is known about the following seven years of his life. We only know that he moved to London, leaving Anne and the children in Stratford, and that by 1592 he was writing plays and working as an actor.

His plays were very popular and he made a lot of money. In 1597 he bought a big house in Stratford for his family, but he stayed in London for a further thirteen years. He continued to write and act and also bought a theatre. In 1611 he finally retired and moved back to Stratford to live in the house he had bought. In total, Shakespeare wrote 37 plays and 154 sonnets (fourteen-line poems). Some of his love poems are addressed to a married woman, and some of them are addressed to a young man. Nobody knows the identity of these two people. Shakespeare died in Stratford on his birthday, on 23 April 1616, and was buried in the church where he had been christened 52 years earlier.

3 Complete the sentences about Shakespeare using one word.

1 Shakespeare was _____ in Stratford-upon-Avon in the sixteenth century.
2 He had _____ brothers and sisters.
3 He studied at _____ but not at university.
4 Susanna was Shakespeare's first _____ .
5 Hamnet and Judith are the names of Shakespeare's _____ .
6 In London, Shakespeare made a lot of _____ .
7 Shakespeare wrote love poems for a man and woman but their _____ is still a secret.
8 Shakespeare returned to Stratford five years before he _____ .

4 🎧 3.32   Listen to the interviews. Which plays from exercise 1 are they studying at school?

1 Leon   2 Maya   3 Riley

5 🎧 3.32   Listen again. Choose the correct options (a–c).

1 Leon went to see a Shakespeare play with his
  a parents.   b English teacher.   c classmates.
2 Leon thinks Shakespeare's language is
  a amazing.   b too difficult.   c quite modern.
3 Maya thinks the stories in Shakespeare's plays are
  a exciting.   b slow.   c difficult to follow.
4 Maya thinks the best way to enjoy the plays is to watch them
  a with a teacher. b in a theatre.   c on film.
5 Riley finds Shakespeare's plays interesting because of the
  a topics.   b characters.   c topics and characters.
6 Where did Riley see *Romeo and Juliet*?
  a In New York.   b In Stratford.   c In London.

6 Complete the sentences with the words below.

Types of literature   plays   poems   novels   short stories

1 A playwright writes _____ .
2 A novelist writes _____ and/or _____ .
3 A poet writes _____ .

7 SPEAKING Name some famous writers from your country. Can you remember any of their works?

> Franz Kafka was a novelist. One of his most famous works is the novel *The Trial*.

1 Look at the photo and read the text. What do you think are the advantages and disadvantages of ebook readers? Use the words below to help you.

convenient light/heavy bookshelf paper
screen space carry lend/borrow

Books: the final chapter?

Printed books have been bought and sold for hundreds of years and during that time, they haven't changed very much. Until now.

The idea of an electronic book with a screen instead of pages has become reality. Ebook readers have been produced and millions of ebooks have been downloaded from online stores.

At the moment, there are about 725,000 ebooks on Amazon – but thousands more will be added every year in the future. So has the final chapter been written? Will printed books be completely replaced by ebooks? They haven't been replaced yet, but perhaps soon 'real' books won't be sold in shops at all – they'll be kept in museums!

2 Underline the passive forms in the text. What tense are they? Complete the table with examples from the text.

The passive
1 present perfect, affirmative Example: _____
2 present perfect, negative Example: _____
3 present perfect, interrogative Example: _____
4 *will* future, affirmative Example: _____
5 *will* future, negative Example: _____
6 *will* future interrogative Example: _____

>>> GRAMMAR BUILDER 10D: PAGE 122–123 <<<

3 Write questions. Use the present perfect passive and *ever*.

1 you / sting / by a bee
   Have you ever been stung by a bee?
2 you / bite / by a dog or a cat
3 you / injure / playing sport
4 your house / burgle
5 your mobile phone / steal
6 your hair / cut / by a family member

4 SPEAKING Work in pairs. Ask and answer the questions in exercise 3.

> Have you ever been stung by a bee?

> Yes, I have. / No, I haven't.

5 Complete the facts. Use the present perfect passive form of the verbs in brackets.

In the last five minutes …

- 635 million unwanted emails *have been received* in the USA and Europe.
- three new books [1]_____ (publish) in the world
- five books [2]_____ (sell) in the USA.
- 15,000 text messages [3]_____ (send) in the UK.
- 5,000 pages [4]_____ (add) to the Internet.
- 300,000 letters and parcels [5]_____ (deliver) by the Royal Mail in the UK.
- 120 hours of video [6]_____ (add) to YouTube.

6 Complete the predictions. Use the future passive form (affirmative or negative) of the verbs in brackets.

Twenty years from now …
1 computers _____ (sell) for $5.
2 housework _____ (do) by robots.
3 smells _____ (include) in the films and TV shows you watch at home.
4 hotels _____ (build) on the moon.
5 all exams _____ (take) online.
6 cars _____ (power) by solar energy.
7 Chinese _____ (spoken) by everybody in the world.
8 wars _____ (fight) to get fresh water.

7 SPEAKING Discuss the predictions in exercise 6 with the class. Do you agree or disagree with them?

> I'm sure hotels won't be built on the moon.

> I think housework will be done by robots.

READING Vampire stories

I can understand a text about vampire novels.

1 SPEAKING Look at the photos. Do you know (a) the author, (b) the book, (c) the actor?

2 🎧 3.33 Read the text quickly. What type of text is it? Choose a, b, c or d.

a an article   c a short story
b a personal account   d an interview

3 Read the text again. Match headings A–F with paragraphs 1–5. There is one heading that you do not need.

A A 21st-century hit
B The first modern vampire books
C Addicted to vampire stories
D Why films are more popular than novels
E The original novel and film
F Why teenagers love vampire stories

4 VOCABULARY Find these words related to novels in the text. Then match them with the definitions below.

<u>Novels</u> chapter characters epilogue female lead plot sequel

1 the people in a novel
2 another book which continues the same story
3 a section of the book
4 an extra bit of story at the end
5 the events of the story
6 the main girl or woman in the story

The Vampires Return

1 They're young, they're rebellious and they have a taste for blood. This description fits not only the characters in modern vampire novels, but also many of the readers. Some teenagers love vampire stories so much, it's almost an addiction. But what is their appeal? Is it the plot or the characters? And why are they so popular with teenagers in particular (apart from the blood)?

2 The modern fashion for vampire stories probably started in 1976, with the publication of *Interview with the Vampire*, a novel by the American writer Anne Rice. This novel and its sequels are known as *The Vampire Chronicles* and about 80 million copies have been sold around the world. They are different from earlier vampire stories in one important way: some of the vampires are likeable characters. For example, the main character, Louis, needs to drink blood to survive, but he hates harming people. There are two different sides to his personality and many teenagers can identify with this. When the stories were made into a film, the part of Louis was played by Brad Pitt.

3 The most successful vampire books of the last ten years are the four novels in the *Twilight* series, by Stephenie Meyer. The books are about the relationship between the female lead, Bella Swan, and a young, sensitive vampire called Edward Cullen. The first novel, *Twilight*, was written in 2003. When the author finished the final chapter, she wrote an epilogue ... and then another, and then another. She realised she had enough ideas for more novels. That is why she wrote the sequels – and millions of teenagers around the world are glad that she did! They love the mix of fantasy, horror and romance. The novels have been made into successful films too.

4 Although *Twilight* is a 21st-century sensation, in fact the popularity of vampire stories is nothing new. In 1897, the Irish writer Bram Stoker wrote a novel called *Dracula*. Twenty-five years later, the film director Max Schreck made the first vampire film, *Nosferatu*. The film was so similar to Bram Stoker's novel that his family took legal action against the film studio – and won. The film studio had to destroy the film, but fortunately a few secret copies survived and in the 1990s, the film was seen again for the first time in seventy years. Like a true vampire, *Nosferatu* came back from the dead! And a lot of the familiar imagery of vampires which teenagers love – pale skin, black hair, red lips – dates back to the original novel and film.

5 Horror stories are particularly popular with teenagers, and that is partly the appeal of vampire novels. But teenagers also enjoy the important themes: the fight between good and evil, or the difference between what you want to do and what you should do. For example, in the *Twilight* books, can Edward show his love for Bella and look after her, or will the 'vampire side' of his personality win? These issues are interesting for teenagers, who are just starting to face life's big questions about love, morality, good and evil. For teenagers in the real world, most problems aren't a matter of life and death, but they often feel like it.

5 Complete the questions with the words below. Use each question word once only.

How many   What   When   Which   Who   Why

1 _When_ was *Interview with the Vampire* published?
2 _____ wrote *The Vampire Chronicles*?
3 _____ copies of the novels have been sold?
4 _____ did Stephenie Meyer write immediately after the last chapter of *Twilight*?
5 _____ did Bram Stoker's family take legal action?
6 _____ themes do vampire stories often deal with?

6 **SPEAKING** Work in pairs. Ask and answer the questions in exercise 5.

> When was *Interview with the Vampire* published?

> In 1976.

7 🎧 3.34 Read and listen to the song. Who is the singer talking to? Choose a, b or c.

a a person she bit and made into a vampire
b a person who bit her and made her a vampire
c a person she danced with who later became a vampire

Bloodletting (The Vampire Song)

There's a crack in the mirror
And a bloodstain on the bed
There's a crack in the mirror
And a bloodstain on the bed
Oh you were a vampire and baby
I'm the walking dead
Oh you were a vampire and baby
I'm the walking dead

I got the ways and means
To New Orleans
I'm going down by the river
Where it's warm and green
I'm gonna have a drink, and walk around
I got a lot to think about oh yeah

There's a rocking chair by the window
Down the hall
I hear something there in the shadow
Down the hall
Oh you were a vampire and now I am
Nothing at all
Oh you were a vampire and now I am
Nothing at all

I got the ways and means
To New Orleans
I'm going down by the river
Where it's warm and green
I'm gonna have a drink, and walk around
I got a lot to think about oh yeah

8 **SPEAKING** Work in pairs. Ask and answer the questions.

1 Would you like to be a writer? Why?/Why not?
2 What kind of book would be most interesting to write, in your opinion? (novel, cookbook, travel guide, etc.) Explain your choice.

> Would you like to be a writer?

> No, I wouldn't.

> Why not?

> Because I think it would be really boring.

I can make arrangements to meet somebody.

1 🎧 3.35 **Read and listen to the dialogue. When and where are Jack and Sophie going to meet?**

Sophie	Hi, Jack. It's Sophie. Are you in town?
Jack	Yes, I am. I'm at the shopping centre.
Sophie	Great! Do you fancy meeting up?
Jack	Yes, OK. What do you want to do?
Sophie	I'd like to see the new Ben Stiller film.
Jack	OK. Why don't we have something to eat first?
Sophie	I'd rather see the film first, if that's OK. It starts in forty minutes.
Jack	Fine. Where do you want to meet?
Sophie	Shall we meet by the bus stop?
Jack	Good idea. I'll be there in fifteen minutes.
Sophie	OK, great. See you later!
Jack	Why don't we go for a pizza after the film?
Sophie	Sure. Why not?

2 SPEAKING **Work in pairs. Practise reading the dialogue, changing the words in blue. Use your own ideas.**

3 **Find three different ways of making a suggestion in the dialogue in exercise 1 and three different ways of responding. Then complete 1–3 below.**

1 _____ meeting up? _____
2 _____ meet by the bus stop? _____
3 _____ go for a pizza after the film? _____

4 **Read the speaking strategy. Who suggests an alternative in the dialogue in exercise 1? What phrase is used?**

SPEAKING STRATEGY

When negotiating you will need to come up with an alternative solution. You can use one of the following phrases:
I'd prefer to … I'd rather … Why don't we … instead?

5 SPEAKING **Work in pairs. Take turns to be A and B. Use expressions from exercises 3 and 4.**

Student A: Suggest an activity below.
Student B: Suggest an alternative activity.
Student A: Accept Student B's suggestion.

Hobbies and interests   go for a bike ride   watch a DVD
listen to music   go shopping   play basketball
have lunch   watch TV   play computer games

6 🎧 3.36 **Listen to the conversation between Lisa and Gary and choose the correct answers (a–c).**

1 Lisa and Gary are both
  a in an entertainment store.
  b on a bus.
  c near the park.
2 Lisa suggests meeting
  a in the park.
  b at the bus stop.
  c in the supermarket.
3 Gary would prefer to buy
  a some food.
  b a present.
  c the new Shakira CD.
4 In the end, they decide to do
  a what Gary wants.
  b what Lisa wants.
  c what they both want.

7 🎧 3.36 **Listen again. Which two phrases from the strategy box do you hear?**

8 **Work in pairs. Prepare a dialogue, following the instructions below. Use phrases from exercises 3 and 4.**

Student A
• You are on the bus to town.
• You need to buy a book for school.
• You want to go for a burger at a café next to the bookshop, so you phone your friend and suggest it.

Student B
• When your friend phones, you are at the sports centre in town.
• You have just finished a game of basketball.
• You need a book for school, too. You don't like burgers – you would rather go for a pizza.

9 SPEAKING **Act out your dialogue to the class. Remember to include expressions from exercises 3 and 4.**

WRITING An informal letter

I can write an informal letter.

1 Read the letter. Answer the questions.

1 Who is Helen writing to?
2 What has she invited her to do?
3 What has Helen just finished doing?

A ....

B ....

Dear Grandma

How are you? I was sorry to hear about your cat. You must miss him. Are you going to get another pet?

Thanks for inviting us all to lunch next Saturday. I'm really sorry, but I can't make it. There's a rehearsal for the school play that afternoon and I really can't miss it.

Guess what? I've just finished reading *The Lord of the Rings*. Thanks so much for giving it to me. I'm not mad about the film, but I love the book.

Have you read *The Hobbit*? If not, I think you should read it. It's quite similar to *The Lord of the Rings* but it's much shorter! I can lend you a copy if you want to read it.

Write back soon!

Love

Helen

PS Do you fancy coming to see the school play? It's next weekend. I can get you a ticket.

2 Underline the expressions in the letter that Helen uses to:

a express a like and dislike.
b make an invitation.
c decline an invitation.
d give advice.
e express sympathy.

3 Match the expressions below with functions a–e in exercise 2. Compare them with the expressions that Helen uses.

1 Are you free to … ?
2 I heard about … . What a shame!
3 I'm really into … , but I'm not that keen on …
4 You ought to …
5 I'd love to, but I'm afraid I can't …

4 Use expressions from exercises 2 and 3 and your own words to:

1 invite somebody to a Halloween party.
2 express sympathy for somebody with a broken arm.
3 give advice to somebody who is starting a new school.
4 decline an invitation to a barbecue.
5 express a like for films and a dislike for sport.

> **WRITING STRATEGY**
>
> Start an informal letter with your address and the date. You do not need to write the recipient's address or his/her title. You don't need to introduce the subject of the letter either.

5 Read the writing strategy. Match A and B at the top of Helen's letter with two of the functions below.

Helen's full name   the date   Grandma's address
Helen's address   a title for the letter

6 You have just received a letter from your English friend. In the letter, he says that he has just failed his driving test. He also invites you to visit him in England next summer. Write a reply (120–150 words). Remember to include information on all of the points and use informal expressions.

- Express sympathy about the driving test.
- Accept or decline the invitation to visit.
- Say what book you've been reading and whether you'd recommend it.
- Invite your friend to come and visit you next year.

> **CHECK YOUR WORK**
>
> **Have you:**
> ☐ laid out the letter correctly?
> ☐ included the information in exercise 6?
> ☐ used informal language and expressions?
> ☐ written 120–150 words?

Unit 9

1 Write the words for the people who commit these crimes.

arson   arsonist

1 burglary _____
2 murder _____
3 vandalism _____
4 shoplifting _____
5 joyriding _____
6 robbery _____

Mark: ___ /6

2 Match the words (1–6) with a–e to make compound nouns.

1 junk   a word
2 computer   b account
3 pass   c programmer
4 bank   d information
5 personal   e email
6 cash   f machine

Mark: ___ /6

3 Complete the email. Use the past perfect form of the verbs below.

not buy   come   not do   drink   drop   spend

Hi Ahmed
My parents got back last night. They ¹_____ the weekend in Brighton visiting my grandma. They weren't too happy with me! I ²_____ any washing up all weekend. I ³_____ all the milk and juice, and I ⁴_____ any food. A friend of mine ⁵_____ round to watch a DVD on Saturday night and he ⁶_____ pizza on the sofa. I'm in big trouble!

Mark: ___ /6

4 Rewrite the sentences using reported speech.

1 'Ellie can use my phone,' said my brother.
2 'It's too cold to play volleyball,' said Laura.
3 'I did my homework,' said my sister.
4 'I'm not laughing,' said my dad.
5 'The soup tastes funny,' said Grace.
6 'I don't want to watch TV,' said Jenny.

Mark: ___ /6

5 Put the lines of the dialogue in the correct order.

a ☐ When did you last have the bag?
b ☐ Yes, I went straight back but it had disappeared.
c ☐ Have you been back to the park to see if it's there?
d ☐ Hello. What can I do for you?
e ☐ About two hours ago in the park.
f ☐ I'd like to report a theft. Somebody has stolen my bag.

Mark: ___ /6

Unit 10

6 Match the titles (1–6) with the types of book (a–f).

1 Quick meals   a textbook
2 My best years   b biography
3 French for beginners   c cookbook
4 Travelling in Africa   d manual
5 How to use your phone   e autobiography
6 Chopin: his life   f guidebook

Mark: ___ /6

7 Complete the text with the words below.

chapter   characters   epilogue   female lead   plot   sequel

All the main ¹_____ are introduced in the first ²_____ . This includes the ³_____ , Tara, a girl with strange powers. The ⁴_____ is full of exciting action. At the end of the book, there's a short ⁵_____ and in it, we learn that Tara actually died 100 years before the story begins! I really loved this book, and I hope there'll be a ⁶_____ soon.

Mark: ___ /6

8 Complete the sentences about London life. Use the present or past simple passive form of the verbs below.

hold   leave   speak   use   visit   wear

1 About 300 languages _____ in London.
2 The British Museum _____ by about 4.5 million people last year.
3 Large black hats _____ by the guards outside Buckingham Palace.
4 About 100,000 mobile phones _____ in London taxis last year.
5 The London Underground _____ by 4 million people a day.
6 The first Notting Hill carnival _____ in 1964.

Mark: ___ /6

9 Rewrite the sentences in the passive.

1 Somebody has stolen my jacket.
2 They'll wash your car while it's in the car park.
3 Somebody will ring a bell when it's time for dinner.
4 They've built a lot of new houses in the capital.
5 They've made cheese in this village for centuries.
6 One day, they'll only sell music online.

Mark: ___ /6

Total: ___ /30

10 Write the missing words to complete the dialogue.

Boy Do you ¹_____ meeting up in town?

Girl Sure. Why ²_____ we meet at the cinema?

Boy I'd ³_____ meet on the other side of town, in the shopping centre. I need to buy a few things.

Girl Fine. ⁴_____ we meet outside the café at 11.30?

Boy OK. ⁵_____ don't we have a drink at the café and then do some shopping?

Girl Sure. Why ⁶_____? See you later!

Mark: ____ /6

Total: ____ /30

Lead-in

1 Work in pairs. How much do you remember about Anna, Dani and Jack? Which event (a–f) did <u>not</u> happen? Put the others in the correct order.

a ☐ Anna went shopping in Leeds.

b ☐ Anna, Dani and Jack planned a fundraising event.

c ☐ Anna, Dani and Jack went to the cinema in Leeds.

d ☐ Jack and Anna went for a drive together.

e ☐ Anna started work at Golden Hills.

f ☐ Jack fixed Anna's mobile phone.

Listening

2 🎧 3.37 Listen to the conversation. How is Anna feeling by the end? Choose two of the adjectives below.

angry   bored   confused   embarrassed   pleased   sad

3 🎧 3.37 Listen again. Choose the correct answer.

1 Anna is leaving Golden Hills to
  a work in Liverpool.
  b find accommodation.
  c start a degree course.

2 She is first going to live
  a in a rented flat.
  b in a house with other young people.
  c in a room provided by her university.

3 Jack is leaving Golden Hills because
  a he's found another job.
  b he's lost his job there.
  c he wants to try a different career.

4 Dani invites Jack to
  a watch a DVD and eat pizza.
  b see a film and have some food.
  c have dinner in a French restaurant.

5 Jack's good mood surprises Anna because
  a he'd been in a bad mood earlier in the day.
  b they had had a big argument the day before.
  c she thought he'd be sad that she's leaving.

Reading

4 Look quickly through the newsletter and find out why Jack is not sad about leaving Golden Hills.

5 Read the newsletter. Match paragraphs A–D with sentences 1–5. There is one sentence that you do not need.

1 Two members of staff are going to leave.

2 Recent fundraising has been very successful.

3 There are plans for improved sports facilities.

4 Golden Hills has had a successful summer.

5 It hasn't been possible to solve a crime.

Golden Hills
Autumn newsletter

A ☐ After three very busy months, the holiday camp is now relatively quiet – until Christmas! Once again, the months of June, July and August have been a great success, with more guests than ever before. We have received excellent feedback. Thanks to everyone for all your hard work.

B ☐ A car was stolen from the Holiday Camp earlier this month. The police are investigating, but so far, no arrests have been made. They have appealed for information and they would particularly like to speak to anyone who was on duty that day. To improve security, new lights will be fitted next week.

C ☐ Thanks to everybody who took part in last month's events for Red Nose Day. The sponsored run raised over £500 and was organised by Dani from the gym. Well done, Dani! And well done to Anna and Jack, who organised the amazingly successful talent show, which raised over £1,000!

D ☐ Unfortunately, we say goodbye to both Jack and Anna in September. Anna is starting a full-time degree course at the University of Liverpool. Jack is starting a job in the IT department of Mersey Software Ltd., which is also based in Liverpool. We wish them both lots of luck.

Speaking

6 Work in pairs. Role-play a telephone conversation between Anna and an English-speaking friend. Talk about:

• some of the things that have happened since Anna started working at Golden Hills.

• how Anna feels about leaving, and her plans for the future.

• an arrangement to meet.

Writing

7 Imagine you are organising a leaving party for Jack and Anna. Write an announcement giving:

• the reason for the party.

• the time, date and venue of the party.

• what will be provided (food, drink, etc.).

1B   Present simple and continuous

1 Work in pairs. Look at the picture. Ask and answer the questions. Use the present continuous. → 1.4, 1.5

1 the girls / wearing / jeans?
  Are the girls wearing jeans? Yes, they are.
2 the dog / sitting down?
3 the girls / standing up?
4 they / drinking?
5 the sun / shining?
6 the girls / chatting / on their mobiles?

2 Make the affirmative statements negative. Make the negative statements affirmative. → 1.1, 1.2, 1.4, 1.5

1 I play chess school after school.
  I don't play chess after school.
2 She's wearing a brown dress today.
3 He doesn't like wearing suits.
4 My dad works in Manchester every day.
5 My sister isn't going out this evening.
6 It's raining at the moment.

3 Complete the questions. Use the present simple or the present continuous. → 1.2, 1.4, 1.5

1 How many languages _____ ?
  She speaks French, German and Italian.
2 Why _____ ?
  I'm smiling because I'm happy.
3 Where _____ his homework?
  He does his homework in his bedroom.
4 Why _____ computer games?
  I'm playing computer games because I'm bored.
5 When _____ on holiday?
  I'm going on holiday at the end of the month.
6 How _____ to school?
  They go by tram.

4 Complete the phone conversation. Use the present simple or the present continuous form of the verbs in brackets. → 1.3, 1.6

Emma   Hi Dan. What [1]_____ (you / do)?
Dan   Nothing much. I [2]_____ (read) my horoscope in a magazine.
Emma   What [3]_____ (it / say)?
Dan   'At the moment things [4]_____ (not go) well. But be patient and optimistic.'
Emma   [5]_____ (you / believe) in horoscopes?
Dan   Not really. Hey, [6]_____ (you / want) to do something this evening?
Emma   OK. What's on at the cinema?
Dan   Only a romantic comedy. I [7]_____ (not like) them much.
Emma   What kind of films [8]_____ (you / like)?
Dan   Action films. I really [9]_____ (want) to see the new Matt Damon film. But it [10]_____ (not come) out until July. That's ages away.
Emma   Well, you'll just have to be patient – like your horoscope says!

1D   Verb + infinitive or *-ing*

5 Match the two halves of the questions. Then answer them. → 1.7, 1.8

1 Do you expect
2 When you were a child, did you spend a lot of time
3 Are you looking forward to
4 Do you mind
5 Do you promise

a playing with cars and trains?
b not to tell anyone my secret?
c leaving school?
d to go to university?
e speaking in front of a lot of people?

6 Complete the sentences. Use the infinitive or *-ing* form of the verbs in brackets. → 1.7, 1.8

1 Kay and Martin agreed _____ (go) and see a film together.
2 Who suggested _____ (see) a film tonight?
3 Why did Kate refuse _____ (help) you?
4 Sara always avoids _____ (ask) her parents for money.
5 I can't help _____ (eat) chocolate when I'm stressed.
6 George decided _____ (take) the bus to town.
7 Jason expects _____ (go) with Sally to the concert.
8 I don't mind _____ (help) my sister with her homework.
9 Do you fancy _____ (come) to my house for dinner tomorrow?
10 We hope _____ (finish) school early today.

1 Grammar Reference

Present simple

1.1 We form the present simple like this:

Affirmative	
I play	we play
you play	you play
he/she/it plays	they play

Spelling: 3rd person singular (he/she/it)
We add -s to the end of most verbs.

+ -s	start → starts	play → plays

We add -es if the verb ends in -ch, -ss, -sh or -o.

+ -es	teach → teaches	miss → misses
	do → does	go → goes

If the verb ends in a consonant + -y, we change -y to i and add -es.

-y → -ies	study → studies	carry → carries

1.2

Negative	
Full form	**Short form**
I do not play	I don't play
you do not play	you don't play
he/she/it does not play	he/she/it doesn't play
you do not play	you don't play
we do not play	we don't play
they do not play	they don't play

Interrogative	Short answer
Do I play …?	Yes, I do. / No, I don't.
Do you play …?	Yes, you do. / No, you don't.
Does he/she/it play …?	Yes, she does. / No, she doesn't.
Do we/you/they play …?	Yes, we/you/they do. / No, we/you/they don't.

1.3 We use the present simple:
- for something that always happens or happens regularly (e.g. every week, often, sometimes).
  Sally cycles to school every day.
- for facts.
  Cows eat grass.
- with certain verbs that are not used in continuous tenses, e.g. *believe, hate, like, love, need, know, prefer, want*.
  I like this music. (NOT – I'm liking this music.)

Present continuous

1.4 We form the present continuous like this:
- the correct form of *be* + the -ing form of the main verb.
  Daniel is eating. / Are you playing?

1.5 **Spelling: verb + -*ing* form**
We add -ing to the end of most verbs.

play + -ing → playing	study + -ing → studying

If the verb ends in a consonant + -e, we usually drop the -e and add -ing.

-e → -ing	write → writing	make → making

1.6 We use the present continuous:
- for something that is happening now.
  Look! It's raining.
- for something that is happening temporarily, not necessarily at the moment of speaking.
  My mum's learning English in the evenings.
- for arrangements in the future.
  We're playing tennis tomorrow.

We don't use the present continuous:
- with certain verbs, e.g. *believe, hate, like, love, need, know, prefer, want*.
  I like this music. (NOT – I'm liking this music.)

Verb + infinitive or -*ing* form

1.7 When we put two verbs together, the second verb is usually in the infinitive or the -ing form.
I want to go home. (infinitive)
John suggested playing chess. (-ing form)
British teenagers like to watch TV. / British teenagers like watching TV. (infinitive or -ing form)

1.8 Below is a list of verbs that are followed by the infinitive, the -ing form, or both.

verb + infinitive		verb + -*ing* form		Verb + infinitive or -*ing* form
agree	offer	avoid	finish	begin
decide	prepare	can't help	imagine	continue
expect	pretend	can't stand	practise	hate
fail	promise	spend time	don't mind	like
hope	refuse	enjoy	suggest	love
manage	seem	fancy		prefer
mean	want	feel like		start

2B Past simple

1 Write the past simple form of the regular (1–8) and irregular (9–16) verbs. → 2.2, 2.3

1	expect _____	9	lose _____
2	compete _____	10	draw _____
3	stop _____	11	do _____
4	equalise _____	12	go _____
5	miss _____	13	make _____
6	carry _____	14	come _____
7	score _____	15	give _____
8	face _____	16	say _____

2 Complete the sentences. Use the past simple affirmative or negative form of the verbs in brackets. Some are regular and some are irregular. → 2.1, 2.2, 2.3, 2.4, 2.6

1 We _____ (leave) the match early because it was boring.
2 My sister was sad because she _____ (not win) her tennis match.
3 Liverpool _____ (not score) a goal – it was Chelsea 1, Liverpool 0 at the end.
4 We _____ (not like) playing table tennis outside because it was too cold.
5 I _____ (run) really fast for the first 300 metres, but was slower over the final 100 metres.
6 You _____ (win) by three sets to one. Well done!
7 My grandad always _____ (prefer) rugby to football.

3 Complete the dialogue with past simple questions and short answers. → 2.4

Ed What [1]_____ (you / do) on Saturday?
Vicky I went to the skating rink to watch ice hockey.
Ed What match [2]_____ (you / see)?
Vicky The New Jersey Devils against the New York Rangers.
Ed [3]_____ (you / enjoy) it?
Vicky Yes, [4]_____ . It was great.
Ed [5]_____ (the Rangers / win)?
Vicky No, [6]_____ . But I like the Devils!

4 Complete the text messages with *was*, *wasn't*, *were* and *weren't*. → 2.5

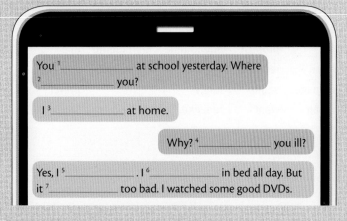

You [1]_____ at school yesterday. Where [2]_____ you?

I [3]_____ at home.

Why? [4]_____ you ill?

Yes, I [5]_____ . I [6]_____ in bed all day. But it [7]_____ too bad. I watched some good DVDs.

2D Past simple and continuous

5 Complete the text. Use the past continuous form of the verbs below. → 2.7

do   not rain   stand   take   think   wait

Everybody in the stadium [1]_____ for the match to start. The players [2]_____ on the pitch. Some of them [3]_____ exercises and others [4]_____ about the game. It was a cold night. It [5]_____ , but the ground was wet. A lot of spectators [6]_____ photos with their mobile phones.

6 Complete the dialogue. Use the past simple or past continuous form of the verbs in brackets. → 2.6, 2.7, 2.8

Officer What [1]_____ (you / do) at 8.30 p.m. yesterday?
Woman I [2]_____ (watch) a film on TV. The film [3]_____ (end) at quarter to ten.
Officer What was it called?
Woman I can't remember. I [4]_____ (not pay) attention.
Officer What [5]_____ (you / do) after the film?
Woman I [6]_____ (make) a cup of tea and [7]_____ (go) to bed. That was at ten o'clock.
Officer How do you know?
Woman Because the church clock [8]_____ (strike) ten when I [9]_____ (turn) off the light.

7 Complete the sentences. Use the past simple or past continuous form of the verbs in brackets. → 2.6, 2.7, 2.8

1 The basketball player _____ (catch) the ball and _____ (throw) it to another player.
2 My dad _____ (arrive) home while I _____ (watch) an ice hockey match on TV.
3 The referee _____ (stop) the match because it _____ (snow).
4 The cyclist _____ (put on) his helmet and _____ (get on) the bike.
5 She _____ (break) her leg while she _____ (ski).
6 The Los Angeles Lakers _____ (score) 30 points in the last ten minutes, but they _____ (not win) the game.
7 It _____ (not rain), so we _____ (play) tennis in the park.
8 Maria _____ (surf) when she _____ (see) a shark near the beach.

8 Complete the text. Use the past simple or past continuous form of the verbs in brackets. → 2.6, 2.7, 2.8

I [1]_____ (arrive) at Sam's party at 9.30 p.m. Lots of people [2]_____ (dance) in the living room. I [3]_____ (go) into the kitchen. Mike [4]_____ (be) there. He [5]_____ (stand) in front of the fridge. He [6]_____ (eat) a pizza. I [7]_____ (say) hello, but he [8]_____ (not hear) me. I don't think he [9]_____ (listen). I [10]_____ (leave) the kitchen and [11]_____ (walk) into the hall. Linda [12]_____ (sit) on the stairs. She [13]_____ (hold) her head in her hands. Her shoulders [14]_____ (shake), but she [15]_____ (not cry). She [16]_____ (laugh)!

2 Grammar Reference

Past simple

2.1 The affirmative form of the past simple is the same for all persons, singular and plural (*I*, *you*, *he*, *we*, etc.).

I watched a football match last night.
She watched TV.
They watched a DVD.

2.2 Spelling: past simple (affirmative) form of regular verbs
We form the past simple (affirmative) form of regular verbs by adding *-ed* to the verb.

| + *-ed* | work → worked | play → played |

If the verb ends in *-e*, we add *-d*.

| + *-d* | dance → danced | smoke → smoked |

If the verb ends in a consonant + *-y*, we change *-y* to *i* and add *-ed*.

| *-y* → *-ied* | study → studied | cry → cried |

If the verb ends in a short accented vowel + a consonant, we double the consonant.

-p → *-pped*	drop → dropped
-n → *-nned*	plan → planned
-t → *-tted*	regret → regretted

2.3 Some verbs have irregular past simple (affirmative) forms. There are no spelling rules for these forms: you need to learn them by heart. See the list in the Workbook.

Irregular verbs behave in the same way as regular verbs in negative sentences and questions.

2.4 In negative sentences and questions, we use *did*/*didn't* + the infinitive without *to* (NOT the past simple form) for regular and irregular verbs. The forms are the same for all persons, singular and plural (*I*, *you*, *he*, *we*, etc.).

Negative	Interrogative
I didn't watch	Did I watch?
he/she/it didn't watch	Did he/she/it watch?
we/you/they didn't watch	Did we/you/they watch?

Short form and full form	Short answer
didn't = did not	Yes, I did. / No, I didn't.

2.5 The past simple forms of *be* are *was* or *were*.

Affirmative	Negative	Interrogative
I was sad	I wasn't sad	Was I sad?
you were sad	you weren't sad	Were you sad?
he/she/it was sad	he/she/it wasn't sad	Was he/she/it sad?
we/you/they were sad	we/you/they weren't sad	Were we/you/they sad?

2.6 We use the past simple:
• for a completed action or event at a definite point in the past.
We played volleyball last Saturday.
• for actions or events that happened one after another.
Joanna got up, had a shower, got dressed and left the house.
• with certain verbs that are not used in continuous tenses, e.g. *believe*, *hate*, *like*, *love*, *need*, *know*, *prefer*, *want*.
The police officer believed his story.
(NOT – The police officer was believing his story.)

Past continuous

2.7 We form the past continuous like this:
• *was* or *were* + the *-ing* form of the main verb
Elizabeth was eating.   The children weren't listening.
Were you playing?
Spelling: verb + *-ing* form
See point 1.5.

We use the past continuous:
• to describe an action lasting for some time or serving as the background to other events.
It was raining.   Some children were playing rugby.

We don't use the past continuous:
• with certain verbs, e.g. *believe*, *hate*, *like*, *love*, *need*, *know*, *prefer*, *want*.
Tim needed a new car. (NOT – Tim was needing a new car.)

2.8 We often use the past continuous and the past simple in the same sentence. The past continuous describes a background action or event in the past; the past simple describes a shorter action or event that happened during the longer action, or which interrupted it.
It was raining when the accident happened.
My friends were watching TV when the fire started.

3 Grammar Builder

3B *some, any, much, many, a lot of, a little, a few*

1 Complete the sentences with *some* or *any*. → 3.1, 3.2

1 There's _____ beautiful scenery around here.
2 It's dangerous to walk along this lane because there aren't _____ pavements.
3 Have you got _____ money in your bag?
4 I'm going to the cinema with _____ friends tomorrow.
5 We haven't got _____ trees in our garden.
6 I'd like _____ information, please.
7 There isn't _____ milk in the fridge.
8 Are there _____ shops near your home?

2 Choose *a little* or *a few*. → 3.3

1 There are **a few / a little** large houses in the village, but the rest are cottages.
2 It's a quiet road, but there's **a few / a little** more traffic at weekends.
3 I bought **a few / a little** books at the airport.
4 I only want **a few / a little** food. I'm not very hungry.
5 I only spoke to **a few / a little** people at the party.
6 I went shopping with **a few / a little** friends last weekend.
7 I spent **a few / a little** time exploring the countryside.
8 My parents were born in Brazil, but I only speak **a few / a little** Portuguese.

3 Replace *a lot of* with *much* or *many*. → 3.4, 3.5, 3.6

1 My dad doesn't like a lot of rock music.
2 Have you got a lot of friends in your village?
3 Have we got a lot of homework this evening?
4 He's a good player, but he doesn't score a lot of goals.
5 It's a terrible place to go surfing because there aren't a lot of waves.
6 I don't spend a lot of time with friends during the week.

4 Complete the dialogue with *some, any, much, many, a lot of, a little* or *a few*. Sometimes more than one answer is possible. → 3.1, 3.2, 3.3, 3.4, 3.5, 3.6

Todd Hi! Are you new to this village?
Katy Yes, I am. We only moved here ¹_____ days ago.
Todd What do you think of it?
Katy It's very quiet. There isn't ²_____ to do at weekends.
Todd No, you're right. I usually go into town with ³_____ friends.
Katy But there aren't ⁴_____ buses after 7 p.m.!
Todd We get a taxi. It only costs ⁵_____ pounds.
Katy That's a good idea. So, where do you go in town? Are there ⁶_____ good nightclubs?
Todd Yes, there are ⁷_____ good ones. My favourite is XTC. They play ⁸_____ great music there.

Katy What kind of music?
Todd Hip hop, mostly. But they play ⁹_____ pop, too. You should come with us next weekend, if you haven't got ¹⁰_____ other plans.
Katy Thanks! I'd love to.

3D Articles

5 Complete the sentences with *a, an* or *the*.
→ 3.7, 3.8, 3.9, 3.10

1 I've got _____ games console and _____ MP3 player, but _____ MP3 player is broken.
2 When we visited _____ USA, we went to _____ White House – but we didn't see _____ President!
3 My friend has got _____ snake and _____ spider. _____ snake is green and _____ spider is black.
4 I had _____ apple and _____ orange for lunch. _____ apple tasted horrible.
5 I bought _____ T-shirt and _____ sweatshirt. I gave _____ sweatshirt to my brother.
6 My dad is _____ actor. He's doing a show at _____ Globe Theatre in London.
7 I was eating a sandwich in the kitchen when _____ door opened and _____ boy walked in.
8 We had _____ amazing holiday in _____ Lake District.

6 Complete each pair of sentences with *a/an* and *the*.
→ 3.7, 3.8, 3.9

1 a There's _____ Italian restaurant in town.
  b I never go to _____ Greek restaurant because it's very expensive.
2 a Please shut _____ door when you leave.
  b The church has got _____ huge door.
3 a I had _____ big dinner before I went out.
  b What's that smell? Did you burn _____ dinner?
4 a No chocolate for me, thanks. I'm going to _____ dentist tomorrow!
  b Ann is studying to become _____ doctor.
5 a I'm tired of taking buses. Let's buy _____ car.
  b _____ car won't start. Let's go by bus.
6 a Sardinia is _____ beautiful island.
  b She was born in Sardinia, but she left _____ island when she was ten.

7 Add *the* once or twice to each sentence. → 3.10

1 Washington, D.C. is capital of USA.
2 He never answers phone when he's at home.
3 I usually get bus to school in bad weather.
4 We took train from London to Paris.
5 Moon goes around Earth about every 27 days.
6 Somebody has dropped rubbish on floor.
7 My cousin enjoys listening to rock music on radio.
8 Nobody tells truth all time.

8 Cross out *the* if it is incorrect. → 3.11

1 My favourite kind of the music is the hip hop.

~~My favourite kind of the music is the hip hop.~~

2 I don't like the zoos because the animals always look unhappy.

3 Take the third road on the right – the church is on the left.

4 I never drink the coffee in the evening.

5 I'm not really into the sport, but I sometimes play the tennis at the weekend.

6 I don't eat the chocolate very often – I prefer the healthy snacks, like the fruit.

7 She wouldn't go in the swimming pool on holiday because the water was freezing.

9 Complete the text with *a*, *an*, *the* or – (no article).

My grandparents live in ¹_____ beautiful cottage near ²_____ sea. ³_____ cottage is in ⁴_____ small village called Frimpton. It's ⁵_____ quiet place – there aren't any cafés or restaurants. But there's ⁶_____ primary school and a church. My grandparents' cottage is next to ⁷_____ church. ⁸_____ tourists often visit Frimpton, especially when ⁹_____ weather is nice in ¹⁰_____ summer.

some and *any*

3.1 We usually use *some* in affirmative sentences and *any* in negative sentences and questions.

There are some traffic lights at the end of the road.
There's some pasta on the table.

The dog doesn't want any biscuits.
They haven't got any money.

Are there any cinemas in your town?
Do you need any help?

3.2 We usually use *some* when we offer or ask for something.
Would you like some tea?
Can I borrow some money?

a little, *a few*

3.3 We use *a little* with uncountable nouns. We use *a few* with countable nouns.
Julia ate a little rice.
Mike ate a few chips.

much, *many* and *a lot of*

3.4 We use *much*, *many* and *a lot of* to talk about quantity. We use *much* with uncountable nouns. We use *many* with countable nouns.
French people don't drink much tea.
Are there many pedestrian crossings in the town centre?

3.5 We use *a lot of* (or *lots of*) with countable and uncountable nouns.
Bill Gates has got a lot of/lots of money.
There are a lot of/lots of roadworks in London.

3.6 We often use *much* and *many* in negative sentences and questions. We don't often use them in affirmative sentences.
We didn't eat much food. or We didn't eat a lot of food.
Were there many people at the party? or Were there a lot of people at the party?
Charlotte's got a lot of money. ✓
Charlotte's got much money. ✗

Articles

3.7 We use *a* before singular countable nouns when we talk about something for the first time.
We use *the* when we talk about something again.
I've got a cat and a dog. The cat's called Joe and the dog's called Sally.
I had a pizza and a coffee. The pizza was great but the coffee was awful.

3.8 We use *the* when it is clear what we are talking about.
Mum's in the kitchen. (the kitchen in our house)
The station is near the park. (There's only one station and one park in our town.)
The man in the yellow jacket is my uncle. (We know which man – he's wearing a yellow jacket.)

3.9 We use *a* when we say what somebody or something is.
Liverpool is a city in England.
Bob is a taxi driver.
Mozart was a great composer.

We use *a* when we say what somebody or something is like.
Scotland is a beautiful country.
That's a nice dress. Where did you buy it?
He's a good-looking young man.

3.10 We use *the* when there is only one of something.
the sun, the North Sea, the sky, the moon, the world

3.11 We don't use *the* when we are making generalisations.
I don't like classical music.
Fiona never drinks tea or coffee.

4B   Comparatives and superlatives

1   Write the comparative form of the adjectives. → 4.1

1. wide _____
2. easy _____
3. wet _____
4. funny _____
5. good _____
6. dull _____
7. hot _____
8. bad _____
9. nice _____
10. scary _____

2   Complete the sentences with comparative adjectives from exercise 1 and *than*. → 4.1, 4.2

1. In my opinion, English is _easier than_ maths.
2. My exam results were _____ your results. I got a B and you got an A.
3. Jason's _____ all the other boys in the class. He never stops telling jokes.
4. In my opinion, historical films are _____ war films. I often fall asleep during historical films.
5. The Pacific Ocean is about 12,000 kilometres _____ the Atlantic Ocean.
6. Last summer was _____ this summer. The sun shone nearly every day.
7. I think basketball is _____ golf. It's more exciting.
8. It rains a lot in Scotland. It's much _____ England.
9. Mr Smith is _____ than Miss Jones. He gives us less homework!
10. Horror films are _____ war films. I can't watch them!

3   Complete the sentences with your own ideas and the comparative form of the adjectives. → 4.1

1. Zac Efron is good-looking, but _Robert Pattinson is better-looking._
2. *Inception* is gripping, but …
3. Action films are often violent, but …
4. Keira Knightley is beautiful, but …
5. Jim Carrey films are entertaining, but …
6. Scarlett Johansson is a talented actress, but …
7. The special effects in *The Lord of the Rings* were spectacular, but …

4   Write the superlative form of the adjectives in exercise 1. → 4.4

1. wide   _the widest_

5   Write the quiz questions. Use superlative adjectives. → 4.4

1. What / large / city / in the USA?
   What's the largest city in the USA?
2. What / far / planet from the sun?
3. Which country in Europe / has got / big / population?
4. What / intelligent / animals in the world?
5. What / long / river in the world?
6. What / hot / planet in the Solar System?

6   SPEAKING   Ask and answer the questions in exercise 5. Check your answers below. → 4.4

1 New York	4 chimpanzees
2 Neptune	5 the Nile
3 Germany	6 Venus

4D   (*not*) *as … as, too, enough*

7   Write sentences with *as … as* and the adjective in brackets. → 4.3

1. Harry hates waiting. Sarah doesn't like waiting, either. (impatient)
   Harry is as impatient as Sarah.
2. Both Fred and Cathy often tell lies. (dishonest)
3. Liam and Sally both love talking. (talkative)
4. George and Ryan both think they're better than anyone else. (arrogant)
5. Joe is very hard-working. You're very hard-working too. (hard-working)
6. Neither Chris nor Simon is very mature. (immature)

8   Rewrite the sentences with *not as … as*. → 4.3

1. Joanna is more ambitious than Peter.
   Peter isn't as ambitious as Joanna.
2. Disaster films are more gripping than comedies.
3. The school in the town is bigger than the school in the village.
4. You're more interested in action films than me.
5. Animated films are usually funnier than normal films.
6. Ian is luckier than me.

9   Complete the sentences with *too* and the adjectives below. → 4.6

inactive   intolerant   predictable   scary   tired   violent

1. Jack never listens to other people's opinions. He's _____ .
2. I knew how the film would end. It was _____ .
3. I hate war films. They're _____ .
4. She needs to get more exercise. She's _____ .
5. I'm not going to stay up and watch the film. I'm _____ .
6. Clare didn't watch the horror film with us. It was _____ .

10   Complete the sentences with *enough* and the nouns and adjectives below. → 4.6, 4.7

computer games   funny   old   patient   people   strong   sugar   time

1. I haven't got _____ to help you.
2. I didn't enjoy the romantic comedy. It wasn't _____ .
3. Yuk! There isn't _____ in my coffee!
4. Julie wasn't _____ to wait for us.
5. I'm not _____ to watch an 18 film.
6. Go to bed. You've played _____ .
7. I wasn't _____ to lift the box onto the shelf.
8. We can't play volleyball. There aren't _____ .

Comparative adjectives

4.1 Spelling

We add *-er* to short (one-syllable and some two-syllable) adjectives.

    + *-er*   long → longer

If the short adjective ends in *-e*, we add *-r*.

    + *-r*   wide → wider

If the short adjective ends in a short vowel + a single consonant, we double the consonant and add *-er*.

    -t → *-tter*   hot → hotter

If the adjective ends in *-y*, we take out the *-y* and add *-ier*.

    -y → *-ier*   friendly → friendlier

If the adjective is long (two syllables or more), we use the word *more*.

    gripping → more gripping

Some adjectives have irregular comparative forms.

    good → better
    bad → worse
    far → further

than

4.2 We use *than* to compare two things or people.

Shrek 3 was funnier than Toy Story 3.

We usually use the object pronoun (*me, you, her, him, us, them*) after *than*.

You're taller than me. ✓
You're taller than I. ✗
but You're taller than I am. ✓

(*not*) *as ... as*

4.3 We use (*not*) *as ... as* to compare two people or things.

not as ... as means *less ... than*.

Jude Law is not as old as Brad Pitt. Brad Pitt was born in 1963, Jude Law in 1972.

as ... as means *equally ...*

Sharon Stone is as tall as Tom Cruise. Sharon Stone and Tom Cruise are both 170 cm tall.

We usually use the object pronoun after (*not*) *as ... as*.

Sarah's as intelligent as him. ✓
Sarah's as intelligent as he. ✗
but Sarah's as intelligent as he is. ✓

Superlative adjectives

4.4 Spelling

We put *the* in front of short (one-syllable and some two-syllable) adjectives and add *-est*.

    + *-est*   long → the longest

If the short adjective ends in *-e*, we add *-st*.

    + *-st*   wide → the widest

If the short adjective ends in a short vowel + a single consonant, we double the consonant and add *-est*.

    -t → *-ttest*   hot → the hottest

If the adjective ends in *-y*, we take out the *-y* and add *-iest*.

    -y → *-iest*   friendly → the friendliest

If the adjective is long (two syllables or more), we use the word *most*.

    gripping → the most gripping

Some adjectives have irregular superlative forms.

    good → the best
    bad → the worst
    far → the furthest

less and *the least*

4.5 *less* and *the least* have the opposite meaning to *more* and *the most*.

Maths is less difficult than English.
What's the least interesting subject that you study?

too and *enough*

4.6 *too* comes before an adjective. *enough* comes after an adjective.

This jacket is too small for him.
This jacket isn't big enough for him.

4.7 *enough* comes before a noun.

He can't buy it. He hasn't got enough money.

5B Present perfect

1 Complete the text messages. Use the present perfect form of the verbs in brackets. → 5.1, 5.2, 5.3

> Lakeside Shopping Centre is great! I ¹_____ (try on) four pairs of trainers and six jackets.
>
> ²_____ (you / buy) anything?
>
> No, I ³_____ . I must be careful – I ⁴_____ (spend) loads of money this month! Is Mum with you?
>
> No, she isn't. She ⁵_____ (take) the car to the garage.
>
> ⁶_____ (Dad / phone) you this afternoon?
>
> I ⁷_____ (not / speak) to Dad today, but I ⁸_____ (send) him an email. And I ⁹_____ (tidy) our bedroom!
>
> Fantastic – thanks! See you soon!

2 What have or haven't you done today? Write an affirmative and a negative sentence in the present perfect for each verb below. → 5.1, 5.2, 5.3

buy eat read watch write

3 Choose *been* or *gone*. → 5.4

1 'Where is everybody?' 'They've **been** / **gone** home. The party's finished!'
2 'Do you like London?' 'Yes. I've **been** / **gone** there twice and I love it.'
3 I've **been** / **gone** to three shops, but I still can't find a present for Harry.
4 'Is Tom at the sports centre?' 'No. He's **been** / **gone** to see his grandparents.'
5 Welcome home. Where have you **been** / **gone** all day?

4 Complete the sentences with *for* or *since*. → 5.3

1 I've been awake _____ five o'clock this morning.
2 My aunt has lived in that house _____ 40 years.
3 It hasn't rained in this part of the desert _____ 1936.
4 I haven't heard this song _____ ages.
5 They've only known each other _____ last summer.
6 She's had an Italian penfriend _____ she was twelve.

5 Write questions using *How long … ?* Write answers. Use *for* or *since* and the information in brackets. → 5.3, 5.5

1 I'm a doctor. (2 years)
  How long have you been a doctor? For two years.
2 I work in a hospital. (2001)
3 I'm ill. (yesterday)
4 I live with my grandparents. (2008)
5 I've got an iPhone. (three months)
6 I play football. (five years)
7 I know Richard. (last Easter)

5D Present perfect and past simple

6 Complete the sentences. Use the past simple form of the verbs given in one sentence and the present perfect in the other sentence. → 5.6, 5.7

1 **go**
  a She _____ to India three times. She loves it!
  b My parents _____ to Egypt before they were married.
2 **not wear**
  a I was cold last night because I _____ a coat.
  b Can I exchange this dress? I _____ it.
3 **not hear**
  a I'm sorry I missed your call. I _____ the phone.
  b Who's this song by? I _____ it before.
4 **buy**
  a I _____ you a present. Do you want to see it?
  b The jacket was half price, so I _____ it.

7 Complete the dialogue. Use the past simple or present perfect form of the verbs in brackets. → 5.3, 5.5, 5.6

Susan That's a really nice top, Karen. When ¹_____ you _____ (get) it?
Karen My mum ²_____ (give) it to me for Christmas, so I ³_____ (have) it for three months.
Susan Really? I ⁴_____ (never / see) you in it.
Karen I ⁵_____ (not wear) it very often. It doesn't really go with anything. I ⁶_____ (wear) it to Tom's party.
Susan Did you? I ⁷_____ (not see) Tom since the party.
Karen Oh, I ⁸_____ (meet) him on Saturday. We ⁹_____ (go) to the cinema to see Orlando Bloom's latest film. ¹⁰_____ you _____ (see) it?
Susan No, I ¹¹_____ (not go) to the cinema for ages.
Karen Come with us next weekend!
Susan Good idea, thanks!

8 Write questions with *Have you ever … ?* Write true answers about yourself. If the answer is yes, add more details in the past simple. → 5.6, 5.7

go / to another country
Have you ever been to another country?
No, I haven't. / Yes, I have. I went to Ireland last summer.

1 eat / shark   4 wear / traditional clothes
2 visit / a beautiful place   5 play / a game online
3 write / a song or a poem

Present perfect

5.1 We form the present perfect like this:

Affirmative	
I've finished	we've finished
you've finished	you've finished
he/she/it's finished	they've finished

Short form and full form	
I've = I have	
she's = she has	

Negative	
I haven't finished	we haven't finished
you haven't finished	you haven't finished
he/she/it hasn't finished	they haven't finished

Short form and full form	
haven't = have not	
hasn't = has not	

Interrogative	
Have I finished … ?	Have we finished … ?
Have you finished … ?	Have you finished … ?
Has he/she/it finished … ?	Have they finished … ?

Short answer	
Yes, I have. / No, I haven't.	
Yes, she has. / No, she hasn't.	

5.2 We form the present perfect with the present tense of the auxiliary verb *have* and the past participle.

Pete has finished his homework.

The past participle of regular verbs is the same as the past simple.

played   danced   studied   dropped

Sometimes irregular verbs have the same past participle as the past simple form but sometimes they are different.

buy – bought – bought

see – saw – seen

For a list of irregular verbs, see the Workbook.

5.3 We use the present perfect:
- to talk about recent events.
  Pete has passed all his exams.
- to talk about experiences.
  I've eaten snails in France.
- to talk about an event or situation that began in the past and continues up to now. We use *for* with a period of time and *since* with a point in time.
  My dad has worked for IBM for 10 years.
  I've had this MP3 player since May.
- to talk about actions that have an effect on the present.
  I haven't finished my homework, so I can't go out.

5.4 We use both *been* and *gone* as the past participles of the verb *go*. We use *been* when somebody has returned.

John has been shopping. (He went shopping but he is here now.)

We use *gone* when somebody hasn't returned.

John has gone shopping. (He went shopping and he is still at the shops.)

5.5 We use *How long* …? and the present perfect to ask how long a situation has continued up to the present.

'How long have you lived in London?' 'Since 2001.'

Present perfect and past simple

See the Workbook for the forms of the past simple.

5.6 We use both the past simple and the present perfect to talk about finished actions.

We use the past simple to talk about completed events at a definite time in the past. The events have no connection with the present.

I visited the USA last year.

We use the present perfect to talk about past events that have a connection with the present. See point 5.3 for a list of the uses of the present perfect.

5.7 We often use the past simple when we ask for or give more details following a *Have you ever* … ? question.

Have you ever been to a pop concert?

Yes, I have. I went to a Blue concert last year.

6 Grammar Builder

6B will and going to

1 Write predictions about technology in ten years' time. Use
I think … or *I don't think …* . → 6.1, 6.2

1 all classrooms / have ebook readers
I think all classrooms will have ebook readers.
2 televisions / be very small
3 ebook readers / be very expensive
4 all computers / be wireless
5 people / use paper
6 watches / include multimedia players

2 Think of offers or promises for the problems below.
Use *I'll …* . → 6.1, 6.2

1 My MP3 player is broken.
2 I need to text my friend, but I left my mobile at home.
3 I want to read, but my ebook reader is broken.
4 I'm going to miss my favourite TV programme tonight.

3 Match sentences 1–5 with decisions a–e. → 6.1, 6.2

1 'Look! Tom's winning the race!'
2 'What would you like to drink, madam?'
3 'My satnav is on the back seat of the car.'
4 'The camera isn't working.'
5 'I'm getting bored with these video games.'

a 'Oh, yes! I'll take a photo of him.'
b 'I'll buy you some new ones.'
c 'I'll have a coffee, please.'
d 'I'll use my mobile instead.'
e 'I'll pass it to you.'

4 Write predictions about the pictures using *going to*. Use the
verbs below to help you. → 6.3, 6.4

eat   fly   throw   chase   fall off   jump   turn on   watch

5 Write three things you intend to do this weekend and three
things you do not intend to do. Use *going to …* . → 6.3, 6.4

I'm not going to get up early on Sunday.

6 Complete the dialogues with the correct form of *will* or
going to. Explain your choice. → 6.2, 6.3, 6.4, 6.5

1 A The red top is £8 and the blue top is £9.
  B I 'll_____ have the red top, please.
  B makes this decision while speaking, so it's 'will'.
2 A Have you got plans for the weekend?
  B Yes. I _____ visit my friends in Brighton.
3 A It's really hot in this room.
  B Don't worry. I _____ open the window.
4 A Is the match nearly over?
  B Yes, this is the 90th minute. Liverpool _____ win.
5 A Do you love me?
  B Yes. I _____ always love you.
6 A See you later.
  B OK. I _____ give you a call tomorrow.
7 A Are you on holiday next week?
  B Yes. I _____ stay in bed all morning on Monday!

6D Zero conditional

7 Match the two halves of the sentences. → 6.6

1 If I eat too much,   a if I don't tidy my room.
2 If it rains,   b you get good marks.
3 My mum gets cross   c I feel ill.
4 If you exercise regularly, d if you turn off the lights.
5 You save electricity   e I take the tram to school.
6 If you study hard,   f you stay fit and healthy.

8 Complete the sentences. Use the correct form of the verbs
in brackets. → 6.6

1 If you _____ two books, you _____ one free. (buy, get)
2 The menu _____ on the screen if you _____ this button
  twice. (appear, press)
3 If dogs _____ chocolate, it _____ them ill. (eat, make)
4 If water _____ , it _____ (freeze, expand)
5 If you _____ water to 100° C, it _____ . (heat, boil)

6D may, might and could

9 Complete the text with *may*, *might* or *could* and the verbs
below. There is one negative form. → 6.7

become   do   happen   prefer   share   want

Sales of CDs are going down because of illegal file sharing,
and film companies are worried that the same thing
[1]_____ with DVDs. More and more people [2]_____
films over the Internet rather than buying them. Buying
DVDs [3]_____ a thing of the past. The music industry
now allows legal downloads from websites like the iTunes
Music Store, and the film industry [4]_____ something
similar. However, if they try to charge too much, people
[5]_____ to pay. They [6]_____ to download films
illegally using one of the many file-sharing programs.

6 Grammar Reference

will

6.1 We use *will* to talk about the future. We form sentences with *will* like this:
- *will* + infinitive without *to*

I will go.

The form of *will* is the same for all persons (*I*, *you*, *he*, *she*, etc.).

Affirmative	Negative
I'll see you later.	I won't tell anybody
She'll be angry.	They won't listen to you.
(full form = *will*)	(full form = *will not*)

Interrogative	Short answer
Will you be at home?	Yes, I will.
Will it work?	No, it won't.

6.2 We use *will*:
- to make factual statements about the future.
  There will be a solar eclipse in 2026.
- to make predictions, especially when they are based on our own thoughts or beliefs.
  I think you'll do well in your exams.
  I don't think England will win the next World Cup.
- to make offers.
  I'll carry your bags.
  I'll lend you my phone.
- to make promises.
  I'll always love you.
- to make instant decisions (decisions that we make while we are speaking).
  Look! There's Tommy. I'll go and say hello.

going to

6.3 We use *be going to* to talk about the future. We form sentences with *be going to* like this:
- present simple of *be* + *going to* + infinitive without *to*
  I'm going to take my driving test next year.
  Roger Federer isn't going to win the match.
  Are you going to be at home this weekend?
  Yes, I am. / No, I'm not.

6.4 We use *be going to*:
- to make predictions, especially when they are based on what we can see.
  Look at that man! He's going to jump in the river!
- to talk about our intentions.
  I'm going to invite her to my party.

6.5 We use both *will* and *be going to* to make predictions and to talk about our decisions.

We use ...	*will*	*be going to*
predictions	based on our own knowledge and opinions: Rooney will score. He always scores in important games.	based on the situation and what we can see: Rooney's got the ball! He's going to score!
decisions	instant decisions that we make while speaking: Show me the menu. Hmm. I'll have chicken.	intentions – things that we have already decided: I'm going to have chicken tonight. I bought it this morning.

Zero conditional

6.6 We use the zero conditional to talk about a result which follows a particular action. We use the present to describe the action and the present simple to describe the result.

If you press this button, the light comes on.

The *if* clause can come before or after the main clause. If it comes after, we don't use a comma.

If you heat ice, it melts.

Ice melts if you heat it.

may, might and could

6.7 The verbs *may*, *might* and *could* are used to talk about something that can happen in the present or future. After these verbs we use the infinitive without *to*.

Where's John? He might be in his bedroom. (now)

Who's that knocking at the door? It could be the postman. (now)

The weather forecast said it may rain tomorrow. (future)

The verb *may* suggests more definite possibility than *might*. Negative forms for *might* and *may* are *might not* and *may not*.

The verb *could* does not have a negative form when it is used to express various degrees of certainty.

I might go out this evening. → I might not go out this evening.

I could go out this evening. → (NOT – I could not go out this evening.)

7B *must*, *mustn't* and *needn't*

1 Match the pairs of sentences. Then complete 1–6 with *must* or *mustn't*. → 7.1, 7.2

1 When you take a taxi in Australia, you _____ sit in the back.
2 You _____ eat with your right hand in many Arab countries.
3 In Japan, you _____ kiss a woman when you meet her.
4 Generally, you _____ point at a person in public.
5 In many Asian countries, you _____ remove your shoes before entering a house.
6 At a meal in Britain you _____ wait until the host starts to eat before you start to eat.

a It is considered rude to keep them on.
b It is not polite to start before them.
c You should sit next to the driver.
d Your left hand is considered dirty.
e You should bow, or shake her hand.
f You should say their name, or describe them.

2 What do the signs mean? Complete the sentences with *must* or *mustn't*. → 7.1, 7.2

1 You mustn't turn left.
2 You _____ stop here.
3 You _____ drive over 120 km/h.
4 You _____ keep left.
5 You _____ watch out for pedestrians.
6 You _____ overtake here.

3 Choose the correct verbs. → 7.1, 7.2, 7.3

How to be polite at a JAPANESE meal

When eating from small bowls, you ¹**must / mustn't** lift the bowl to your mouth, so that you don't drop any food on the table. You ²**mustn't / needn't** leave your chopsticks in a bowl of rice. Put them on the table, next to the bowl. When you drink soup, you ³**needn't / must** drink it quietly. It's OK to make quite a loud noise! You ⁴**mustn't / must** pour a drink for yourself. That's very impolite. You ⁵**needn't / must** wait for someone else to pour it, and in return you ⁶**must / mustn't** pour drinks for other people. You ⁷**needn't / must** wait until their glass is empty. In fact people often fill the glasses every few minutes. You ⁸**must / mustn't** belch. In some Asian countries it is considered polite, but not in Japan.

7D First conditional

4 Match the two halves of the sentences. → 7.4, 7.5

1 If he doesn't phone her,
2 They won't buy a new car
3 If you give me your number,
4 If it rains tomorrow,
5 Where will we sleep
6 If you don't tell your parents where you are,

a if it costs too much.
b they'll be worried.
c if we can't find a hotel?
d she'll be disappointed.
e I'll call you tomorrow.
f what will we do?

5 Complete the superstitions. Use the present simple form of the verbs in brackets. Are any of them familiar? → 7.4, 7.5

1 If you _____ (eat) bread crusts, you'll have curly hair.
2 If you _____ (not cover) your bald head, it will start raining.
3 If a cat _____ (wash) behind its ears, it will rain.
4 You'll catch a cold if a cat _____ (sneeze) three times.
5 If you _____ (not believe) bad things will happen, they won't!

6 Complete the superstitions with the *will* form of the verbs in brackets. Are any of them familiar? → 7.4, 7.5

1 If you sing before 7 a.m., you _____ (cry) before 11 a.m.
2 If you _____ (not take) down the Christmas decorations before Twelfth Night, you'll have bad luck.
3 If you have an itchy nose, you _____ (have) an argument with someone soon.
4 In Russia, if you aren't married and you sit at the corner of the table, you _____ (not marry) anyone in the next seven years.
5 In Ireland, you _____ (not have) bad luck if you put a penny in your shoe.

7F should and ought to

7 Give advice to these people. Use *should* or *ought to* and the phrases below. → 7.6, 7.7

ask her out   report it to the police   see a doctor
smoke   take an aspirin   wear something smart

1 I've got a headache. You should / ought to ...
2 I fancy a girl in my class.
3 I've lost my mobile.
4 Liz has got a temperature.
5 I don't know what to wear to my job interview.
6 I've got a bad cough.

8 Give advice to these people. Use *I think* / *I don't think* and *should* or *ought to*. Use the verbs in brackets or your own ideas. → 7.6, 7.7

1 I found €100 in the street. (keep)
2 I bought this DVD and it's scratched. (take back)
3 I'm feeling really tired. (stay up)
4 My bedroom is a complete mess. (tidy)
5 I've put on a lot of weight recently. (eat)
6 I want to go out, but I haven't got any money. (borrow)

must and mustn't

7.1 The form of *must* or *mustn't* is the same for all persons (*I*, *you*, *he*, etc.).

Affirmative	Negative
I must go home.	You mustn't tell anybody.
You must tell the truth.	They mustn't be late.
	(full form = *must not*)

Interrogative*	Short answer
Must you leave so early?	Yes, I must.

*We do not often make questions with *must*. It is more common to use *Do you have to ...?*

7.2 We use *must* + infinitive without *to* to say that something is necessary, and it is very important to do it.
In some Asian countries, you must eat with your right hand.
You must be quiet in the school library.
We use *mustn't* + infinitive without *to* to say that something is prohibited, and it is very important not to do it.
We mustn't be late for school.
You mustn't use a mobile phone in the cinema.
We often use *must* or *mustn't* to express rules and laws.
In the UK, you must be 17 to drive a car.
You mustn't smoke on aeroplanes.

needn't

7.3 We use *needn't* + infinitive without *to* to say that something is not necessary but isn't against the rules.
You needn't bring a towel. There are towels at the swimming pool. (But you can bring one if you want.)
You needn't take sandwiches as lunch is provided. (But you can bring them if you want.)

First conditional

7.4 We use the first conditional to predict the result of a future action. We use the present simple to describe the action and *will* + infinitive without *to* to describe the result.
If you go to bed late, you'll be tired tomorrow.
     (action)   (result)
If I miss the bus, I'll take a taxi.
     (action)   (result)

7.5 The *if* clause can come before or after the main clause. If it comes after, we don't use a comma.
If you drink too much coffee, you won't sleep well.
You won't sleep well if you drink too much coffee.

should and ought to

7.6 The form of *should* and *ought to* is the same for all persons (*I*, *you*, *she*, etc.)

Affirmative	
You should go to bed.	You ought to go to bed.
They should leave now.	They ought to leave now.

Negative	
He shouldn't eat so much.	He oughtn't to eat so much.
We shouldn't stay up late.	We oughtn't to stay up late.

Interrogative	
Should we tell him?	*
When should I phone you?	

*We do not use *ought to* to form the interrogative.

7.7 The verbs *should* and *ought to* are used to give advice and talk about things that are or aren't important.
If you've got a headache, you ought to take an aspirin.
You shouldn't talk with your mouth full.
The verbs *should* and *ought to* are often used in expressions with *I think ...* and *I don't think ...*.
I think you ought to go to bed.
I don't think we should spend all our money. (NOT – I think we shouldn't spend all our money.)
Do you think we should phone Chris?

8B Second conditional

1 Match the two halves of the sentences. → 8.1, 8.2

1 If the buildings were stronger,
2 If everybody cycled more,
3 If people didn't have barbecues in the forest,
4 If it rained more in this country,
5 If we had more sun in this country,
6 If these people had clean water to drink,

a they'd use their cars less.
b we'd be able to grow crops more easily.
c they wouldn't get so many diseases.
d we'd use more solar power.
e they wouldn't fall down during earthquakes.
f there wouldn't be so many fires.

2 Complete the *if* clauses in sentences 1–4 and the main clauses in sentences 5–8. Use the correct form of the verb in brackets. → 8.1, 8.2

1 If I _____ (know) his address, I'd go and visit him.
2 We'd live in the city centre if we _____ (have) enough money.
3 If I _____ (have) a tablet PC, I'd watch films on the bus.
4 You wouldn't be so tired all the time if you _____ (go) to bed earlier.
5 If you didn't get a few horrible presents, it _____ (not be) Christmas!
6 We _____ (not use) our car so much if we didn't live in the countryside.
7 He _____ (have) more money if he didn't buy so many clothes.
8 If it didn't rain so much, the countryside _____ (not be) so green.

3 Write second conditional sentences. → 8.1, 8.2

1 I'm not very good at ice hockey. I can't skate very fast.
If I could skate faster, I'd be better at ice hockey.
2 I go to bed late. I'm always tired in the morning.
3 I'm not going to watch the World Cup final. I don't like football.
4 I'm not taking a coat with me. It's warm outside.
5 She isn't sending any postcards. She hasn't got her address book with her.
6 I don't understand this exercise, so I can't do it.

8D *I wish ...*

4 Complete the wishes. Use the correct form of the verbs in brackets. Then match them with the people in the pictures. → 8.3, 8.4

1 I wish I _____ (have) my bike.
2 I wish I _____ (not be) on my own.
3 I wish I _____ (can) buy that dress.
4 I wish I _____ (know) her.
5 I wish I _____ (have) my swimming costume.
6 I wish it _____ (be) warmer.

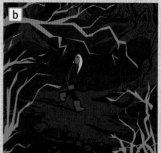

5 Write sentences starting with *I wish*. → 8.3, 8.4

1 I can't play the piano.
2 I don't like pasta.
3 I can't ride a horse.
4 I don't have a pet.
5 I'm not very tall.
6 I've got a lot of housework to do.
7 I'm not very good at football.
8 I don't speak Spanish.

Second conditional

8.1 We use the second conditional to talk about situations that are unlikely or unreal. It can refer to the present or the future.

We use the past tense to describe the unlikely, unreal or imaginary action or situation, and *would* + infinitive without *to* to describe the result.
If I had a lot of money, I'd visit the USA.

8.2 The *if* clause can come before or after the main clause. If it comes after, we don't use a comma.
If I lived in the country, I'd have a dog.
I'd have a dog if I lived in the country.

I wish ...

8.3 We use *wish* + past simple or past continuous to say that we want something to be different from how it is now.
The present situation: Alison has brown eyes.
Wish: Alison wishes she had blue eyes.
The present situation: It's cold. I am wearing a jacket.
Wish: I wish I was wearing a coat.

8.4 After *if* and *wish* we sometimes use *were* rather than *was* with *I/he/she/it*. *Were* is more formal than *was*.

9B Past perfect

1 Complete the sentences. Use the past perfect form of the verbs in brackets. → 9.1

1 He was upset because somebody _____ (steal) his watch.
2 They were shocked that he _____ (murder) his wife.
3 I was happy that the police _____ (catch) the vandals.
4 We couldn't drive to London because somebody _____ (vandalise) our car.
5 We heard that an arsonist _____ (burn down) a school in London.
6 After they _____ (rob) the bank, they escaped in a BMW.

2 Look at the pictures and complete the sentences. Use the past perfect negative form of the verbs below. → 9.1

finish   fly   lock   have   play   tidy

1 Tom was nervous. He _____ before.
2 It was obvious that Kate _____ tennis before.
3 Jake didn't pass his driving test because he _____ enough lessons.
4 Sam wanted to go out, but she _____ her homework.
5 Harry's mum was cross. He _____ his bedroom.
6 Sally realised that she _____ the windows.

3 Complete the sentences. Use the past simple and the past perfect form in each sentence. → 9.1, 9.2

1 After Tom _____ (eat), he _____ (read) the news online.
2 When I _____ (turn on) the TV, the match _____ (already / start).
3 Jason _____ (not live) in a capital city before he _____ (move) to London.
4 We _____ (play) tennis after school _____ (finish).
5 I _____ (not can) go out because I _____ (not do) my homework.

9D Reported speech

4 Complete the reported speech sentences. Use the past simple, *could/couldn't*, past continuous or past perfect. → 9.3, 9.4

1 'I hate drug dealers,' said Amy.
   Amy said that she _hated_ drug dealers.
2 'Some boys are vandalising a car!' said James.
   James said that some boys _____ a car.
3 'Every year burglars break into hundreds of houses in the city,' said the journalist.
   The journalist said that every year, burglars _____ hundreds of houses in the city.
4 'A thief stole my wallet,' she said.
   She said that a thief _____ her wallet.
5 'A shoplifter stole three CDs,' said the shop manager.
   The shop manager said that a shoplifter _____ three CDs.
6 'The murderer is in the police car,' said the police officer.
   The police officer said that the murderer _____ in the police car.
7 'Burglars can easily break into your house if you don't lock all the doors and windows,' said the police officer.
   The police officer said that burglars _____ easily break into their house if they _____ lock all the doors and windows.
8 'Joyriders took my car from my garage,' the man said.
   The man said that joyriders _____ his car from his garage.
9 'You can go to jail if you deal drugs,' said Becky.
   Becky said that he _____ go to jail if he _____ drugs.
10 'Two men robbed the bank,' the bank manager said.
   The bank manager said that two men _____ the bank.

5 Complete the sentences with the correct pronoun. → 9.4

1 'You're annoying me!' she told me.
   She told _____ that _____ was annoying her.
2 'I like playing games on my mobile,' he said.
   He said that _____ liked playing games on _____ mobile.
3 'I'm going out,' said Catherine.
   Catherine said that _____ was going out.
4 'She never texts me,' said Tony.
   Tony said that _____ never texted _____.
5 'They failed their exams,' said Tom.
   Tom said that _____ had failed _____ exams.
6 'We all go to the same school,' she said.
   She said that _____ all went to the same school.

6 Rewrite the sentences in direct speech. → 9.3, 9.4

1 She said that I wasn't helping.
 'You aren't helping,' she said.
2 She said that he was feeling fine.
3 You said that you were going to the cinema this evening.
4 They said that they couldn't come to our party.
5 He said that he'd seen the drug dealers dealing heroin.
6 She said that last month someone had burgled her house.
7 You said that you'd had something to eat.
8 She said that she wanted a drink.
9 He said that I was late.
10 She said that she could ski really well.

Past perfect

9.1 We form the past perfect like this:

Affirmative
I/you'd gone
he/she/it'd gone
we/you/they'd gone

Short form and full form
'd = had

Negative
I/you hadn't gone
he/she/it hadn't gone
we/you/they hadn't gone

Short form and full form
hadn't = had not

Interrogative
Had I/you gone ... ?
Had he/she/it gone ... ?
Had we/you/they gone ... ?

Short answer
Yes, I had. / No, I hadn't.
Yes, she had. / No, she hadn't.

The past participle of regular verbs is the same as the past simple.
finished   danced   studied   chatted

Sometimes irregular verbs have the same past participle as the past simple form, sometimes they are different.
go – went – been/gone
buy – bought – bought
see – saw – seen

For a list of irregular verbs, see the Workbook.

9.2 We use the past perfect to talk about an event in the past which happened before another event in the past.

Time line

the robbers left the bank   the police arrived   Now
When the police arrived, the robbers had left the bank.

Reported speech

9.3 When we report somebody else's words, the tense of the verb usually changes.

Direct speech	Reported speech
Present simple →	**Past simple**
'I don't like dogs,' Ben said.	Ben said (that) he didn't like dogs.
'My dad is at work,' Becky said.	Becky said (that) her dad was at work.
Present continuous →	**Past continuous**
'He's wearing a blue top,' Michelle said.	Michelle said (that) he was wearing a blue top.
Past simple →	**Past perfect**
'We moved to London in 2000,' Phil said.	Phil said (that) they had moved to London in 2000.

It is not necessary to use *that* in reported speech.

9.4 The pronouns sometimes change, depending on the context.
'My name's Jill,' she said.
She said that her name was Jill.

'We went to the cinema,' Mark said.
Mark said that they had gone to the cinema.

'I'll meet you after school,' Becky said.
Becky said she'd meet me after school.

10B   The passive (present and past simple)

1 Underline the past participles in this sentence. Then complete the rule about regular past participles. → 10.1

When the final Harry Potter book was published in the USA, 12 million copies were printed in one go!

> The past participle of regular verbs is the same as the _____ simple form.

2 Complete the table with the irregular past participles below. Write the two missing base forms too. → 10.1

bought   kept   seen   sent   sold   taken   taught   written

Base form	Past participle
send	
keep	
write	
teach	
buy	
sell	

3 Choose the correct words to complete the present simple passive sentences. → 10.1

1 Portuguese **is** / **are** spoken in Brazil.
2 Shoes **isn't** / **aren't** worn in Japanese homes.
3 Pork **isn't** / **aren't** eaten in Muslim countries.
4 Ferraris **is** / **are** made in Italy.
5 Most Internet pages **is** / **are** written in English.
6 Champagne **is** / **are** drunk on special occasions.

4 Complete the text. Use the present simple passive form of the verbs in brackets. → 10.1

CELEBRITY MAGAZINE INTERVIEWS

First, the celebrity ¹_____ (contact) by the magazine. If the celebrity agrees to the interview, a reporter ²_____ (send) to their house. The celebrity ³_____ (interview) and lots of photographs ⁴_____ (take). Then the article ⁵_____ (write) – it's always a very kind one – and a lot of money ⁶_____ (pay) to the celebrity!

5 Complete the past simple passive sentences with *was* or *were* and the names below. → 10.3, 10.4

Beyoncé   JK Rowling   Johnny Depp   Levi Strauss   Marie Curie   Peter Jackson

1 Radium _____ discovered by _____ .
2 *The Lord of the Rings* _____ directed by _____ .
3 Jeans _____ invented by _____ .
4 The Harry Potter books _____ written by _____ .
5 The song *Single Ladies* _____ recorded by _____ .
6 The part of Jack Sparrow _____ played by _____ .

6 Rewrite the text in the passive. Use the present and past simple. → 10.4

They launched the website Amazon.com in 1995. They chose the name 'Amazon' because it's the biggest river in the world. At first, they only sold books. Soon, they added CDs and DVDs. Today, they offer all kinds of products on their website. People download thousands of ebooks every day from the Kindle store. Last year they sold goods worth $25 billion!

The website Amazon.com was launched ...

10D   The passive (present perfect and future)

7 Complete the second sentence so that it means the same as the first sentence. Use the correct form of *be*. → 10.4

1 a Somebody has stolen my bike!
   b My bike _____ stolen!
2 a Brazil has won the football World Cup five times.
   b The football World Cup _____ won by Brazil five times.
3 a They've built that house too near the cliff!
   b That house _____ built too near the cliff!
4 a People have grown olives for thousands of years.
   b Olives _____ grown for thousands of years.
5 a Scientists have discovered a new planet.
   b A new planet _____ discovered by scientists.

8 Rewrite the sentences in the passive. Use *by* if necessary to say who has done the action. → 10.3, 10.4

1 They've broken a window.
2 They've burgled our house.
3 They've stolen four paintings.
4 The police have questioned three people.
5 They've arrested a man and a woman.
6 The local newspaper has contacted us.

9 Complete the advertisement. Use the future passive form (*will*) of the verbs in the brackets. → 10.4

Send us the story of your life.

We will publish your autobiography!

Don't worry if you can't write very well. The text
¹_____ (read) by one of our expert editors
and mistakes ²_____ (correct).
The final text ³_____ (email) to you before
printing. The cover ⁴_____ (design) using
a photo of you. Then your book ⁵_____
(print) on high quality paper and a hundred copies
⁶_____ (send) to your home.

What a perfect gift for friends and family!

10 Complete the questions. Use the correct passive form (present simple, past simple, present perfect or future) of the verbs in brackets. → 10.4

1 How many Harry Potter books _____ (write)?
2 Where _____ polar bears _____ (find): the Arctic or the Antarctic?
3 Where _____ the next Olympic Games _____ (hold)?
4 Which kind of food _____ (sell) at a baker's shop?
5 Can you name one novel that _____ (make) into a film?
6 In which century _____ computers _____ (invent)?
7 What language _____ (speak) by ordinary people in Ancient Rome?
8 _____ Scotland ever _____ (hit) by a tsunami?

11 Work in pairs. Ask and answer the questions in exercise 10.

Passive (present simple)

10.1 We form the present simple passive like this:
• present simple of *be* + past participle of the main verb.

Affirmative
This newspaper is published daily.
These grapes are grown in Italy.

Negative
This wine isn't made in France.
Cars aren't used on the island of Tresco.

Interrogative
Is your bicycle serviced regularly?
Are your clothes washed by hand?

Short answer
Yes, it is. / No, it isn't.
Yes, they are. / No, they aren't.

10.2 We use the passive when we want to focus on the action, not on who performs it, or when we don't know who performs it. We often use the present simple passive to describe a process. First, the bottles are washed. Then they're sorted into different colours. Next, they ... , etc.

10.3 When we want to say who performed the action, we use *by*.
My exams are marked by the teachers.

Passive (other tenses)

10.4 We form other tenses of the passive like this:
• correct tense of *be* + past participle of the main verb.

Tense	Example
past simple	This house was built in 1850. My friends were robbed in Mexico last year.
present perfect	Our car has been stolen! The Twilight books have been read by millions.
future simple (*will*)	His first novel will be published next year. The pyramids will be closed next week.

Part 1

1 Label the pictures with the adjectives below.

arrogant   clever   generous   impatient   lazy   nasty
shy   talkative

1 _____

2 _____

3 _____

4 _____

5 _____

6 _____

7 _____

8 _____

2 Write adjectives with the opposite meaning to those in exercise 1.

3 Choose the correct adjectives.

1 He's **funny** / **serious**. He never tells jokes.
2 He's **honest** / **dishonest**. He never tells the truth!
3 She's **lazy** / **hard-working**. She always does her homework on time.
4 She's **rude** / **polite**. She never says 'please' or 'thank you'.
5 He's **strong** / **weak**. He always thinks for himself.

Part 2: extension
Negative prefixes: *un-*, *in-*, *im-*, *ir-* and *dis-*

LEARN THIS!

Negative prefixes: *un-*, *in-*, *im-*, *ir-* and *dis-*
The prefixes *un-*, *in-*, *im-*, *ir-*, and *dis-* are negative. When they come before an adjective, they make its meaning opposite.
kind – unkind   patient – impatient
honest – dishonest   responsible – irresponsible

4 Choose the correct words.

1 **An honest** / **A dishonest** person always tells the truth.
2 An **ambitious** / **unambitious** person tries very hard to be successful.
3 A **sensitive** / **An insensitive** person doesn't think about other people's feelings.
4 A **rational** / **An irrational** person thinks clearly and carefully.
5 A **loyal** / **disloyal** friend says nasty things about you when you're not there.
6 A **tolerant** / **An intolerant** person doesn't listen to other people's opinions.
7 An **active** / **inactive** person gets a lot of exercise.
8 A **lucky** / **An unlucky** person often has bad luck.
9 A **mature** / **An immature** person behaves like a child.
10 A **friendly** / **An unfriendly** person makes a lot of friends.

EXAM STRATEGY

The most common negative prefix is *un-*. If you are completing an exercise and can't decide which prefix to use, choose this one!

5 Complete the sentences. Use the adjectives below with or without the prefix *un-*.

attractive   believable   fair   fit   grateful   safe

1 He's very _____ . He could be a model or a film star.
2 She's very _____ . She can run ten kilometres.
3 Don't touch that electric cable. It's _____ .
4 Thanks for the present. I'm very _____ .
5 England are beating Brazil 8–0. That's _____ !
6 My parents give my older sister more money than me. It's really _____ .

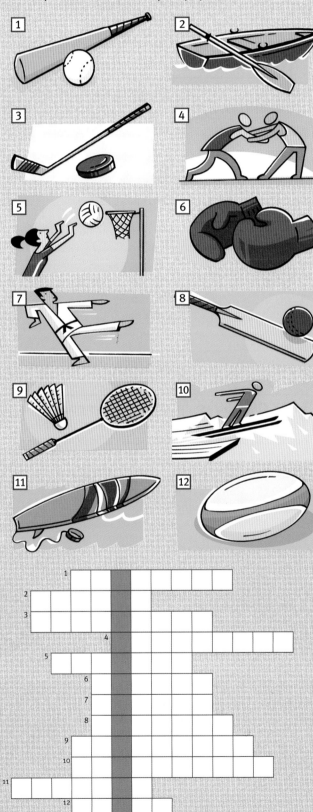

Part 1

1 Do the puzzle. What is the mystery sport?

2 **SPEAKING** Work in pairs. Ask and answer questions to find out what your partner thinks of the sports in exercise 1.

> What do you think of ... ?

> I love it. / I like it. / It's OK. / I'm not very interested in it. / I hate it.

Part 2: extension
Collocations: sports and games

3 Read the dialogue. Then complete the chart with the words below.

kick lose miss pass score win

Suzie	I played netball yesterday.
Kevin	How did it go?
Suzie	Well, I scored 25 points, but we didn't win the game.
Kevin	That's a shame. We lost our football match. And I missed a really easy goal!
Suzie	Oh dear. What happened?
Kevin	Dylan passed the ball to me and I kicked it straight at the goalkeeper!

Verbs	Nouns
compete in / lose / win	an event / a race
_____ / win	a match
lose / _____	a game
lose / _____ / win	a point
_____ / score	a goal
miss / score	a penalty
hit / _____ / _____ / throw	a ball

4 Complete the sentences with the verbs below. Change the verbs into the past simple if necessary.

compete   hit   lose   miss   score   win   win

1 He was so disappointed – he _____ a penalty in the last minute of the match!
2 In badminton, you need to _____ 21 points to _____ a game.
3 He isn't one of the biggest baseball players, but he _____ the ball very hard.
4 She _____ in her first rowing event when she was 43, and amazingly she _____ it by more than ten metres!
5 I'm pleased that we played well, but I'm sad that we _____ the match.

Part 1

1 Complete the sentences with the words below.

cottage   field   gate   lane   pavement   pond
road signs   rubbish bin   street lamps   traffic lights

1 I can't read the _____ – they're all in Welsh!
2 We drove along the _____ and into the village.
3 The horse escaped from the _____ by jumping over the _____ .
4 If you don't want that sandwich, put it in the _____ .
5 The town centre is very dark. They need more _____ .
6 Stay on the _____ when you're waiting to cross the road.
7 Why are the _____ always red when I'm in a hurry?
8 My aunt lives in a beautiful old _____ in a small village.
9 She threw the ball and it landed in the _____ with a splash.

2 Write the words in the correct order to make directions.

1 straight / on / go
2 end / to / go / the / the / road / of
3 first / take / the / right
4 traffic / turn / lights / the / at / right
5 stop / go / past / bus / the
6 South / along / Street / go

3 SPEAKING Work in pairs. Look at the map.

Student A: Give your partner directions to:
  a the school.   **b** the park.
Student B: Give your partner directions to:
  a the clothes shop.   **b** the train station.

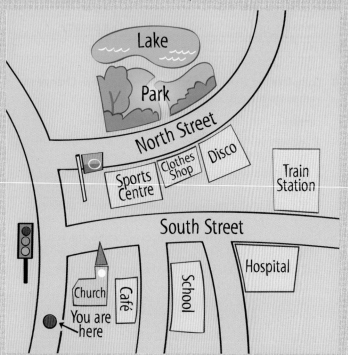

Part 2: extension
Compound nouns

LEARN THIS!
1 We can form compound nouns from two nouns.
2 We usually write them as two words (e.g. *post office*), but sometimes as one word (e.g. *postbox*). You need to check in a dictionary.

4 Read the *Learn this!* box. Then complete these compound nouns from Lesson 3A.

bin   box   crossing   lamp   lights   path   pole   sign

1 pedestrian _____   5 street _____
2 post _____   6 telegraph _____
3 road _____   7 traffic _____
4 rubbish _____   8 foot _____

5 Match 1–8 with a–h to make compound nouns. (Four of them are written as one word.)

1 basket _____   a teacher
2 head _____   b work
3 week _____   c tennis
4 home _____   d pool
5 sweat _____   e shirt
6 shopping _____   f end
7 swimming _____   g centre
8 table _____   h ball

LOOK OUT! Stress in two-word compound nouns
The main stress is usually on the first word (e.g. post office), but sometimes the stress is on both words (e.g. pedestrian crossing).

6 🎧 1.31 Listen and repeat the compound nouns from exercise 5. Underline the stress.

7 Complete the sentences with compound nouns from exercise 5.

1 _____ is a game for two teams of five players.
2 My brother plays waterpolo at our local _____ .
3 We go for bike rides in the countryside at the _____ .
4 I finished my _____ , but I left it on the bus!
5 I usually wear shorts and a _____ when I do athletics.
6 There's a fantastic new clothes shop in the _____ .
7 Is the _____ at your school a man or a woman?
8 We sometimes play _____ at school during the lunch break.

4 Vocabulary Builder

Part 1

1 SPEAKING Work in pairs. Think of examples of all the types of film below.

action film   animated film   comedy   disaster film
documentary film   historical drama   horror film   musical
romantic comedy   science fiction film   thriller   war film
western

> *Kill Bill* is an action film.

2 Read the sentences. What types of film are the people talking about? Choose from the list in exercise 1.

1 I liked the songs, and the acting was OK, but the actors couldn't sing!
2 I love films about the Wild West, especially ones with cowboys and Indians.
3 It was the most exciting and gripping film I've ever seen. You didn't know who the murderer was until the very end.
4 I'm really interested in that period of history, but I don't think the film was very accurate, so I didn't enjoy it.
5 The special effects were amazing. I almost believed that it was 2050 and people actually lived on the planet Mars.
6 It was about the Battle of Britain in 1940. Very exciting, but also quite violent.
7 It was very funny, and the ending was hilarious!
8 It was probably the scariest ghost story I've ever seen.

3 Choose the correct adjectives.

1 I can't stand romantic comedies. They're too **predictable / serious**.
2 The special effects were absolutely **spectacular / moving**.
3 I didn't find the characters or the story interesting. It was a very **gripping / dull** film.
4 It was a really **entertaining / serious** film – the audience clapped at the end.
5 It was a very **slow / moving** film. Not much happened in the first hour.
6 I'm not keen on war films. They're too **slow / violent** for me.
7 The ending was very **predictable / moving**. Lots of people were crying as they left the cinema.
8 The film was too **scary / gripping** for the children. They hid behind the sofa!

Part 2: extension
-ed and -ing adjectives

4 Complete the table.

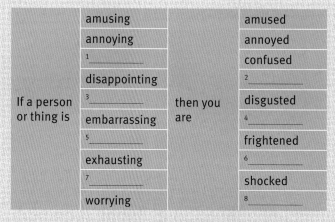

	amusing		amused
	annoying		annoyed
	1_____		confused
	disappointing		2_____
If a person or thing is	3_____	then you are	disgusted
	embarrassing		4_____
	5_____		frightened
	exhausting		6_____
	7_____		shocked
	worrying		8_____

5 Can you add any more -ed and -ing adjectives to the table?

6 SPEAKING Describe the people in the photos. Use -ed adjectives from exercise 4.

> I think he looks …

> I don't think he looks …

7 Work in pairs. Use -ing adjectives to describe these things and experiences in your life.

1 a sports event
2 a war film
3 a day out with your friends
4 your last maths lesson
5 an argument with a family member
6 Christmas Day

> A sports event. It was exciting. It was also disappointing, because my team lost.

8 Complete the adjectives.

1 I don't like this film. It's bor_____ .
2 I can't do this calculation. It's confus_____ .
3 Try not to get annoy_____ with your little sister.
4 I fell over in the canteen. It was so embarrass_____ .
5 I'm worr_____ about my exams. I hope I don't fail.
6 The pictures of the earthquake on TV were shock_____ .
7 We were disgust_____ at his bad language.
8 They were exhaust_____ at the end of the 10 km race.

Part 1

1 Label the pictures with the words below.

baker's   chemist's   DIY store   electrical store
estate agent's   garden centre   jeweller's   stationer's

1 _____   2 _____

3 _____   4 _____

5 _____   6 _____

7 _____   8 _____

2 Look at Gina's shopping list. How many shops does she need to visit? Which ones? (There is no supermarket in her town!)

2 kg chicken   the new Hilary Duff CD
a car magazine   'The Independent' newspaper
1 kg sausages   8 burgers
1 kg carrots   a new Wii game

3 SPEAKING Write a shopping list with eight different items. Then swap with your partner. Say which shops your partner needs to visit.

Part 2: extension
Verbs: shopping and money

4 Complete the sentences. Use the correct form of the verbs below.

borrow   charge   cost   lend   owe   pay for   save
sell   spend

1 Please _____ those DVDs at the till.
2 'I've _____ all my money at the cinema. I need to _____ some for the bus.' 'OK. I'll _____ you £1.'
3 I need to work at the café this weekend. I _____ my parents £100.
4 My sister's really careful with money. She _____ most of her pocket money every week – she never buys anything!
5 They _____ sweets and chocolate at the newsagent's.
6 The console was expensive. It _____ nearly £300. But they didn't _____ me for the games.

Talking about prices	
We write	**We say**
75p	Seventy-five p
£15	Fifteen pounds
£4.99	Four pounds ninety-nine or four ninety-nine

5 PRONUNCIATION Study the information in the box above, then say the prices.

1 £2.50   4 £45
2 50p   5 £10.99
3 £19.95   6 95p

6 SPEAKING Complete the dialogue. Use the correct form of verbs from exercise 4. Then read it aloud in pairs.

Customer   Hello. I [1]_____ this surfing magazine about five minutes ago. I think you made a mistake.
Assistant   Really? What's the problem?
Customer   Well, I gave you £5, but I only got £1.05 change.
Assistant   How much does the magazine [2]_____ ? Let's see … £2.95.
Customer   So you [3]_____ me too much.
Assistant   You're right. I [4]_____ you £1. Here you are.
Customer   Thanks.
Assistant   Have you seen this new surfing magazine? If you buy it today, you [5]_____ £2.
Customer   It looks interesting. But I can't [6]_____ any more money. I need to [7]_____ it for the bus home!

Vocabulary Builder

Part 1

1 Complete the names of the electronic devices with the words below.

book   console   frame   nav   PC   player   recorder   TV

1 tablet _____
2 hard disk _____
3 note_____
4 satellite _____
5 MP3 _____
6 games _____
7 sat_____
8 digital photo _____

2 What electronic devices should these people buy?

1 I like books, but they take up too much space.
2 I want to listen to music while I'm walking to school.
3 I want to make a film of my grandad's 80th birthday.
4 I love watching films on television. But I want a really clear and high-quality picture.
5 My mum is always getting lost in her car.
6 My laptop is a bit old, and quite heavy.

3 SPEAKING Work in pairs. Match the sentences with the devices below. More than one answer is possible.

camcorder   digital radio   digital photo frame
ebook reader   games console   HD TV   hard disk recorder
MP3 player   notebook   satnav   satellite TV
smartphone   tablet PC

1 You can listen to music on it.
2 It helps you to find your way.
3 You can store photos on it.
4 You can record or watch moving pictures on it.
5 You can read stories on it.
6 You can play games on it.

Part 2: extension
Phrasal verbs

4 Look at the pictures and phrasal verbs. Match the opposites.

 1 turn on / switch on   a put away

 2 turn up   b turn off / switch off

 3 take out   c take off

 4 plug in   d turn down

 5 put on   e pull out

5 Complete the sentences with the prepositions below.

away   down   off   on   out   up

1 Can you pick _____ my MP3 player? I dropped it on the floor.
2 Can you turn _____ the radio? There's a really good music programme on in a minute.
3 When I switched _____ the light, I couldn't see anything.
4 Can you please put _____ the DVDs when you've watched them?
5 She took _____ her mobile phone and turned it on.
6 Can you turn _____ the TV? It's too loud!

6 Read the *Learn this!* box. Then rewrite the sentences using the object pronoun in brackets.

> **LEARN THIS!**
>
> When we use this type of phrasal verb with an object pronoun (*me, him, it, them*, etc.), we must put it between the verb and the preposition.
> *Please switch off **your mobile**. Please switch **it** off.*

1 Please put away that DVD. (it)
2 He picked up his baby son. (him)
3 He took out his wallet. (it)
4 Can you turn up the music? (it)
5 They put on their coats. (them)
6 She put down her MP3 player. (it)
7 Turn on the lights! (them)
8 Take off those dirty trainers! (them)

Part 1

1 Label the pictures with the words below.

cross your legs   fold your arms   give a thumbs up
hold hands   pat somebody on the back   shake hands
shake your head   shrug your shoulders

1 _____   2 _____

3 _____   4 _____

5 _____   6 _____

7 _____   8 _____

2 Write the correct gesture. Choose from the phrases below. Sometimes more than one answer is correct.

beckon   bow   hold hands   hug   kiss   nod
pat somebody on the back   point   shake hands
shake your head   shrug your shoulders   wave   wink

What do you do when you:
1 want to say 'no'? shake your head
2 want to say 'Come here'? _____
3 want to say 'yes'? _____
4 say goodbye to someone? _____
5 say 'well done'? _____
6 want to comfort a family member? _____
7 meet a Japanese person for the first time? _____
8 want to say that you are joking? _____
9 want to show something to somebody? _____
10 want to say that you don't know? _____

3 SPEAKING Work in pairs. Take turns to be A and B.

Student A: Choose a gesture from exercise 1 or 2. Do it or mime it.
Student B: Say what Student A is doing.

> You're shaking your head.

Part 2: extension
Phrasal verbs

4 Label the pictures with the phrasal verbs below.

bend down   hold out your arms   lie down
lift up your foot   put up your hand   sit down   sit up
stand up   turn over   turn round

1 _____   6 _____
2 _____   7 _____
3 _____   8 _____
4 _____   9 _____
5 _____   10 _____

5 Choose the correct phrases.

1 John always **lifts up his foot / puts up his hand** to answer in class.
2 When you're on a bicycle, don't **lift up your foot / bend down** before you start moving!
3 My little daughter **held out her arms / put up her hand** so that I could pick her up.
4 I heard someone call my name, so I **bent down / turned round** and looked.
5 He **bent down / lay down** and picked up his shoes from the floor.
6 Uncle Stanley **lay down / stood up** on the sofa because he wasn't feeling well.
7 Go into the classroom, **sit up / sit down** and get out your books.
8 My mum says my dad keeps **turning round / turning over** in his sleep and waking her up.

Part 1

1 Label the pictures with six of the natural disasters below.

avalanche   disease   drought   earthquake   famine
flood   forest fire   hurricane   landslide   tornado
tsunami   volcanic eruption

1 _____

2 _____

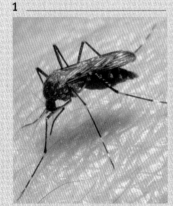

3 _____

4 _____

5 _____

6 _____

2 Match the headlines with natural disasters from exercise 1.

a Lava destroys town
b Water levels still rising as rain continues
c Road buried under tonnes of rock and mud
d Snowboarders found alive under 5m of snow
e Two years without rain
f Heat and smoke force people from homes

Part 2: extension
Word formation: noun suffixes *-ion*, *-ation* and *-ness*

LEARN THIS!

We can form nouns by adding suffixes (word endings) to verbs or adjectives. Sometimes the spelling changes.
1 verb + *-ion* / *-ation*
   oppress → oppression
   organise → organisation
2 adjective + *-ness*
   sad → sadness
   tired → tiredness

3 Read the *Learn this!* box. Then complete the table below. (The spelling changes in one of the nouns.)

Verb	Suffix	Noun
inform	-ation	1 _____
react	-ion	2 _____
educate	-ion	3 _____
protect	-ion	4 _____

Adjective	Suffix	Noun
dark	-ness	5 _____
good	-ness	6 _____

4 🎧 3.15 Listen and repeat. Underline the stress on the verbs, adjectives and nouns in the table above. When is the stress on the noun different from the stress on the verb or adjective?

5 Complete the sentences with nouns from exercise 3 and the *Learn this!* box.

1 T_____ is dangerous when you're driving. You should rest.
2 After years of o_____ , the people have finally been able to vote in an election.
3 You can find more i_____ about these issues by looking online.
4 Young children who have to work need the p_____ of the government.
5 So far, there has been no r_____ from the government to the protests.
6 The sounds of war continue all day, and even during the hours of d_____ .

Part 1

1 Complete the crimes with the endings below.

-ary -bery -ding -eft -er -ging -ism -ling
-on -ting

1	joyri_____	6	rob_____
2	drug dea_____	7	mug_____
3	burgl_____	8	murd_____
4	vandal_____	9	ars_____
5	shoplif_____	10	th_____

2 Read sentences 1–10. What kinds of criminal are they? Choose from the words below.

arsonist burglar drug dealer joyrider mugger
murderer robber shoplifter thief vandal

1 She killed her husband.
2 She takes things from shops without paying for them.
3 He sells cocaine and heroin to teenagers.
4 He got into the house through an open window and took some cash and jewellery.
5 Some teenagers broke three shop windows in the town.
6 He took his neighbour's car and drove it around town late at night with his friends.
7 She took a wallet from somebody's bag during the lunch hour.
8 They stole £1 million from a bank in Bristol.
9 She set fire to an old house near the village.
10 He attacked two girls in the street and took their mobiles and their handbags.

3 Match the crimes in exercise 1 with the types of criminal in exercise 2.

4 Complete the sentences. Use the correct form of the verbs below.

burgle deal go murder rob set steal vandalise

1 Robin Hood _____ from the rich and gave to the poor.
2 Armed criminals _____ two banks in Bristol last week.
3 Somebody _____ this telephone box six times since last March. The phone never works.
4 Somebody _____ my aunt's house last weekend. They took jewellery and a DVD player.
5 Jason sometimes _____ joyriding at the weekend. His parents don't know about it.
6 A drug dealer _____ a man in Manchester yesterday. The police have arrested him.
7 Mark uses drugs, but he doesn't _____ them.
8 If he _____ fire to any more buildings, he will go to prison for sure.

Part 2: extension
Word formation: noun suffixes -er/-or, -ist and -ician

5 Read the *Learn this!* box. Find five more words with the -er suffix in the list in exercise 2.

> Words that describe a person who does a particular activity often end in *-er/-or*, *-ist* or *-ician*.
> 1 Words that end in *-er/-or* are often connected with a verb:
> *A mugger is somebody who mugs people.*
> *A film director is somebody who directs films.*
> 2 Words that end *-ist* are often connected with a noun:
> *An arsonist commits arson.*
> *A novelist writes novels.*
> 3 Words that end *-ician* are often connected with an *-ical* adjective or a noun:
> *An electrician does electrical work.*
> *A magician does magic.*

6 Complete the words with *-er/-or*, *-ist* or *-ician*. Use the information in the *Learn this!* box to help you.

1 He's a polit_____. He makes political decisions.
2 He's an act_____. He acts in plays and films.
3 She's a software programm_____. She programs software.
4 She's a reception_____. She works in reception at a big hotel.
5 As a child, my sister was always good at maths. Now she's a mathemat_____.
6 She's a scient_____. She works in a science laboratory.
7 He's a violin_____. He plays the violin.
8 She's a clean_____. She cleans offices.

7 Match pictures a–h with the people in exercise 6.

Part 1

1 Complete the crossword.

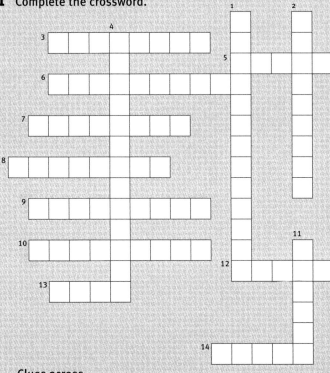

Clues across

3 A _____ often contains photos and articles about famous people.

5 A _____ uses pictures and speech bubbles to tell stories.

6 A _____ contains words and their definitions.

7 A _____ tells you how to cook particular dishes.

8 A _____ is a book that you use in lessons at school or college.

9 A _____ is a book about a person's life, written by another person.

10 A _____ gives information about recent events in the world.

12 An _____ is a book of maps.

13 A _____ is a show that you see at the theatre.

14 A _____ is a long, fictional story.

Clues down

1 An _____ contains information about lots of different subjects.

2 A _____ provides information about a place you are visiting.

4 An _____ is a person's story of his/her own life.

11 A _____ tells you how to use something.

2 Think of one real example of a play, a novel, a textbook, a magazine, a dictionary and a newspaper.

Part 2: extension
Books and text

3 Label the pictures with the words below.

author   back cover   chapter   contents page   front cover
hardback   page number   paperback   publisher   spine
title

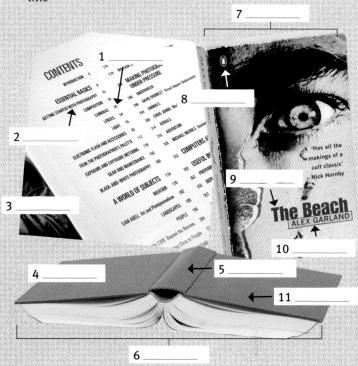

LOOK OUT!

Nouns can function as adjectives when put in front of other nouns, e.g. *front cover*. They work as adjectives to give more information about the noun.

---

4 Read the *Look out!* box and find examples of three other nouns functioning as adjectives in the word list above. Can you think of any others?

5 Answer the questions about your copy of *Solutions 2nd edition*.

1 Is it a hardback or a paperback?
2 How many words are on the front cover?
3 How many website addresses are on the back cover?
4 What colour are the page numbers?
5 What information is on the spine?
6 How many contents pages are there?
7 What are the authors' names?
8 What is the name of the publisher?
9 In what parts of the book does the title appear?

ACKNOWLEDGEMENTS

Illustrations by: Adrian Barclay pp14, 24, 71, 90, 114, 116, 120, 124 (ex 5), 125, 126, 129 (ex 2); Claude Bordeleau/Agent 002 p111; Simon Gurr pp5, 17, 37, 77, 85, 87, 91, 118, 124 (ex 1), 128, 130; Sean Longcroft p64; Andy Parker pp55, 59, 78, 79, 97. 129 (ex 4).

Cover: Alamy (O2 Arena hanging lamp display/Graham Salter/© Lebrecht Music and Arts Photo Library).

The publisher would like to thank the following for the permission to reproduce photographs: Alamy Images pp4 (Kristen Stewart in *Twilight*/Summit Entertainment/AF Archive), 6 (Girls grooming donkey/WoodyStock), 7 (Oblivion ride, Alton Towers/LifeStyle), 8 (Cowgirl holding guitar/Tetra Images), 8 (Female punk rockers/Gaertner), 11 (Portrait of teen boy/Johner Images), 21 (Friends bowling/Profimedia International s.r.o.), 21 (A shuttlecock in flight over a badminton net/Simon Gill), 23 (Yorkshire Dales/ICP), 28 (Playing online video game/David J. Green - Lifestyle), pp31 (Water park/Stephen French), 39 (*The Matrix Reloaded*/Pictorial Press Ltd), 43 (knights/imagebroker), 44 (Mobile phone shop/Ace Stock Limited), 44 (Shop mannequins/Johnny Greig UK), 46 (Restaurant interior/JTB Photo Communications, Inc.), 49 (Ebay website/ICP-UK), 49 (Man using laptop at home/Fancy), 51 (Teenager shouting at mobile phone/RubberBall), 54 (Nintendo DS/Hugh Threlfall), 54 (HD video camera/Judith Collins), 54 (Sat nav device/ICP), 54 (MP3 player/D. Hurst), 54 (DAB radio/Hugh Threlfall), 56 (Woman looking at Facebook website/David J. Green - lifestyle themes), 57 (Computer polygraph lie detector test/Mark Burnett), 57 (Apple iPhone 4 smartphone/Oleksiy Maksymenko Photography), 58 (transport map/Mim Friday), 60 (Friends on sofa/moodboard), 61 (Woman reading memos/avatra images), 63 (shopping/Frances Roberts), 67 (Cat sitting on wooden fence/legge), 70 (Information desk/Eddie Gerald), 74 (Avalanche), 80 (Fundraising/Sally and Richard Greenhill), 80 (Charity run/Mark Bassett), 80 (Fundraising bake sale/MShieldsPhotos), 80 (Shaving head/Ann E Parry), 81 (Litter on street/Michael Kemp), 83 (Comic Relief 2007), 84 (burnt out car/Joe Fox), 84 (house fire/Sandra Baker), 85 (cash machine//Machin), 88 (PIN theft/Ray Grover), 93 (Lunch in jail/Spencer Grant), 94 (Stack of British newspapers/ICP), 95 (1960's secretary with typewriter/ClassicStock), 95 (Graphic designer/Blend Images), 95 (Amazon website/NetPhotos), 98 (Teen girl reading *Twilight* novel/Ben Molyneux People), 98 (Brad Pitt/Photos12), 103 (Yorkshire Dales/ICP), 104 (Walking a dog/Myrleen Pearson), 127 (Stressed woman/Brownstock), 130 (Couple holding hands/Cultura), 130 (Legs of woman under desk/Image Source), 130 (Woman shrugging her shoulders/Blend Images), 131 (warning signs/George & Monserrate Schwartz), 131 (Mosquito/Graphic Science), 132 (US President Barack Obama/Jan Socher), 132 (Female office worker/amana images inc.), 133 (Book lying open on floor/UpperCut Images), 133 (Book index/Gaspar R Avila), cover (Lamp display in concert auditorium/Lebrecht Music and Arts Photo Library); BBC Worldwide Ltd p68 (flying penguins); Corbis pp9 (Dance party/Julian Smith), 11 (Teen girl smiling/Edith Held), 11 (Teen boy portrait/Hans Bjurling/Johnér Images), 14 (Argentinean footballer Lionel Messi/Andres Kudacki), 14 (Jamaican sprinter Usain Bolt/PCN), 14 (Tennis player Caroline Wozniacki/Hugo Philpott/epa), 15 (tortoise/Vstock/Tetra Images), 16 (The World Bog Snorkeling Championships/

Andrew Fox), 21 (Baseball bat and ball/TongRo Image Stock), 26 (Fox hunt/Nathan Benn), 27 (Dubrovnik coastline/Thom Lang), 35 (Actress Keira Knightley/Jorge Uzon), 47 (Harrods department store/Phil O'Connor/Loop Images), , 52 (The Barber of Seville/Robbie Jack), 54 (iPad tablet computer/Ron Royals), 63 (market/Strauss/Curtis), 66 (Christmas tree in shopping mall/Benelux), 68 (Spaghetti Harvesting April Fool's/BBC), 74 (Tornado/Eric Nguyen), 74 (Volcanic eruption/Martin Rietze/Westend61), 74 (Homes destroyed by landslides and flooding/Paul A. Souders), 74 (Drought/HU YANHUI/Xinhua Press), 95 (The Thomas Jefferson Building/William Manning), 96 (Portrait of Shakespeare/Bettmann), 97 (Kindle 2 e-book reader/James Leynse), 98 (Bram Stoker/Hulton-Deutsch), 130 (Thumbs up sign/Ken Seet/Spirit), 130 (Senior basketball players/Patrik Giardino), 131 (Earthquake damage/Carlos Barria/Reuters), 131 (Flooding/Cameron Davidson), 131 (Refugees/Bettmann), 132 (Scientist in laboratory/Noel Hendrickson/Blend Images), 132 (Woman at concierge desk/Mark Edward Atkinson/Blend Images), 132 (Woman writing on blackboard/C.Devan); Getty Images pp36 (Hilary Swank accepting Academy Award/Kevin Winter), (Jamie Foxx with Academy Award/S. Granitz/WireImage), 40 (Queue in cinema/Eli Dreyer/Taxi), 43 (rugby/Julian Finney), 46 (Lily Allen And Sarah Owen Open Pop-Up Store 'Lucy in Disguise' at Selfridges/Dave M. Benett), 52 (Jennifer Lopez/Neilson Barnard), 84 (shoplifting/Steven Puetzer), 89 (Identity theft crime/Heath Patterson/Photographer's Choice), 93 (Women at cafe/Eileen Bach), 94 (A Spider-Man Marvel comic book/Jonathan Alcorn/Bloomberg via Getty Images), 95 (Young woman posting a letter, c 1930s./SSPL via Getty Images), 96 (Teen girl laughing/Ron Levine/Digital Vision), 132 (Violinist/Alvis Upitis); iStockphoto pp17 (crushed paper/Duncan Babbage), 23 (crushed paper/Duncan Babbage), 25 (park/A-Digit), 26 (old card/Mike Bentley), 28 (wooden signs/Tatiana Georgieva), 28 (old card/Mike Bentley), 29 (landscape/MerggyR), 31 (seasons/korpas), 45 (Woman shopping for shoes/YinYang), 46 (Covent Garden market lamp/essxboy), 49 (Vintage map of Texas/Daniel Stein), 54 (Digital picture frame/Victor Martello), 58 (linen paper/Sandy Jones), 68 (Twelve O'Clock/Joseph Gareri), 74 (torn newspaper/Trevor Hunt), 88 (binary/geopaul), 136 (seasons/korpas), 136 (crushed paper/Duncan Babbage), 137 (torn newspaper/Trevor Hunt); Kobal Collection pp4 (Heath Ledger in *Batman: The Dark Knight*/Warner Bros/DC Comics), 4 (Nicole Kidman in *The Golden Compass*/New Line Cinema), 4 (Johnny Depp in *The Pirates of the Caribbean: Curse of the Black Pearl*/Walt Disney Pictures), 34 (*Knight and Day*/New Regency Pictures), 34 (*Saving Private Ryan*/Dreamworks LLC/David James), 34 (*Mamma Mia!*/Universal/Playtone), 34 (*Avatar*/Twentieth Century-Fox Film Corporation), 34 (*Troy*/Warner Bros/Alex Bailey), 34 (*Valentine's Day*/New Line Cinema), 38 (*The Man with the Golden Gun*/DANJAQ/EON/UA), 39 (*Rush Hour*/New Line/Roger Birnbaum/Bob Marshak), 86 ('*Robin Hood*' 1922, United Artists), 86 ('*The Adventures of Robin Hood*' 1938/Warner Brothers), 86 ('*Robin Hood:Prince of Thieves*' 1991/Morgan Creek/Warner Brothers), 86 ('*Robin Hood*' 2010/Universal Pictures), 94 (*Lord of the Rings: The Return of the King*/New Line Cinema), 94 (*Oliver Twist*, 2005/R.P. Productions/Runteam Ltd/Guy Ferrandis), 94 (*Alice in Wonderland*, 2010/Walt Disney Pictures), 94 (*Sherlock Holmes*, 2009/Silver Pictures); Mary Evans Picture Library p17 (1912 Stockholm Olympics/IBL Collections); Masterfile p50 (Woman pointing out flaw to sales clerk/Al Accardo); Moviestore Collection p94 (*The Twilight Saga: Eclipse*/Summit Entertainment); OUP pp10 (Teen couple/Brand X Pictures), 12 (Teenagers drinking coffee/Gareth Boden), 20 (Teens talking in corridor/Image Source), 21 (Tennis racket and ball/Photodisc), 30 (Train ticket queue/Photodisc), 30 (Street cafe/Chris King), 30 (Commuters/Photodisc), 68 (Big Ben), 73 (Restaurant waiter/BananaStock), 73 (Waiter at table/Photodisc), 73 (Bush fire/imagebroker), 84 (graffiti/Stockbyte), 92 (Polar bear/Digital Vision), 96 (teen boy/Chris King), 96 (teen boy/Digital Vision), 127 (Woman not enjoying food/Image Source), 127 (Frightened man/Brownstock Inc.), 130 (Man with arms crossed/Image Source), 130 (Portrait of teen boy/Red Chopsticks), 130 (Shaking hands/Imagebroker), 131 (Hurricane/Stockbyte), 132 (Shakespeare play/Stan Fellerman); Photolibrary pp6 (Girl rock climbing/Corbis), 8 (Teen boy singing/Blue Jean Images), 8 (Teen girls singing in bedroom/Blend Images), 21 (Close-up of weights/Radius Images), 29 (Farmer/Monty Rakusen/Cultura), 49 (Euro bank notes/Creativ Studio Heinemann/Westend61), 65 (Man arriving at a dinner party/Fancy), 84 (burglar/moodboard), 85 (eating chocolate rabbit/Radius), 87 (teenage girl/Big Cheese), 89 (Computer hacker/Nick Rowe/White), 100 (Teen with mobile phone shopping/Moodboard), 127 (Student asleep in class/Image Source), 132 (Office cleaner/Jacobs Stock Photography); Press Association Images pp17 (A 'mystery player', Karl Power pictured in the Manchester United Team/Valeria Witters/Witters), 43 (James Blunt/Goncalo Silva/Demotix), 101 (First edition of '*The Hobbit*'/Sang Tan/AP); Rachelle Strauss p76 (Strauss family bin); Rex Features pp4 (*The Simpsons Movie*/c.20thC.Fox/Everett), 4 (Daniel Craig in *Quantum Of Solace*/c.MGM/Everett), 7 (Thorpe Park/Jonathan Hordle), 14 (Formula One driver Lewis Hamilton/Canadian Press), 16 (World Snail Racing Championships/Geoffrey Robinson), 18 (Surfer Bethany Hamilton/Sipa Press), 19 (Surfer Bethany Hamilton/S Robertson/Newspix), 32 (*Dancing on Ice* figure skaters/Ken McKay/ITV), 34 (*The Day After Tomorrow* film still/c.20thC.Fox/Everett), 34 (*Up* film/c.W.Disney/Everett), 58 (French Policeman on Segway Personal Transporters/Sipa Press), p41 (*Paul* - 2011/Universal/Everett), 58 (The electric Uno motorbike/MotorcycleMojo), 58 (Sir Clive Sinclair with Sinclair C5 motor car/Steve Blogg), 75 (Olivia Wilde/NBCUPHOTOBANK), 84 (drug dealing/Paul Brown), 133 (*The Beach* paperback book); Robert Harding World Imagery p31 (Wray Castle/James Emmerson); SuperStock pp25 (Flat interior/View Pictures Ltd), 44 (Sports shop/Photononstop), 116 (Woman eating noodles/Asia Images).